GROUNDS FOR MARRIAGE

Marilyn Funt · GROUNDS

FOR MARRIAGE

Dodd, Mead & Company

New York

Acknowledgment is made to Rick Bard, publisher of *Manhattan*,
for permission to reprint the lines from his interview with Carly Simon on page 281.

Published by Dodd, Mead & Company, Inc.
71 Fifth Avenue, New York, N.Y. 10003
Manufactured in the United States of America
Designed by Kay Lee
Text set in 11/14 Caledonia

First Edition

1   2   3   4   5   6   7   8   9   10

Library of Congress Cataloging-in-Publication Data
Funt, Marilyn, 1937–
   Grounds for marriage.

   Includes Index.
   1. Marriage—United States. 2. Married
people—United States—Interviews.
3. Celebrities—United States—Interviews.
I. Title.
HQ734.F95   1988   646.7′8   88–1202
ISBN 0-396-09086-9

To my children, Juliet and William Funt. I hope that in some way my more positive feelings about marriage will help to diminish some of the emotional pain that they weathered as children of divorce.

Contents

Foreword

Grounds for Marriage is, first of all, a thoroughly enjoyable book to read. Reading about how people feel and how they relate to each other also provides a surprising amount with which to identify. Glimpses of private lives have a universal appeal, especially when we're made privy to the lives of famous people. Indeed, Marilyn Funt has written both a highly entertaining book and, more importantly, a very useful book. The vast majority of texts on relationships tend to focus on severe "problems" and offer possible solutions. This book is unique, because it examines healthy, constructive, and cooperative relationships.

All of the marriages described in this book demonstrate the commonality among long-standing, fruitful unions. It's inspirational because it gives all of us hope. The couples—be they celebrities or your next-door neighbor—all share the human condition and are seeking that most gratifying of all human conditions—a happy marriage. Cooperative relating can occur in an endless variety of ways. This remarkable book provides another unique perception: that there is no one, two, or fifty ways to achieve an harmonious blending of two separate identities. Each relationship has its own special problem areas, but none is insoluble where there is motivation and goodwill.

To me, the book is especially gratifying because the heart of the cooperative process is the satisfaction derived from self-realization— one's own and one's partner's. Marilyn Funt, through her unique ability to draw out honest feelings, presents a rare portrait of mutual joy. Actual case material of this kind is rare. People speak with remarkable candor as they talk about their struggles, their problems, and the solutions they found. How they view themselves, each other, and the world they live in teaches us about constructive compromise, without which no relationship can long endure.

So many sustained relationships are adversarial, largely compet- itive, and often antagonistic. So many are sadomasochistic. Marilyn Funt's cooperative partners show us that we can in fact give to each other without depleting ourselves. They demonstrate that mutual help can and often does result in strengthening of self. Relating of this kind, whatever the unique lifestyle may be, is an essentially antinar- cissistic device. Narcissism is always self-corrosive. The people in this book, through long relationships, demonstrate how they have them- selves escaped the traps of narcissism to become more fully devel- oped people.

In closing, let me say that Marilyn Funt is a superb interviewer. She knows how to get people to talk about the real substance of their lives. She knows how to get out of their way when they talk. She knows how to listen so that we can listen, too. She knows that people can and do change and grow in healthy directions. Through her book, Marilyn shows us how cooperative, sustained relating makes a major contribution to healthy growth and fruitful living. This is a remark- able collection of data. I don't know of another like it. It will be most useful for already married couples and for those contemplating remarriage, or for those marrying for the first time.

Theodore Isaac Rubin, M.D., P.C.

Acknowledgments

I first want to thank the wonderful variety of married couples that I was given the privilege to meet. I was always surprised when they said yes, but feared the yes would not guarantee any true openness. I was delighted to be wrong so many times. These couples seemed to welcome the interview as an opportunity to talk to each other with a third party present. This way, they avoided many of the normal breakdowns of communication and perhaps reached a new height of intimacy and friendship. If that took place, this book is a success for that reason alone.

A big hug to John Malone, author of *Straight Women—Gay Men—A Special Relationship*, the only non-Jewish non-neurotic I have ever worked with. Without his organization and writing ability, the book would still be in little pieces all over the living-room floor. No matter how scrawled my notes were, he always found them "perfectly clear."

Thanks to Rhoda Lukin who was my first editor at *New York Womens Week*. When I handed in my first assignment, I asked her, "Is this writing?" Rhoda's reply: "Once I go over it, it will be." She is still "going over it," and without her encouragement I might have stopped a long time ago; to Lillie Balinova, who started helping to edit the extra load of tapes, and has since become a close friend and creative ear. Her instinctual feel for what sounds right became an invaluable aid in judging the interviews and picking the ones to go with; to Dr. Theodore Isaac Rubin, for making a commitment to me and standing by it, even when his own work became "too much"; to my editor, Cynthia Vartan, whose crisp, clear way of looking at the material gave *Grounds for Marriage* its definite shape and style. She is in control, wants things a certain way, but if it is important to the author she can let go without it being a big deal or ammunition for future encounters. She is the total professional, and I felt secure in her hands, yet never threatened; to my agent, Bill Adler, for thinking of me and giving me the opportunity to do this book.

A special thanks to Julie Rosner for putting up with all the difficult parts of getting this project off the ground.

Thanks, too, to my sister Elaine Laron, lyricist and television writer, and one of the original participants in *Free to Be . . . You & Me*. Her brilliant and very creative ideas were always available for me to "steal."

A big thanks to my children, Juliet and William Funt, for being so involved with their own lives that they did not make me feel guilty for being as involved with my own, and with my work. I would also like to thank Allen Funt for still "being around" and interested in what I am doing. Upon returning from a trip to Africa, he offered me an interview that he did of a Maasai couple (through a translator) that he thought I could use for my book. A brief excerpt follows with a note from Allen.

A: Ask him how much he paid for his wife.

T: Twenty cows.

A: Is he a good man?

T: Yes, he is—but she must always do what he says.

A: If she did something that upset him, would he punish her?

T: Yes—he has punished her—by hitting her with a stick.

A: He hit her with a stick! Did she cry?

T: Yes—but he only hit her a few times—he is not a bad man.

July 5, 1987

Marilyn:

Here is a man in Kenya who beats his wife with a stick after buying her for twenty cows, and you think I was a bad husband!

Allen

Finally, thanks to MY PORT in a storm.

Introduction

Grounds for Marriage is based on interviews with more than 150 couples who have created successful, lasting marriages. These are couples who believe in marriage and were determined to find their own ways of making their relationships work. That is their common bond; in other ways they are often very different from one another. Some are rich, some poor, the majority middle-income. Their marriages reflect a wide range of cultural and ethnic heritages—Italian, German, Irish, Jewish, Polish, Hispanic, Afro-American, American Indian. There are couples who may seem as familiar as the people next door, as well as people whose names are constantly in the newspapers or whose faces regularly light up television and movie screens.

But whether they are self-made millionaires or small shop owners, secretaries or movie stars, housepainters, lawyers, therapists, or ex-cops, they reveal with extraordinary candor and intimacy the secrets of their private lives. They talk not only about how they love but also how they fight, what makes them cry as well as what makes them laugh. Some asked that only their first names be used so they could speak more freely, but most were willing to let the world know what they have felt and experienced in their marriages, no holds barred. They were willing to be interviewed and quoted because they are proud of having made their marriages work, and liked the idea that their personal histories might be helpful to other couples who face the same kind of problems they faced.

Make no mistake, they have had their problems. The stories in this book are not touched-up portraits that make it all seem easy. These couples don't look at their marriages through rose-colored glasses. They tell what really happened, the ways they hurt one another as well as the ways they nurtured one another. Because they admit their failures and are frank about what caused trouble in their marriages, their experiences take on the real value of lived truth.

There have been many books about how to have a good relationship or a good marriage. But most such books depend upon rules or formulas that few couples could really follow without becoming somebody else entirely. *Grounds for Marriage* is definitely a book to learn from, but it is not a book of rules. In fact many of these couples have made their marriages work by breaking old rules and creating new ones of their own—tailored to their specific needs as individuals married to one another.

Trying to live your own marriage by somebody else's rules is as fruitless as Cinderella's stepsisters trying to cram their feet into the glass slipper. The idea that there is some single magic formula for a good marriage is a fairy tale. There are in reality hundreds of different ways of making relationships work, thousands of grounds for marriage. As one husband put it, "we learned to face our problems and deal with them our way, never mind what the rest of the 'happily married' were thinking or doing, never mind the rest of the world." Every good marriage is unique in some way, just as the individual partners are.

Can a woman with a Ph.D. really make marriage work with a housepainter? Can people who scream at each other when they are angry have a happy and fulfilling relationship? Can a couple who see one another only two weeks out of every month maintain a stable marriage? The answer in each case is yes. It's not the surface circumstances that count, it's how the couple handles those circumstances.

The couples I interviewed made their marriages a success by doing things in very different, even opposite ways. The housewife, the career woman, the woman who returns to work after her children are grown—these are very different lives, but they all result in terrific marriages because both partners feel comfortable with the situation. In a period during which tensions are high concerning the career/family choices faced by so many women, the personal solutions of the husbands and wives in *Grounds for Marriage* offer a wide range of illuminating perspectives.

More controversial is the matter of sex. There are couples who are strictly monogamous, others who choose to ignore the issue of fidelity, and a few who forthrightly sanction infidelity by their partners. Would a man with a low sex drive really say to his wife, "Go and have an affair if you want to?" Would a man in medical school really allow his wife to work as a high-priced call girl to pay the bills? Can these possibly be good marriages? You may change your mind.

Couples who have agreed upon ways of living that others might regard as highly unusual or even extreme can in fact tell us a lot about making marriage work, throwing into high relief the issues that may be submerged in more straightforward relationships. But the many fundamentally conventional couples here also show how varied the solutions can be within seemingly similar marriages. They've all made it happen their own special way.

During my interviews with these one hundred-plus couples, I asked about work and money, probed feelings about children and in-laws, and challenged people to be frank about sexual fidelity and fulfillment. I wanted to know how disagreements were handled and what techniques couples used to communicate with their partners. I did not make use of a specific questionnaire, agreeing with the many experts who feel that questionnaires often narrow the focus in a way that lets the truth slip away between the lines. I took a relaxed, personal approach, asking specific questions when necessary to nail down the facts, but encouraging the couples to engage as much as possible in a dialogue between themselves.

The majority of these couples have been married for at least fifteen years, and many for upward of twenty-five years. Some who have been married for less time provide particularly telling insights precisely because they are still in the process of creating a relationship that fully addresses the needs of both partners. A few couples who have been married a relatively short time have also been included because of a special commitment to marriage they demonstrate and because they serve as examples of how to get off on the right foot. And what about the celebrities? Are they "different"? Yes, from each other—and not at all necessarily because they are celebrities.

The book itself is divided into eight chapters, beginning with an overview of long-term marriages, then focusing on work and money, children, the influences of in-laws and friends, the importance of sex, communication, and concluding with chapters on remarriage and on the varying seasons of marriage. Some couples naturally had much more to say about some subjects than others, depending on the focus of their own marriages. Thus many couples will appear in only one chapter; others had important things to say in a number of areas, and their comments will appear throughout the book.

Good marriages are made on earth, not in heaven. You won't find the perfect couple here. What you will find are enduring couples, people who fell in love and remain in love. Their marriages remain vibrant not only because they love one another, but also because they have a healthy respect for one another's needs and dreams. They respect both themselves *and* the partner. Based on that respect, they have hammered out personal rules with mutual trust, interest, and fondness.

Recent studies have shown that good marriages are good for you. Happily married people have fewer health problems and live longer—perhaps because they have more to live for. But it is also true that good marriages are not a matter of arriving at a plateau of understanding that will serve to the end of one's days. As Dr. Clifford J. Sanger, clinical psychiatrist at New York Hospital, says, "If there is no conflict, something is wrong with the marriage." Good marriages keep growing. People change, ideas change, circumstances change, and societal influences change. If change is viewed as threatening, people withdraw, and withdrawn people make for static and eventually unhappy marriages. When change is welcomed for the vitality and richness it brings to marriage, the partners can use it as a stimulant, inspiring one another to new explorations of themselves and the relationship itself. That is what the couples interviewed for this book have done and are still doing, each in their own way. The vitality of their marriages serves as both an inspiration and an objective study of how marriage as an institution can and does work. These couples show that the vast hunger for commitment that has developed in the 1980s can be successfully satisfied. We do continue to have grounds for marriage.

List of participants

Martin and Bella Abzug
Joey and Cindy Adams
Steve Allen and Jayne
   Meadows
Jim and Denise Amato
Arthur and Elaine*
Marlene and David Barnaby
Don and Rachel Barton
Robert "Kool" and Sakinah Bell
Harry and Lou Bendak
David and Debbie Black

Joseph Bologna and Renee
   Taylor
Brad and Libby
David and Helen Gurley
   Brown
Carl and Willy Burkhardt
Sid and Florence Caesar
Roger and Gail Calloway
George and Brenda Carlin
Eric and Edie Chandler
Spencer and Diane Christian

Kari Clark
(married to Dick Clark)
Gary Collins and Mary Ann
Mobley
Jackie and Barbara Cooper
Dan and Laurie
Lester and Babs David
George and Edith Denny
John and Bo Derek
Bruce and Andrea Dern
Doug and Nancy Ellis
Brendan and Sally Dunn
Malcolm and Helen Elliot
Jeff Endervelt and Polly
Bergen
Jim and Terry Englisis
Mel and Eleanor Erlich
Juan and Zoila Fernandez
Lou and Karla Ferrigno
Arthur and Marcy Forest
Rod and Marilyn Gist
Jeffrey Goidel and Harlene
Cooper
Stu and Judith Goldblum
Eydie Gormé
(married to Steve Lawrence)
Lorne and Nancy Greene
Peter Greenough
(married to Beverly Sills)
Monty and Marilyn Hall
Warren and Jane Hamilton
Elbert and Lauresteen
Hatchett
Betsy and George Heath
Harry and Leona Helmsley
Brian and Suzanne Henry
Gary and Sandy Hewitt
Howard and Jeanne
Fred and Ruth Howard

Marty Ingels and Shirley Jones
Jason and Carole
Waylon Jennings and Jessi
Colter
Jim and Nora
Joe and Vicky
Casey and Jean Kasem
Ray and June Kerns
Larry and Susan Kirstein
Stephen and Rose Kovac
Jack and Elaine LaLanne
Alan Lansburg and Linda Otto
Larry and Jane
Richard Leibner and Carole
Cooper
Len and Roberta
Benjy and Jay Lenart
Hank and Cindy Lewis
Simon Liberman
(married to Jean Liberman)
Cesar and Marianna Lopez
Luis and Maria Lopez
Henry and Ginny Mancini
Mario and Dave
Pat and Marcy Marks
Ross and Erica Marlowe
Mike and Julia Martinson
Arthur and Lois Marx
William Masters and Virginia
Johnson
Jim and Cara McClellan
Robert and Marion Merrill
Alan and Joan Miller
Marvin and Marcella
Mitchelson
Joe and Audrey Minerva
Thomas Muller and Elizabeth
Hanson
Terrence and Lillian Mullins

Roy and Ginny Nevans

Bob and Ginny Newhart

Jackson and Karen North

Jay and Sandy Originer

Paul and Linda

Brad and Norene Peck

Toby Perlman
(married to Itzhak Perlman)

Peter and Sharon

Martin and Gladys Poll

Vincent Price and Coral
Browne

Larry and Susan Prince

Leon and Idelle Rabin

Menshulam Riklis and Pia
Zadora

Robert and Sarah

Smokey and Claudette
Robinson

Louis Rodriguez and Judy
Gherke

Kenny and Marianne Rogers

Mickey and Jan Rooney

Malcolm and Arlene Rose

Jack and Sylvia Roseman

Mel and Maxine Rosenblum

Theodore Isaac and Ellie
Rubin

Bill and Marylou Sanford

Bill and Cindy Shoemaker

Norman Sheresky and
Elaine Lewis

Harold and Gwen Simpson

Richard Singer and Cynthia
Malmuth-Singer

Bill and Karen Spofford

Stan and Judy

Stan and Magda

John and Diane Stratta

Alan and Peggy Tishman

Al and Neile Toffell

Edward and Linda Villella

Todd and Lisa Washburn

Herman and Violet Weiss

Ted and Barbara Wilkes

Richard and Wendy Willis

Neil and Ann Yarbro

*Some of the participants requested that only their first names be used.

GROUNDS FOR MARRIAGE

ONE

I have the feeling that Ginny and I have walked through a mine field, and we've arrived at
twenty-three years because we went through
all that crazy period—sexual revolution, open
marriage, all that stuff—and survived.
—*Bob Newhart*

There are times in every marriage: Joe will say,
"What's the matter, don't you love me?" I'll say,
"I love you but I don't like you today."
—*Audrey Minerva*

Long-term marriages: A lifetime together

In a time in which there are half as many divorces as there are
marriages each year, the phrase "long-term" has become somewhat
devalued. Couples who make it to their tenth anniversary receive
fulsome, and sometimes premature, congratulations for their stability. In this chapter, however, you will meet couples who really have
been married a long time, from a low of seventeen years to a high of
forty, with most well past the thirty-year mark.

How did they do it? That's what I wanted to find out. The
answers they give are varied, but there are a number of words that
keep cropping up: love, of course, but also friendship, patience,
understanding, tolerance, hard work, comfort, fulfillment. They are
common words, and ones you might expect to hear. But each couple,

1

each person, gives those words a slightly different spin, special meanings that jump out at you in the context of each relationship. What's more, those words can hold different meanings for a couple at different stages of their marriage.

A good marriage evolves. It doesn't reach a certain point of balance and hold that position. Change is always taking place, in circumstances, in perceptions, in feelings. Some things do get settled in a long-term marriage, but others do not, and they create a tension, often a healthy one, that is part of a never-ending dialogue. There are always new issues, too; some of them can be settled according to agreed-upon approaches, but many others require the couple to improvise, to seek out new solutions. Thus the finish line is never completely known in any marriage. The starting line, however, is clearly marked.

And so, always, the question: What did you expect from marriage?

One husband answers, "A good companion, a good sex life, a lot of fun."

"Same thing," says his wife. "I was brought up believing that was what life was—marriage, children, home."

"And it turned out boring, no sex, no fun," concludes the husband, laughing.

This is Mel and Maxine Rosenblum talking. They've been married thirty-four years, have two sons, a daughter, and two grand-children. After retiring from the New York Police Department, Mel bought a gas station, then changed to a taxi business, and is now in trucking. They live on Long Island in New York, and you could call them an average couple—except that that always misses the point. Average is a dull, statistical word, and every couple is different, every marriage compounded of the quirky individuality of two human beings trying to make one life together.

No matter how long they've been married, couples vividly remember the beginnings. How they met, what they thought about one another. They may have grown up together, met at college or at a party, worked together, or even stumbled across one another by accident. But the memory of it is always sharp.

"I was attracted to Maxine before I was introduced to her," Mel says. "I used to see her in a restaurant, but she wouldn't talk to me.

She was quiet and shy, and I think she thought I was maybe not for her—that I was of a different faith."

"I did think that," Maxine admits, "but it really didn't have anything to do with it. He tried to pick me up a couple of times, but I ignored him."

"I said, 'Hello, smiley,' because she never smiled."

"He was being cute. Finally a friend introduced us. We went to Coney Island and right away we knew we were for each other."

Right away we knew. In this book you will meet a lot of couples who felt that way. But you will also find couples who circled one another warily, couples who became friends long before there was any real romantic interest, and even the occasional couple who initially couldn't stand one another. Knowing right away is nice, and fun to be able to say twenty or thirty years later, but it isn't in itself any prescription for a good marriage. A great many divorced couples have also felt an instant rapport, only to find it turn sour over the passing years.

Even in good, long-lasting marriages, people have gone through the same kinds of problems that break other marriages up. Mel and Maxine admit that they argue. "Ninety percent of the time, it's my fault," Mel says. "We both know it, but she puts up with it."

"He's moody. And short-tempered."

"We argue about stupid little things. But she can holler and scream and then the next minute ask if I want something. And I can do the same thing."

"There were times I thought about divorce. Not because I hated him, but because he was so stubborn, I thought he'd never change. But I never followed through on those feelings. I might've wondered how my life would be different if I'd married someone else. But only when I was angry."

Maxine has said something important here. *Not because I hated him.* There are couples I interviewed who say they argue very little. But there are many who do not hesitate to "holler and scream." There are even those who think that's important, a sign of caring. But what couples in good marriages do not come to is hating one another. Some have come close to that line during certain traumatic periods, but they have never crossed it. They'd be in a book about divorce if they had.

For Mel and Maxine, some of the arguments were about his work. She tried to discourage him from joining the police. "But at the time I was very young, and I didn't discourage too much. He was very happy doing that. You have to be a certain kind of lady to live with a cop. I was always concerned—worried—until he came home. But you get used to it."

Then she remembered an incident. "The first time he came home with a revolver, it was loaded, and he cocked it. I was beside myself."

"I didn't know what to do. I said I'd fire it into the mattress, and she went screaming into the bathroom. 'Don't you dare. Don't you dare.'"

They both laugh. People who have been married a long time love to tell stories on each other, and even themselves. "Years ago," says Mel, "I was saving money for a surprise for Maxine. I went to the bathroom to count it, but she said she had to come in. So I hid it under the dress of a knitted doll that covered an extra roll of toilet paper. Then I forgot about it. Around a week later, Maxine called me at work. She said she was running the tub and fifty-dollar bills were coming out of the drain. My daughter, Leslie, was screaming and using the plunger, trying to get more. I asked how much they had and Maxine said four hundred and fifty. I said, 'Put the plunger down. You've got it all.'"

And it's Maxine's turn. "Mel got drunk at a New Year's Eve party when we first married. We were walking home in a snowstorm, and he said . . ."

"'Do you love me?'"

"I was angry at him for getting drunk and wouldn't reply. He said, 'If you don't say you love me, I'll . . .'"

"'Stick my head in the snow.'"

"And he did. He kept throwing himself into a snowbank . . ."

"She finally said she loved me, and I dried up."

This last has been bantered back and forth like a vaudeville routine. It seems a kind of celebration of survival.

Maxine and Mel are proud to have gotten through so many years. And they are proud of their kids, pleased with the way they turned out. But they don't pat themselves on the back too much. "A lot was luck," says Maxine. "I don't know. Hopefully, besides luck, it was because of what we did. We didn't specifically say, 'Do this, do that.' Just being in the house, listening to our conversations and the talks we had around the dinner table, they sort of got a picture of the way we saw things."

"We were lucky. We never told them to work hard or be honest. We told them when we didn't like something or we got disgusted with something. I think they just picked things up from watching us. If they didn't do their homework, they went to school the next day and had to take responsibility for it."

"We were strict in ways like that, but we were affectionate. If the kids were bad, they knew they might get hit. But ten minutes later, Mel was right up there giving them a kiss and a hug. I did the same thing."

"I thing it was important that Maxine was in the house when the children came home from school."

"Our kids grew up at a time when there were a lot of problems, like drugs. Mel was in the narcotics division then, and a lot of people we knew called him and said, 'What should we do with this kid?' I know a lot of people whose kids went astray because the parents had no time for them."

"I may be changing my opinion about women working while raising families. I didn't want that; I'd rather have taken two jobs. But now it's a necessity for a lot of people. But I think it's hard on the kids."

You will meet other people in this book who had good marriages, but problem kids. Perhaps the Rosenblums were just "lucky." But it seems more likely that they always had a special feeling about children, and that they communicated it to their children. For Mel and Maxine, kids were the center of their marriage. "Without them, our lives wouldn't have been full," says Mel. "It'd be dull. We might have gone more places and done more things, but we wouldn't have enjoyed our lives. We enjoyed our children. We always did things with our children and they always wanted to do things with us. For us, marriage meant children."

Now there are grandchildren, and they love that. Maxine takes care of them sometimes, as her mother and Mel's mother did of her children years ago. "But I don't want to have them on a full-time basis," Maxine says. "I did my job and I have my life now. Take care of them? Absolutely. If my daughter wants to go on vacation, I'm more than happy to watch them. But I wouldn't want her to go to work with me watching the children. It was the same with our parents. None of them wanted to take care of the children on a full-time basis. But they'd be more than happy to watch them for a week."

And so in a way it is full circle. But the Rosenblums still have a life of their own to lead, including an ongoing sex life. "Recently," Mel says, "we had sex at two o'clock on a Sunday afternoon. My son, Michael, called and interrupted us. He said he was glad that I was still sexually active at my age. Young people still think you're over the hill at fifty, I guess. But I'm not even near the hill."

"Sex isn't like it was when we first got married, but it's sustained with love and romance."

"It's not a bell ringer every time. But it's great."

"I just feel very comfortable with Mel. I feel that he's good in any kind of situation. I was quite upset when he gave up his gas station to go into the taxi business, and it affected me physically. I don't like rocking the boat too much. But it keeps it interesting. Mel's never afraid to do anything, go anywhere. And, I've trusted him implicitly our whole married life. I never put my foot down. We don't have the kind of marriage where I could say, 'You cannot do this.' And he couldn't say that to me."

"Maxine's a good wife and mother, a good cook, a good house-keeper. And she's very devoted. Maxine took care of my mother before she died, and she was so gentle with her. Even when my mother wasn't ill, she made her feel that she wasn't alone. She called her every single day, and I'll always appreciate it."

"For our twenty-fifth anniversary, he got me a gold medal, because he said I deserved a medal for living with him. The medal had the words *Thanks* in diamonds. Even now he gets moody and people don't know how I stand it. But I know the better side of him."

"That's it," says Mel. "I want a divorce. But I don't have time; I have to go play ball."

BILL SANFORD: Our marriage was successful because it just had to be. In our day there was no such word as divorce. It just wasn't in our vocabulary forty years ago. You took your marriage vows and you stood by them. If kids nowadays understood that you have to work at marriage, learn to compromise, bend a little instead of jumping up and quitting before a relationship even has a chance to bloom, we wouldn't be having the divorce rate in this country that we have now.

MARYLOU SANFORD: Bill and I had our problems. There were rough spots, especially in the beginning. But he's right. We never considered divorce. I remember talking to my mother about some little fight Bill and I had—more than once. She usually took his side, and I knew I had to work things out because there was no going home to mother. I'm sure that if there had been something seriously wrong she might have been more sympathetic. But that wasn't the case, and she was right.

Ginny and Roy Nevans of Cleveland, married for twenty-four years, met at a party on New Year's Eve and were married on New Year's Eve two years later. "Neither of us had been particularly interested in marriage, though all our friends were doing it and Ginny's family was putting a little pressure on her."

"We began a sexual relationship," says Ginny. "On my part that was a tremendous guilt trip. There was a certain feeling that because I did have sex with him that I should marry him."

But they also had strong mutual interests. "Ginny knew sports, which was very important. I was a New York kid who lived around Madison Square Garden, Ebbets Field, and the Polo Grounds. And Ginny also loved to go out. We both loved the theater and doing all those New York things."

Roy's family had been involved in the theater, and his love of show business has led him to produce both Broadway shows and some television. But that is an avocation. Primarily he is an executive in the food business. As part of his work he's away from home at least two weeks out of every month. "I recently went around the world, and it's not unusual for me to do that. Since the children were born, Ginny hasn't been able to travel with me very much."

While many husbands and wives travel a great deal these days in the course of their jobs, it is more usual for the separations to be only a few days at a time, not whole weeks or more. It makes for a different sort of marriage.

"When Roy is away, I'm running my own household and my own

show. The problem is that when Roy comes home there's a transference of authority. He feels then that he has to be head of the household, especially when it comes to the children. It's very difficult. The kids will start to ask me something, and then they'll remember that they have to ask Roy if he's home that week. Of course, all the confusion can be funny, too."

Roy smiles, but doesn't deal directly with this issue. "I do more with Ginny and the kids than a lot of people who are home all the time," he says. "Because I'm away so much, when I'm home I really take the time to be with them."

"We do things with the children then, yes, but they're the superficial fun things. When he comes home, the kids are ready to go, go, go, and Mommy's the bad guy if I bring things like homework."

They both agree, however, that there are advantages, too. "We can eat TV dinners when Roy's away," Ginny says without apology, "and if the house is a mess, it doesn't matter that much, either. We have much more freedom of movement to do what we want on the spur of the moment. When Roy comes home it's more organized. He gets a chart, and in two weeks we've got to do this and this and talk to that one and fix the roof."

"I'd find it hard to live with a regular routine like my neighbors do," Roy says. "I have an apartment in London, and if I want to leave anything lying on the floor and bring in take-out food, or go out and get drunk, I can. Here, I find it difficult to do what I'm supposed to sometimes. I don't know if I could live with a normal type of lifestyle."

Inevitable tensions grow out of the Nevanses' lifestyle, but the one that you might expect to be the most potentially troublesome, infidelity, appears to cause them no concern. By mutual consent, they ignore the issue. "Our neighbors worry about it more than we do," says Ginny. "We haven't discussed it, and I've always felt that if something happened, it happened. It wouldn't have anything to do with me particularly. I still have a great belief that what would be most threatening is intimate conversation rather than intimate sex. We're both too busy to really think about these things."

"I agree with Ginny. I don't think it would really affect me. The marriage is too solid."

"I think people who worry too much about these things get in more trouble than they anticipate—they build it up into something that didn't exist. Many sexual encounters today are very casual."

And in terms of sexuality, separation again brings a bonus. "After twenty years," Roy says, "there's no way it's going to be like the honeymoon, but I certainly come home with much more interest in my wife's sexuality than I would if I were here all the time. I'm always very glad to see her."

There is another way, Roy feels, in which their lifestyle keeps the marriage fresh. "I see too many people who have nothing to say to each other. We have too much to say and not enough time. I'm making a movie now, and I discuss everything with Ginny and bounce everything off her. She's also been very helpful in my food business. Of all the partners I have, I'm the only one whose wife is involved, and my partners hold her in very high regard. She comes across very well with people."

Ginny Nevans is clearly something more than "the little woman back home." She has not had a career of her own, but she has participated in her husband's career in a variety of ways, and has his respect for the value of her contributions. Ginny, in fact, is considering doing something on her own. "I've been talking with some women about opening a shop together. We could trade off time and I'd be free to travel as the children are more on their own or off to college."

"I'd be happy to finance it," Roy says. "I'd prefer that she travel with me, but I'd support whatever she wants to do."

Ginny feels that the main thing they both lose out on because of the way they live is their relationships with friends. "We can't see them on a regular basis. Everything's slotted into a calendar and arranged. We have no time for impulse things. But I think if Roy had to do it any other way, he'd be impossible to live with."

Roy nods in agreement. "I think I'd be a very poor husband in a traditional marriage. I have this great wanderlust. If I were tied to a nine-to-five job, commuting, I'd go up the wall. I'm very lucky that I'm married to someone who can live the life that I live."

Over the last two decades of their twenty-five-year marriage, Marcella and Marvin Mitchelson have spent even more time apart than the Nevanses. It works for them, too, in a different way. She is in her late forties, he in his late fifties. Marvin has established himself as the premier Hollywood divorce lawyer, and has been involved in many headline cases, particularly since he pioneered the concept of palimony.

When they met on Capri, where Marcella was playing a small part in the Sophia Loren/Clark Gable film, *It Started in Naples*, she barely spoke English and he didn't speak Italian. Marvin was on vacation, came on the set, and asked to be introduced to her. Since the English and Italian weren't working, Marcella says, "We tried Spanish, and he asked me to meet him for lunch the next day. Everyone meets in the square in Capri, and he told me a time, but I didn't pay any attention to him and did not go. The next day I was in the square at a different time and he ran after me, calling me 'Señorita.' I apologized for not keeping the other appointment—I really hadn't expected him to be there—and we had lunch. He wanted to go shopping and insisted I try on some clothes in a boutique. While I was trying them on, he had already paid for them. I said no, I didn't want them. I didn't want to be obligated. I think that is why he began to take me seriously. He sometimes says, jokingly, 'I wish you had taken those clothes.'"

Marvin proposed the next day, bringing a half-carat diamond ring. "Gable's wife had to interpret the proposal. I said no. He went back to the States and then returned a month later and said that in three months he would send me a ticket to come see the States. I arrived in New York and he met me with a two-and-a-half-carat ring. We came to Los Angeles for his work, and I took an apartment on the same street as his. We both went to Berlitz to learn each other's languages and were married a year later."

Marcella and Marvin had a son and first led a fairly quiet life, although Marcella even then was studying painting and dance. Now they are a major part of her life. When Marvin won a two-million-dollar settlement for Pamela Mason four years later, he was on his way to great success, and their lives changed. "He was always traveling, and his social life became all business. So we each have our own friends. It is important for a woman who is married to a successful man to make her own life. I have to have my own friends and interests. If he is here, that's better, but if he is not, I have to know I have some kind of life. Marriage is an attitude, and too many of my friends just try to please their husbands, and that makes them unhappy and frustrated."

Marcella says that she never really wanted a career as an actress. "I have my painting. It's me. It comes from within myself and it gives me a great deal of satisfaction. I have had a few shows in the States and in Rome. And I also have my Greek dancing, which helps me stay in very good shape."

Marvin very much approves of his wife's separate interests. "She had to adjust to my being away so much, but she has turned out to be someone with strong individual interests, and if she had married a more typical man, who needed a lot of attention, she would not have had the opportunity she has for self-expression." Marvin feels that the most significant element in most divorces is boredom—far more than adultery. "Marcella never bores me. She is a vital, alive woman, and she gets me going when I'm home. When the romance winds down, after a couple of years of marriage, then couples must cultivate their marriage like gardens—one day at a time. That is hard to maintain. In our case, I think the separations help. They have allowed Marcella to become more interesting to herself and to me. Although some of our friends may talk about our relationship in a disparaging way, we feel this works best for us."

Marcella agrees. "I want to be married, yet I am a very independent woman, and being married to Marvin allows me to develop parts of myself that I might not be able to in a more confined structure. When I get upset with him, I tell him to go, but he won't leave. I tell him I'm prepared to be without him because I'm alone so much. Actually that is true—more women should be prepared, because you never really know what will happen. So many women are just lost when their husbands are not around, they just don't know what to do with themselves. Life for two people is hard, I think. It is always difficult to live with another person. Marvin is very easy to live with. It is easy to stay married to Marvin—as long as I am in his bed when he is home, he is okay."

While Marcella is out of the room briefly, Marvin talks about how much she means to him. "I need to be married," he says. "I need to know I have a truly understanding friend—Marcella is that to me. She knows me much better than anyone else and accepts me. I travel so much, I need to have a home and a home life. I like being a parent and I have a good relationship with our son. Marcella has been a good mother as well as a good wife. She has stuck by me during all the difficult times. She has a deep sense of loyalty. She is lively and interested in many things. I like her looks and still find her very attractive in miniskirts—she takes good care of herself, and I appreciate that."

What wife wouldn't be happy to hear herself talked about in such glowing terms! But Marcella doesn't have to be there to hear it; she knows how he feels.

Marilyn and Monty Hall both came from poor families, but at the time they met, Marilyn was doing better than he was, working as a teenage radio actress. Her mother wanted her to marry a rich man and was always putting Monty down. "But," she says, "I loved him and I knew he'd make it." The beginning was tough economically, however. They had two children before Monty began to be successful, and he was constantly having to go away to try to find work. "Marilyn had to be both mother and father," Monty admits.

But when success did come with Monty's show *Let's Make A Deal*, another price had to be paid. Superficial as a game show may seem, it involves very hard work and very long hours. He was usually unable to get home until ten o'clock at night.

"The key was," Monty says, "that I did come home at ten o'clock. And there was always a hot dinner waiting, and Marilyn sitting there for me."

"When Monty came home, he went through a decompression period. I had people over for coffee and dessert, but things were tough."

Marilyn made the decision to keep herself busy in creative ways. "I was writing a cookbook, a children's book. I wrote *Love American Style*, a special for Monty. Then I went back to UCLA for my master's in fine arts."

"She did two award-winning documentaries. She wasn't just waiting around for me. One night we were being grabbed by photographers who physically separated Marilyn from me. Later, she told me in no uncertain terms that she wasn't an appendage, but her own person. I respected that, but it was a problem for me when she went for her master's degree and dinner wasn't on the table every night at ten."

"Also when I was working on a picture. I remember coming home one night at nine and Monty and my daughter and the housekeeper—whom I hadn't told what to prepare—were all angry. They couldn't figure out what to do."

"She gave us all a lecture in self-sufficiency."

After Marilyn had started her own career, she and Monty had a surprise. "Twelve years after my second child was born, a miracle happened. I had a baby, even though I'd been told I couldn't. So I was also very involved in the baby. I called her my magnificent bondage."

But the career continued, and Monty wasn't always pleased with what that meant. "I wasn't too happy when she went to Israel to do *A Woman Called Golda.* After nine weeks, I went to visit her for five days. I flew across the world and didn't even get to see her really. She got up at six A.M. and said, 'Want to take a plunge in the Mediterranean? That's your only chance to see me.'"

Yet, after thirty-five years of marriage, despite the tensions caused by career conflicts, they remain close in ways that many couples are unable to sustain. Sex is as important as it ever was. "All the emotions are there," Monty says. "She's still my best friend. She's still my girlfriend, and I'm her lover. No matter how tired we are, we do hold each other while we sleep."

"We have electric beds," Marilyn notes with a wry smile, "and they're separated. I lie in the crack."

"She comes over to my side and sleeps half there and half in the crack. That's devotion."

A lot of women would agree that in the end it is usually up to them to make the extra gesture—lying in the crack—that keeps things running smoothly. But you won't encounter any women in this book who are patsies. Even those few who let their husbands lead the way are what might be called "willing conspirators." And there are many more who made the marriage work in the long run by drawing a line when the time came, insisting that they had to be a partner in making the rules.

The marriage of David and Debbie Black, for example, involves an ongoing struggle for individual fulfillment that often causes trouble for couples of the "baby-boom" generation. Married for seventeen years, David is an author and Debbie is a teacher. Their story begins in a way inconceivable to couples of earlier generations.

It was the very end of the 1960s. An MIT engineering student developed a computer dating service for use by East Coast college students. It was through the service that David and Deborah, children of their times, first met while he was a student at Amherst and she at Smith.

"The main preoccupation," Debbie Black explains, "was finding boyfriends and dates. Using the service was a reaction to mixers. They were horrible."

"She was first on my list, and after we met that was it. I was completely snowed. I had a big beard, which I'd been growing for three years, and when I got back to the dorm I told my roommate I was in love, and then I looked in the mirror and saw part of the hot fudge sundae Debbie and I had had clotted in my beard. So I hacked it off and showed up clean-shaven the next day. We went to see a Gilbert and Sullivan show. She was the first person I'd met at school who knew anything about their work. And when we went to a French restaurant, she ordered in French. I was a goner."

"He was very intense and very impressive, and I was very sorry that he shaved off his beard. But I felt very self-conscious because of his intensity."

"Horniness. All I wanted was to read her my latest novel and get her into bed. Yes, in that order. I wanted her full attention while reading to her. If I had to make a choice, it was reading to her."

"I was just uncomfortable. I was still a virgin, and though I hadn't really been conscious of it, I was not ready for any kind of sexual experience. I didn't want to see him, and I started avoiding him—even though he was bribing me with great theater tickets. After a while I changed shcools and started dating someone else."

"She went to a black college."

"I couldn't stand Smith. That incredible preppie attitude. I felt useless. It was the 1960s. I wanted to be part of the civil rights movement. There were a few other white students at the black college, too."

It was more than two years before David and Debbie got

together again. A girl David had been living with walked out on him. He knew Debbie was in town and called her.

"This time," Debbie says, "we got sexually involved right away. I was no longer a virgin, but I still felt you should be serious about sex, and my assumption was that this was true love. So we began living together. I was cooking and he was writing. We wanted to travel once I graduated, so we decided it would be easier if we were married. That's what we told ourselves to propel us into the marriage, which we were not prepared for. All he knew was how to type."

"Not type. Write!"

Debbie ignores this, saying, "I was open to an untraditional marriage where I would support the family."

"The marriage had really taken place before we actually married."

"We felt bonded to each other. We used to sign our name as David Deborah."

"So we had a wedding. I was dressed as Tolstoy and Debbie wore her grandmother's dress. We wrote our own marriage vows. It wasn't anything like the traditional service. We traveled across the country with a couple of hippies. Took a trip on the Queen Elizabeth with a steamer trunk filled with books. We are both heavy readers and we love to read to each other. It is part of family life, part of lovemaking. We were in our hippie phase when we returned. Lived in the East Village, and in the summer communally with friends in the country. Debbie was absolutely supportive; she never asked me to do a job while I was writing. She was a social worker. Worked at the Bank Street School for a few years and then she started teaching, and about that time my income started matching and then surpassing hers. So I was finally supporting us."

"I thought I was pretty hot stuff—supporting him and also doing everything around the house. He was pampered from head to toe."

Although David says that he had once thought they would lead a Bohemian life forever, money and possessions became more important as his success grew. They had a daughter, and for the first three years after her birth, Debbie stayed home. But she is now back teaching. And that has raised some new issues.

"My fantasy has always been that I would spend ten hours a day writing, with my family around for emotional support. For a long time that's how it was. but with our child and Debbie working again, that has changed."

"Aside from my own needs, one of the reasons I am working now is to take the total responsibility from David's shoulders."

"I know that I can always make a living from my writing. I haven't taken a vacation in twelve years. But I have a three-book contract set at this time. We just bought a home in the country and for the first time I have started taking a month off in the summer."

"Maybe he will even start to take a couple of weeks at a time so we can travel—enjoy the warmer climates in the winter—have experiences with our daughter. My main indulgence is getting all the therapy I can. I've always gone—I go twice a week now. Next year my income will increase about four thousand dollars. Teaching is not only for a second income, it is for my future growth."

"I really think Debbie should be doing what she wants, but I definitely miss and regret the fact that she doesn't read my work as she used to. My fantasy is Sonja Tolstoy writing every word in longhand."

"I don't have the time I used to, with the teaching and our daughter to look after, and, yes, I am more into myself. I give David credit. He has really come a long way. He is trying to change very much."

"And I love Debbie more and more all the time. She is really more of a person this way."

"We are both developing. That is what makes it so interesting and profound to be a part of someone else's life, and actually know we do help each other. That is what keeps us together and makes it so worthwhile."

"I want her to fulfill her potential within the marriage, and I often feel guilty because I am louder—take up more emotional space."

"You are a great adversary. It helps to make me stronger."

David smiles. "Emotional isometrics or marital isometrics. You push against each other and get stronger."

Emotional isometrics, pushing against one another and getting stronger, is fine when both partners are strong to begin with. But in some marriages it is necessary for one partner to acquire new strength, or for the other partner to develop new insight, or for both things to happen, if the union is to survive.

Television star Bob Newhart, fifty-six, and his wife Ginny, forty-five, have been married twenty-four years and have four children. Bob was an accountant before becoming a comedian, and Ginny worked briefly as an actress.

"I met Bob when I was twenty, and we married two years later. Until he was twenty-nine, Bob had really been struggling—living at home—and didn't have much time for dating. I'd been dating Buddy Hackett's agent, but Buddy didn't quite approve. He told me about a nice Catholic boy he knew, never married, a young comic. I met Bob at Buddy's and we had a great time."

"I thought Ginny was very nice, very comfortable. We laughed together, but it wasn't love at first sight for either of us."

"He called and asked me to a party, but I had a date with this other person. I saw Bob from time to time, but we'd usually just go to see his show or something. But he was always there for me. I could call him at three in the morning, hysterical over something, and he'd listen. I liked his stability. Then it all came to a head on Bob's birthday. He was playing golf with Bing Crosby's son Phil. Bob said he was going to this party with his girl, Ginny Flynn, and Phil said that couldn't be, because she was going with his agent."

"When I found that out I realized that I cared for Ginny a lot more than I thought I did. All those emotional things that scared the hell out of me surfaced. I was afraid that we wouldn't be together, and it was then that she first saw my emotional side."

"I went to his house that day with his gift, and he was just horrible. He said he wouldn't share—that I had to stop seeing this other man or he wouldn't see me anymore. I was devastated, and I'd never seen him so upset. I left him and went to a gas station and called this other man. I was hysterical and in no condition to drive. But he was in a meeting and didn't want to drop everything to pick me up. I realized that if I married him I'd probably come second the rest of my life. Bob called the next day to make sure I wasn't going to be at a party where Hackett was fixing him up with a girl. I told him I wasn't sure how I felt about him, but I was breaking up with the other person. The next day, Bob and I were engaged."

"That sounds sudden, but in the back of my mind I knew it was going to happen," Bob says. "I just hadn't found the right time or place to say anything. I think finding out about the other man speeded up the process. I was ready for marriage, and I knew Ginny was the kind of woman I wanted to marry."

Despite their mutual show-business backgrounds, Ginny was a virgin and lived at home until the day she married. "I think my being a virgin was important to him. The very beginning of our marriage was fun and romantic. But it was a big adjustment, and we had some fights. I had a baby right away and Bob was on the road a lot. I was also Bob's secretary and valet and the wife of a celebrity. I was immature and Bob was a little bit, too. I had to learn to run a home. But we really had a partnership. I listened to all his routines and made suggestions. I was a part of it all."

"I trusted her judgment," Bob says. "She was going to know me warts and all, my frailties and strengths and weaknesses. She's been right a lot."

"But after Bob started his first television show, our life together was kaput. He had that life out there and I had no input. I felt discarded. At that time, Bob was a very private person and he didn't always let me in on things. After our third child was born I got very depressed. I had a breakdown, really, and rarely left the house. I did what I had to do as far as the children went, but that's all. Finally, I started in therapy and they put me on medication, but it took three years to get better. At first Bob didn't understand it and we didn't discuss it with anyone. One day, Don Rickles came over and said I looked like I'd been hit by a truck. I started screaming at him. He said, 'God Almighty, that's what I do for a living—I insult people.' Anything would trigger me off. We laugh at it now."

"It was a strange, difficult time. But I don't think you leave because things are a little rough."

"At one point my therapist told me to leave Bob, and Bob did leave for a week or two. The advice was wrong. Bob didn't really know what to do. But eventually he began to understand what I was going through—like the feelings I had when we'd go out and people would shove me aside to get to Bob."

"I was able to open up more and give her what she needed emotionally. We both changed as a result of this period. I loved her and I felt for her. I was far less sensitive before. Looking back, I don't really know why she married me. I was a jerk, though I thought I was wonderful at the time."

"Bob did become much more sensitive to my feelings. I hadn't had friends to share what I was going through. Bob's friends were older and their wives couldn't relate to what I was feeling. Then we started making mutual friends like the Rickleses. His best friends are my best friends, and we both have the same interests, like travel. We never get bored when we're together. His observations are always amusing, and he's bright. I'd vote for him if he ran for President. And since he's become more confident in his work and in himself, he's become even more terrific. We can express our feelings toward each other."

"We get along so well because our values are the same, but we're different. She does things that I could never do, and I do things that she could never do. Being a comedian is a form of Russian roulette every time you go on stage. Maybe that's why we do it. I think comics require a very special understanding of what they do from their wives. So, in a funny way, the stability that she wanted from me, I get from her. She's always there saying, 'Don't get too impressed with yourself.'"

"Bob knows that I know what's right for him professionally. He knows I'm one of the few people who'll tell him if something's horrible. I do the business now. With the new television show, I read the script and watch them rehearse and we discuss what works and what doesn't."

Ginny's involvement in Bob's professional life is unusual for a star's wife, but it is very much by mutual consent. When he goes on the road to make appearances in Las Vegas or elsewhere, Ginny goes with him. She's fully aware that a lot of women are likely to come on to him. But he clearly doesn't object to her being there. "I remember calling her from Las Vegas once when she wasn't there. I said, 'You'd better get up here. I'm a strong man, but I'm not that strong.' And she came the next day."

Ginny says that Bob is very much the nice guy he appears to be on television. "He does dumb things sometimes. His driving is terrible. He doesn't know what he's doing in the morning and moves around very slowly. I have lots of nervous energy, so he sometimes irritates me, but we haven't really argued in a long time. We pretty much agree on things. We used to have problems when Bob didn't want to be involved in child-rearing, but much later on he realized that he'd been wrong. Now he's a very involved parent."

"We've worked at it, but sometimes we have to get away alone. When the kids ask why, we say, 'Because we want to.' That's preparing them for their own lives if they have children. It doesn't mean we don't love them."

Bob has little use for people who have their priorities wrong. "There are men who have everything—money, cars, beautiful homes, but they think they're not happy. That's because their priorities were cars, homes, money. And when they got them, there was still something missing. The wives get the blame. I have the feeling that Ginny and I have walked through a mine field, and we've arrived at twenty-three years because we went through all that crazy period—sexual revolution, open marriage, all that stuff—and survived."

"Our own sex life has gotten better because we're more comfortable. I used to be pretty naive, and now I'm not. Now there is an ease. You don't think about things—it just happens. I don't just mean sex. Whatever it is, it's spontaneous. We had children so quickly that we really didn't get to know each other. Now we have more time for each other, busy as we are. We're more sensitive to each other's needs. Sexually, as in other areas, we can talk so much more openly."

"It may sound corny," says Bob, "but we were very lucky to find each other."

"At the start we were friends. I loved him, but it wasn't like bells going off. But there was something special about Bob. Suzanne Pleshette told me that he just wears well. I must've had that feeling all along. I wouldn't trade my life, my age, for anybody's in the whole world."

Some people seem almost destined to marry—or at least feel that way about it. John and Diane Stratta are the same age, both in their mid-forties, and have also been married for twenty-four years.

MARILYN: I understand you've known each other since childhood.

JOHN: We were supposedly thrown in bed together at three months of age. Our mothers were friends.

DIANE: We lived in the same area. Our backgrounds were very similar and we were together a lot as children. When I was ten, my family moved to Los Angeles and I grew up there. But the families were always in touch, and I saw John again during high school on a trip back east.

JOHN: Looking back, it seems as if the closeness has always been there. Even when we were separated all those years, we were always aware of each other.

DIANE: I just knew I would end up being married to John. I dated lots of men, but I had this inner feeling about him. We had the kind of friendship where we had a ball together. It wasn't romance as such, though, until I came back to New York to work after college.

MARILYN: How did the romance get started?

JOHN: One day I realized she was very good-looking. I saw her differently.

MARILYN: Did you have a sexual relationship before marriage?

JOHN: Not really. Not in those days, from our kinds of families.

MARILYN: Did you discuss your roles before marriage?

DIANE: Yes, he even said, "Oh, you'll be just like my mother. You'll always want to work."

JOHN: I tend to be withdrawn, and Diane is very expressive. I always admired that, and she was happiest doing something on her own. I wanted her to be whatever she wanted to be. She had modeled, designed clothes, worked on TV production. I knew she needed to be involved in something.

MARILYN: When you married, who was earning the major income?

DIANE: I was. John was still in dental school. I was teaching adult education. Believe it or not, in 1954 I was being paid fifteen dollars per hour. John worked weekends and we were able to manage.

MARILYN: As a married couple, what was different for you than all those years of friendship?

JOHN: The closeness we felt was enormous.

DIANE: As much as I felt I should visit my parents after we married, I could not leave John, even for a short time.

MARILYN: Were you worried about leaving him alone?

DIANE: No, it wasn't that. It was just the loss of not being with him.

JOHN: I experience the same feeling if I have to go away. To this day I drag her along.

MARILYN: Is it a severe mutual dependency?

JOHN AND DIANE (simultaneously): No, no.

JOHN: We are both independent types. It is just a true friendship. We can discuss anything about anything. Most of the time we agree. We have so many of the same thoughts.

DIANE: As soon as something happens, whether it is good or bad, I have to tell him immediately. Sometimes I drive him crazy, but I would never think to call a woman friend or anyone else.

MARILYN: No real arguments?

JOHN: We seldom fight. When we fight it is all hell let loose, but it lasts a short time. A lot of screaming. I have a mother who is the epitome of being able to put in the knife and twist it, and if I let it, all that conditioning comes out. I can be real mean. She throws things.

MARILYN: Will you be mean enough to force Diane to do things she does not want to do?

DIANE: No, he will never do that. His cruelty is momentary, and I know he is not a cruel person. I am not frightened. We both bend when we feel the other person truly wants it that way.

MARILYN: How about money?

DIANE: There has never been any talk about money, other than his telling me I am too cheap about myself and should buy more just for me. He is very generous.

MARILYN: How has having a child fitted in?

JOHN: Susanne was an accident. We were planning to wait a lot longer. But after Susanne we tried for years to have another child and could not.

MARILYN: When two people are so close, is a child an intrusion?

JOHN: She was not. She just fit in, but I always wondered if because we are as close as we are she felt as if she was intruding. She was always part of the triangle.

MARILYN: When two people are so close, is a child an intrusion?

DIANE: Not when Susanne was young, but after that in and out of various jobs—teaching, home economist, now as a Mary Kay representative. I also went back to get my master's degree.

JOHN: She would have been wonderful on stage. She has such

style, such vitality. The kids loved her, and she loved what she was doing. That's one of the main areas of appeal for me, because I tend to confine myself to my four little walls. She is my contact with the outside world, without my having to be there.

MARILYN: Why do you think that after more than twenty years the pull to each other is still so strong? So few people have that.

DIANE: We have grown together, but we have not outgrown each other.

Growing together has also been a strong element in the marriage of Zoila and Juan Fernandez, who have been married for thirty-one years. They have lived in New York City for all but the first two years of their married life, but both were born in Cuba. Zoila works as a sample maker for Calvin Klein Jeans, while Juan has been employed as a general helper at a bank in recent years. Zoila begins their story.

"When I left my hometown, my desire was to be independent and on my own. I had no family in Havana and had to fend for myself. I've been working ever since I can remember. I met Juan at work. I worked at a dry cleaning store, and he worked at a grocery store right across the street. It was love at first sight. Even though I was just seventeen years old, alone in the big city, he never took advantage of my innocence. He admits that he wanted to."

"She looked so sweet and innocent. I knew she was alone. I wanted to help her out. We would sneak out at lunch and talk. I would walk her home after work. We both love to dance, and whenever there was a party, I would invite her."

At the time, Juan's stepfather had recently died, and he was head of the family. Although his mother resented Zoila, two years later they were married. They did not even consider moving in with his mother. "I know trouble when I see it," Juan exclaims. "I was young, not stupid."

"We moved into a small apartment near his family's house. He had to live up to his macho image, so he never did any housework. But that only lasted until we moved to New York two years later."

"When we came here in 1956, we only had each other. No relatives or friends. We didn't know the language. Moving was cultural shock. But that's when our marriage really started to come together."

"We had to learn together," says Zoila. "We made friends

together, everything. We were always together, except for work. I have never really had any desire to go out with the 'girls.' Our friends are other couples."

"I feel the same way," says Juan. "Zoila is everything to me. She knows what I'm thinking and feeling. I have a habit of calling her even when I go out shopping or to cut my hair. I think about her when I'm away. I miss her."

"I went to Cuba a couple of years ago to visit and it was hard for me. Even though I was so occupied with all my relatives, Juan was in my thoughts at all times. I was always talking about him. I wanted him to be there to share it all."

"The separation was harder for me," Juan says. "I had made a schedule of things I wanted to take care of around the house. But then, when I would come home after work and she wasn't there I began to get very depressed. Having dinner by yourself is not easy if you are used to having someone with you for so many years. After the first couple of days I just ate out."

"When Juan came to pick me up at the airport, we made such a scene. He stood by the gate, and as soon as I walked out we embraced one another. He gave me a passionate kiss. We both began to cry. It was quite a spectacle."

This degree of togetherness may have had an influence on their decision not to have children, although Juan gives other reasons. "We wanted children at the beginning of our marriage, but there were two reasons why we didn't. First, we were in a different country—we only had each other. In Cuba you always had relatives who would take care of children if you worked. The second reason was money. We couldn't afford for Zoila to be out of work to raise a child. Also, we didn't feel it was wise to bring a child into a situation that would be difficult for us to handle."

"To have children just for the satisfaction of having a child was not what we wanted. It's a lot of responsibility to bring up a child, and we felt it was not for us," Zoila says.

Satisfaction is a word that both Juan and Zoila use often in talking about their life together. They are still sexually very active because, as Zoila puts it, "Sex expresses how we feel about each other." In a very romantic gesture they were remarried in the church on their twenty-fifth wedding anniversary, renewing the civil vows they had originally taken. "We are both Catholic," Zoila notes, "but Juan had never been one to go to church. Little by little we have accepted it. Now we share going to church together."

But romantic as they are, Juan and Zoila are not naive. She puts it very directly. "You have to work at marriage. You have to feed it constantly. You can't take the other person for granted. You form a union out of love, and this love goes through stages. We never stop growing as human beings, and the marriage also grows. The outside world is very hard. In a marriage you give each other support, and that makes it easier. To sum it up, you have to be friends first."

Friends first. That is an oft-repeated theme in good marriages. Couples who *like* one another from the start frequently seem to have an edge in making the relationship work. Love seems to find a fertile ground in the soil of friendship; the plant may not bear flowers as exotic as those sown in passion, but the roots go deeper. Yet in that friendship garden, you may find some unexpected long-lasting blooms.

"We met at a party, found out that we had many common interests, and became instant friends. We didn't move in with each other until two years later, when we felt that we were ready to make a serious commitment. I think our relationship has endured for more than twenty years because we are two mature people who are flexible and who are able to understand and forgive each other's foibles."

The partners in this relationship are not legally married. In fact, they are homosexual. But aside from the legalities, Dave and Mario are as much "married" as any couple in this book. They came out of the closet before it was fashionable to do so, and have no qualms about people knowing what their relationship is. They own a comfortable house in a "straight" Hollywood neighborhood, and most of their friends are straight. Both are in their fifties, well educated, and successful in their careers.

Dave was born and raised in New York, the only child of an attorney and a college professor. His parents gave him a love of fine arts, music, ballet, and theater. They realized he was gay when he was a teenager and accepted that fact, but he has not been able to have a close relationship with them. He is now a CPA with a large auditing firm and travels extensively.

Mario was born and raised in the Napa Valley, one of four children. His parents didn't know he was gay until he was in his late twenties, and although initially mortified, came to see things differently over time. His brothers and sisters are all married with children, and the family as a whole accepts both Mario and Dave, who spend holidays and some vacations with them. Mario is a gourmet cook, a wine expert, an art collector, and travels with Dave whenever he can. He owns an art gallery in Los Angeles.

They have been faithful to one another since they started living together. "We are not interested in casual sex," says Dave. "We consider ourselves to be married and are faithful; you remember that old-fashioned concept. We do patronize restaurants and shops owned by our gay friends, but we definitely avoid pickup places. Actually, there are many gay people who establish long-term relationships. It's just that the unstable ones get more publicity, just like the divorce rate among straights."

It used to disturb Mario that his lifestyle was considered unnatural by many people, but not any more. "I went to a shrink, more to satisfy my family than anything else. I struggled with myself and felt guilty for having disappointed my parents, who are strict Catholics. But that was before I met Dave. Once I realized that loving him was as natural for me as my mother's love for my father, I left the guilt and the self-torture behind."

"People sometimes ask if we would have preferred to be straight. But that's an unfair question. I've spent the major part of my adult life with a person I know to be one of the kindest, gentlest, most loving people in the world. I can't imagine any woman giving me more love than I've been privileged to have from Mario. About five years into our relationship we decided to make it 'legal' in our way. We had a marriage ceremony, performed by a clergyman. Our closest friends were there, and Mario's family attended. That was very important to us. Like any straight couple, our feeling of commitment was much more intense after that."

Their only regret concerns children. "I love children," Dave says. "Mario's nieces come down to visit during the summer, and we have the best time. We look forward very much to seeing them. There are so many unloved, unwanted children in the world that someday maybe gay couples will be allowed to adopt them. I don't think we'll see that day in our lifetime, but I do think we'll see legal marriages for gays."

In fact, Dave does have a son, but one whose childhood he was unable to be a part of. Dave cites the story of what eventually happened as a prime example of how deeply Mario cares for him. "A few years before I met Mario, I tried to go straight. I met and married a girl in New York. She was young, pretty, sweet, but not very worldly. She became pregnant, but the marriage wasn't working. I confessed that I was a homosexual and she threw me out. She even got a restraining order forbidding me to see my son. I tried to fight it, but it was hopeless. Soon afterwards I moved to California. I tried to contact my son many times through the years, but she never so much as let me talk to him. I told Mario about it a few years ago. Without telling me why he was going, he flew to New York to see my ex-wife and son. I don't know how he managed to get through to her. My son thought I was dead—which is what she had told him. Two years ago, he came to Los Angeles and we met for the first time. It was awkward, but we are communicating. He's been out to see us several times, and I flew in to see him last month. Mario's family doesn't know about him yet, but we are to introduce him to everyone at Christmas. Without Mario, it would never have been possible."

Dave and Mario's relationship has flourished in a fundamentally disapproving society. They met that challenge simply by showing other people that they had as much right to care for one another in their way as anyone else does. By accepting themselves, they smoothed the way to acceptance by others.

But long-time relationships often require couples to accept circumstances that could not in any way be anticipated. Adversity can strike anyone, even the strongest or most talented, and when it does it presents challenges for a couple that test even the best of marriages.

Joe and Audrey Minerva have three children, three grand-children, and have been married for thirty-four years. Audrey has always been a housewife, while Joe was a New York City police officer for eighteen years. Then he contracted multiple sclerosis and has been in a wheelchair ever since.

What does that do to a marriage? For a lot of people it would lead to divorce, or at least serious consideration of it.

"Not for me," says Joe.

"Not that I considered divorce . . ." Audrey trails off.

"You considered leaving me."

"Yeah. But I couldn't imagine that being permanent."

"I see. You were just going out for the night." Joe can't repress a grin.

"Now I can look back and say, what a traumatic experience it must have been for a man who was so active. But I was going through a traumatic experience myself. Aside from the fact that he was in the wheelchair, I had just had a child and was coping with two teenagers. And he was very depressed. In my whole marriage that was the only low that was bad. He followed me around, telling me what to do and what not to do. 'See the fingerprints on that wall.' Little picky things that he would never have noticed before. I told him, 'I can take your illness without any qualms, but I can't take you.' It was a total reversal of his personality. Finally, I blew up and said, 'You have a problem, so what? A lot of people are worse off than you. You have to come to terms with this, or I can't live with you.' Thank God he came round to his normal charming self."

"It was tough. I was very bitter. At the beginning, there's all these syndromes—why me, what have I done to deserve this. You feel sorry for yourself. I was frightened. I wondered how in the world we'd survive. We had a thirteen-year-old, a sixteen-year-old, and a newborn. I was unable to work. You have to make a decision. Am I going to go on, or am I going to quit? I didn't want to quit. But I couldn't have made it without Audrey."

"I just said, 'Cut the crap.' And I found out there's humor in everything. Like, sometimes Joe's leg will go a little spastic, and I'll say to him, 'Oh, boy, let's get the castanets. We're doing our José Greco bit.' We all do it."

"I almost fell out of this chair one night watching Henny Youngman on Johnny Carson. He told this sick joke about a wheelchair. I laughed so hard. I repeat the story whenever I can. I find myself reassuring people who don't know me that I'm fine."

"We have very supportive friends and family. Our friends never treated him any differently. They didn't act like he was an egg that was going to break. If they wanted to tell him he was full of shit, they did. We have a very normal life."

"We pay out bills, we have food on the table. Earlier this week I said, 'I'm a very lucky person. I'm fifty-seven and with all the hunger in the world, I've never known a hungry day.' Nor has my family. I have good kids, good family, a nice house. We used to engage in more activities. That's the only change. But we have a social group that meets every month at all our homes, round robin. We go out to dinner, or friends visit. Audrey goes out a couple of nights a week with the girls. If the weather's good, I get out on my own every day for three or four hours, so she can get her act together."

"He has to have his hours to himself, and I do, too."

Has infidelity ever entered the picture? Audrey laughs. "I'd cut it off and there wouldn't be any more problems. For me, infidelity would be unthinkable. I have everything I want right here. I never felt that I lacked anything sexually."

"I think we revolted before the sexual revolution. We were never afraid to experiment and learn. What makes one person better than another person? I think that after people have been making love together for over thirty years, they really know how to satisfy one another."

Audrey does not feel that her life has been limited by not working. "I guess it's old school, but I have a career as a mother and housewife."

"Do you know how many hats she wears now? She's a mother, grandmother, a housewife, a cook, a nurse, a lover, a chauffeur. People can't appreciate what Audrey does for me. They see me sitting in this chair. It's almost three hours of constant care to get me here. A bed bath, lotion all over my body so the skin doesn't break down, exercising in bed. She's not a big person, but she lifts me off the bed, puts me in this chair. Then it's breakfast, getting me into the bathroom, back in the chair, then finally dressing me. That's why I go out every day; she deserves a rest."

And what do they like most about one another?

"Joe is very much a man, yet he is very gentle. He's never been afraid to cry."

"She'll laugh at the drop of a hat. And her great compassion for people. You could put her on a desert island and a week later she'd have a group of friends."

In the end, they both agree, it comes down to mutual respect. "And, yes," says Audrey, "you have to be able to laugh—laugh at yourself occasionally. There are times in every marriage: Joe will say, 'What's the matter, don't you love me?' I'll say, 'I love you, but I don't like you today.'"

"People will tell you they've been married twenty years and have never had an argument. They're in trouble."

"There's no emotion there."

"If they haven't had an argument, they're just ignoring each other."

"Sometimes you've got to have a blowup—even if you call each other the most horrendous names. So what?"

"We sometimes have an argument as I'm going out the door, and I'll swear to myself that I'll never talk to her again. Then I come home and say, 'What're we eating for dinner?'"

Audrey Minerva looks at her husband and laughs.

Joe Minerva's adversity was thrust upon him—an accident of fate. But some people bring their own problems upon themselves, and seem bent upon self-destruction. Audrey Minerva simply had to accept what had happened to her husband—it was an irreversible condition of life. But sometimes one partner has to watch the other disintegrating, knowing that it doesn't really have to happen.

Florence Caesar, wife of the almost legendary star of the 1950s television classic *Your Show of Shows*, had to deal with such a situation. Florence and Sid Caesar have now been married for more than forty years. But there was a long period during which Sid slowly, and then more rapidly, fell apart.

"The pressures of television got to Sid," Florence remembers. "It was gradual—he started by drinking after a show or a rehearsal, but then it became before, and it affected him more and more. When he was drinking too much, the doctors put him on pills. He wouldn't feel good, so he took more drugs, and he was drinking, too."

"I was very strong physically," Sid says, "and it took years to hurt my work. But it did happen. The bottom came when I was appearing in a play in Canada, and I couldn't remember a line. I couldn't remember where I was supposed to stand. Nothing."

Florence insists that they did have happy times even when he was drinking. "When he saw me getting too fed up he'd try to be a little better. I had endurance. I had to keep the kids okay. I went to psychiatrists for a while. Sid had been going for years. I had a nice home and clothes and money and kids. I was married to a star. What else did I want? He had to worry about supplying all this." Florence shakes her head. "I did consider leaving him, and I told him about it, but he never believed me. Young people today would never put up with it. Maybe it's rationalizing, but I felt because of his talent I had to keep him creating. I admired his work so much. It might have ended differently if that hadn't been so. And I truly loved him."

"I wouldn't be here if it hadn't been for this marriage," Sid says. "I might not be dead, but I'd be very sick. You can't come out of something like that by yourself. I was in therapy twenty years and I never got anything out of it. They got me functioning, but that's not living. Enjoying, appreciating, is living. I got better at home, with Florence to help me."

There is no doubt that Florence's patience, understanding, continued admiration for her husband's talents, and quite simply her love, helped Sid recover. But that was his safety net. Climbing back up on the tightwire of sobriety had to be his own doing.

"To get better you have to start to learn from your own mistakes, instead of making the same ones over and over. I was ready for it. I'm my own worse enemy, and I realized I had to make friends with myself. Nobody's mad at me but me. I'd say, 'Hey schmuck, you're really gonna do this?' And I'd reply, 'You're an idiot—you won't do this.' I'd verbalize it. But to get well is also to get back to your family. I was away from them for twenty years. I made friends with myself, then I had to make friends with Florence and the children. I knew it wouldn't happen overnight. I said, 'Sidney, this has gotta happen. You ain't got it yet—but it's starting to happen.' I kept talking to myself. I'd play it all back and hear what I was saying. You're a better psychiatrist for yourself."

"When he got off everything, he was very vulnerable. He knew he couldn't manage by himself. That's where I could really help."

And so they came through. Sid changed in the process. He still has ambitions and ego. "You don't get rid of it altogether. What you do is put it in perspective. I don't need to be on top of the world. I want to enjoy what I'm doing. If I'm playing at a beautiful place, I want

Florence to be there. If you don't share it with somebody, who cares if you see the moonlight or you don't. The person I want with me is Florence."

With the quiet strength that is her hallmark, Florence Caesar says, "Even during the bad times, I've always known that the love was there."

Merely surviving several decades together is not what good marriages are all about. It is getting there with the love and caring still intact, wanting the other person to be at your side—as Sid and Florence Caesar do. It's not just "sticking it out" through bad times— it's doing it because you know that something deeply worthwhile continues to exist. Some people are luckier than others, of course, and there are many long-term marriages that have never been faced with bad trouble. But those also require a real intensity of caring, a true cherishing of the other.

It was thirty-four years ago, and they didn't know one another yet. The only thing they shared was a maid, whose name was Gussie. Their lives were both involved in music; he was already a star at the Metropolitan Opera. She was a concert pianist just beginning to make a professional career.

They were having very different feelings about life, feelings that would make them right for each other.

HE: I'd just been divorced, and I was angry at myself for the failure. I came from a close family, and all my friends were married and having children. One part of me wanted all of that, and another part just wanted to have a ball.

SHE: After seeing Van Cliburn perform one night, I ran into one of my most revered teachers standing on 122nd Street and Broadway at eleven P.M. Here was this dried-up biddy in her late sixties waiting for a bus by her lonesome. I knew that wasn't for me. I didn't want to be married to my piano.

Their mutual maid Gussie thought they were made for each other, and tried to fix up a date. They both resisted.

HE: I thought if I married someone else in the same field it'd be like going to bat with two strikes against me. I didn't want to listen to Gussie.

SHE: One day Gussie called my apartment and just put him on

the phone. He asked me to the opera that night, but I had to work. He was so stunned I turned him down that he never called back. I thought, "You get one call from Merrill and you're supposed to drop dead."

But Gussie didn't give up. She finally got Robert Merrill and his future wife Marion together ten months later.

So how did this first meeting go?

MARION: He was the opposite of the conceited guy I'd expected him to be. We could talk like old friends right away.

BOB: I felt Marion was the most honest person I'd ever known. Sincere and very real. I felt like I could talk to her for hours.

MARION: On our first dinner date I didn't think twice about going to his apartment afterward to listen to records. I was that comfortable.

I assume a big part of that feeling of comfort came from your shared love of music?

BOB: Of course. But there were other things. She loves baseball, and I'm a baseball nut. It was one of those marvelous accidents. She was a Detroit fan then, and we went to Yankee games together. We still do. She keeps scorecards and statistics at the games. She's a part of the organization, sitting in George Steinbrenner's box and letting everyone who comes in know what happened in the last inning. Several years ago I was asked to manage the Old-Timers' Game, and Billy Martin gave me a uniform with the number 1½. I sang the national anthem at home games during the 1978 World Series. Every time I sang we won, and the Dodgers manager told me if I went out on the field again, he's shoot me. Many wives resent their husbands' going to a game, but Marion looks forward to it. Some nights when I'm tired she just drags me to Yankee Stadium.

What do you disagree about?

MARION: The only major disagreement we've had recently was about building an indoor swimming pool. Bob couldn't swim, so he didn't want one. I had to take care of the whole thing myself. But now Bob has taken swimming lessons, and he swims around the pool like a little dolphin. I knew he'd end up enjoying it, and he has.

All performing artists have egos. Has there ever been a problem about that?

MARION: When Bob had big performances coming up, I understood what he was going through. I'd handle the kids and everything else so he could concentrate on the performance.

BOB: It's great for an artist to have a wife who understands the instabilities and concerns of the profession. I had two lives—one at the theater and one at home. I left my work at the theater. Those nights that I did come home unhappy about my performance, Marion understood.

MARION: We have very few problems because we know how to react to each other's moods.

BOB: Too many people work at having common interests, at knowing each other. It just has to be there.

MARION: I tell my daughters that when they're dating and think "He's great, *but* . . ." that you have to find someone where there are no buts.

Leon Rabin begins with a speech.

"We came here to be interviewed by you because we thought this was important. We live in a time when the values of society have changed radically, and people seem to accept it. Well, wait a minute. We won't accept it. We won't accept that marriage is a failure, we won't accept that marriage won't work. I have heard learned rabbis talking to young people, saying that the age of the family is over. I pulled my hair out."

"You certainly did!" says his wife Idelle, looking at his bald pate.

"Yes. That's how I lost it." And Leon smiles.

Leon, sixty-nine, and Idelle, sixty-two, have been married for thirty-seven years and have been in business together since 1952. They met during World War II when Leon, a graduate in psychology from Penn State, went to Dallas as a professional community organizer for the USO. Idelle, a fine arts graduate of the University of Texas at Austin, became a volunteer.

"In the beginning," says Leon, "we were not dating, we were working together. We enjoyed each other's company."

"Leon and I would have remained friends even if we hadn't married. We had common goals, common values. We had a working friendship instead of a courtship."

But then the relationship began to shift. "We were putting together a memorial program for Roosevelt after his death," Leon remembers. "Our common feelings for him as President and about his death gave us our first joint emotional experience."

Idelle remembers something else, too. "It was at the same time that I found out about his whimsy, which is how he handles everything. I heard some of the women talking about this awful man Leon Rabinowitz, who had a wife and three children but came down there on weekends dancing and playing around with all the girls. Obviously, I was upset. I went up to him, shaking my finger in his face. 'How could you . . . ?' He said, 'Have I done anything embarrassing, not in good taste?' And I really couldn't think of anything. Then all of a sudden he starts cracking that laugh of his, just like he's doing now. And I realized he was pulling people's legs. He used it as a defensive mechanism to keep a lot of overanxious girls off his back."

"All my life it's been that way. When I'm bored or don't want to get involved in a real discussion, I become very whimsical."

"I immediately thought, this guy's really got something. And I went home wondering why he was explaining it to me and not any of the others."

They continued to grow closer to one another, but there was no sexual relationship before their marriage. "It would have been difficult for me to push for it," Leon says. "She was a Jewish broad. I knew her values. And I was too friendly with her father."

So far as Idelle was concerned, it was a given that she would be a virgin when she married, as was common among young women of that time. "I was totally naive sexually. I was a sophisticated, worldly, well-traveled woman of twenty-three, but I knew nothing in that area."

"Middle-class Jewish broads were all like that," Leon teases.

"We had so many projects we were working on, I never thought about marriage. It just sort of happened. He asked me, but it wasn't really asking. We knew we were going to."

"Being able to do things together, work together, that was the important thing. If our relationship had been primarily sexual, we probably wouldn't have gotten married. If that's all there is, watch out."

They were married within a year after they first met. "At first, I stayed home and tried to play out the role of the young married

Jewish princess. Mah-jongg, bridge, luncheons. Boredom led to desperation, which finally led to inspiration. I just didn't fit in. I didn't really know why, but I knew I was unhappy. That lifestyle was not for me. But I had a talent for making embroidered and beaded blouses. That led to an accessories business that later became Leon's and mine. My mother was involved, and the name we gave it was DeLann's—a contraction of Idelle and Anne. It started to become successful when Leon joined in with us. His organizational ability was terrific."

"When I came in, the dollar volume was twenty-five thousand. It's now close to two million. But Idelle sets the tone for the entire business. Her style, her manner, makes DeLann's—"

Idelle interrupts. "Leon's management is the bottom line."

They smile at one another.

Don't they ever argue, running a business together?

"We don't always agree when we start out, but we come to agreement through discussion, through breaking it down."

"It's not all soupy-silky, though. I will become disturbed with him, so I might sulk or become quiet. He never lets it last. We have problems, I get angry, but we talk it through. After all, we are running a business that is a big success; we both want to work out the differences, and we do."

After the business was fully launched, the Rabins adopted a daughter. "I was determined to have a child," Idelle says. "I did not feel I would be a nice Jewish girl if I was not a momma. When we realized I would not become pregnant, we adopted Charlene. She knew she was adopted from the start, and she had a lot of emotional problems about it. When she was just seven or eight, with her little legs dangling from the kitchen table, she would say, 'Mommy, how can anyone give up a baby?' That's why today she does an expert job of mothering. It was a difficult time for a while with her, but I never felt guilty. Leon and I worked very hard at what we thought was good parenting. Having the business to run, and Leon and I being so close, may have added to Charlene's difficulties as a child. But it's turned out fine—she's now joined the business herself."

In addition to running their business, the Rabins have many outside interests. Leon is a national officer of the American Jewish Committee, and they both serve on the boards of the Dallas Opera,

Symphony, and Ballet. Idelle is also on the Chamber of Commerce Cultural Arts Committee and is a trustee of the Dallas Historical Society. Idelle cherishes their involvement with the arts. "My father thought an actress was just as bad as a prostitute, so as the nice Jewish girl, I never got to pursue those goals. But I've made up for it." As for Leon, he makes it clear that Idelle offered him the "one thing I didn't have"—class. "Her family's style was foreign to me in my personal experience growing up. Idelle's mother was American-born, unlike my parents, and extremely well educated. She was a social snob, but she admired my level of education, the fact that I'd gone for a master's degree. I learned a lot from Idelle and her family, though."

"And Leon represented so many things that I needed, the strength, the support system, the integrity. I needed an ally I could trust. He was that man."

"I only wanted her to be happy. I have always felt that a person has a right to do what they need to do. It was my task to help her achieve that."

"He truly has the highest sense of tolerance of anyone I have known. We have the kind of partnership that makes it hard for me to understand what couples are talking about when they express their need for separate vacations and so on. I would be devastated to travel without Leon. Half of me wouldn't be there. He is my closest friend. Our single biggest thread is our verbalization. We love to tell each other everything. We sleep together, eat together, and work together. That is a lot of togetherness. At this age I try to push myself to do some things without him, because I know if anything happens to him I must be able to function on my own."

"Life is never boring with Idelle. Boredom kills more people than anything else. I will never be bored."

"I want to grab it all while we can, and while we are together," says Idelle Rabin. "When he says he is getting a cold or is too tired to go out, I yell, 'Take two aspirins and let's go.'"

If you have to ask every time you want a hat,
you're out of your mind.
—*Cindy Adams*

At a time when she could have shown great
disappointment in me, due to our financial
problems, she built me up and became successful with her own work.
—*Jay Originer*

Work and money: Who's the boss?

For Betsy and George Heath, money, work, and confusion about the
provider's role almost brought an end to their marriage.

Both were in their mid-twenties when they were married
nineteen years ago. George was a successful television producer and
Betsy an entrepreneur in children's market research. The marriage
began with a sense of rightness, of mutual approval, that created a
kind of emotional and sexual high. But things changed quickly.
George found himself out of work for the first time, and Betsy
established a new and immediately successful business.

"Betsy became the steadier earner," George notes. "I did freelance work, and it was the beginning of my being out of work for
periods of time. I took charge at home. I enjoyed cooking and was

very good at it. Our first fight, in fact, was over an egg. I liked a four-minute egg, and one day Betsy made breakfast and cooked a two-minute egg. But the fight wasn't really about the egg itself. What we were fighting about was territory—who was going to control the kitchen."

"Our marriage had gone through several phases," Betsy explains. "The first was a highly shared one of great peace. The second was a determination of territory and assigning roles. George assumed the more dreaming/fantasy role. He enriched my life with great style and I enriched his with practicality. His territory became marvelous acts of love from the kitchen."

They led a busy social life, orchestrated by George, but even as he enjoyed creating it, he felt it was in some ways a sham. "I always thought of myself as rich and successful even if I was not, and it was always important to me to mix with rich, successful people. That was the main weakness in my character. It began to impinge on our conscious life when Betsy would say, 'Where is your income to sustain this lifestyle?'"

They took a long time to face what was going on in their relationship, and in the meantime the marriage was becoming increasingly rocky. Even having a child did not really alter the fact that Betsy was the provider and George the dependent person. He came to feel that he was a child himself in his relationship to Betsy. "I began to resent her," he admits. "I took some job that wasn't right and then I had an affair to prove something, prove I was still a man. At home we were angry in bed, and I began to realize that Betsy's frequent trips to California involved another man. We confronted that, that we were proving ourselves sexually outside of marriage."

But solving that issue still left other problems unconfronted. Betsy was torn about George's working—or not working. "There was a part of me that didn't want George to be successful. I had total freedom under the guise of providing." But it was also her feeling— simply part of her conditioning—that a man must provide. "It became apparent that while he didn't have to provide for me, he did have to provide for himself."

On top of everything else, George developed a drinking problem. It was almost too much. "Betsy said to me, 'Why don't we split up? What do I need you for? You're no fun. You're always depressed.

Someone else can take care of the house.' I entered therapy then. I was scared she was going to leave me. Betsy also came along to the therapist."

In therapy, George came to accept that traditional role values were not that important. The therapist made him feel good about the contributions he *was* making. "As we got down into our deeper needs, we both found that we wanted to stay married, and married to each other. But it was crazy the way we were married. I learned that constant complaining about problems doesn't really help. Focusing on the positive, the good stuff we had, was reemphasized. We had found many joys in living together—we had to get back to that."

George then went to work and produced a show that he regarded as the best of his career. Around the same time, his parents died and he was left a comfortable amount of money. "That meant that while I was trying to keep working, I also had the wherewithal to write my own checks."

Even though the money came from his parents, it helped him a lot in terms of his ego. Betsy states it succinctly: "He did not have to come to me as a child."

"Then, as the money began to run out, I started to work on projects that were less grandiose and closer to reality."

Gradually, their perspective changed again. "I think we both realized that together we were much more than we were alone," George says.

Betsy adds, "I asked myself, 'If this marriage is not going to be right, what are the alternatives? To live alone? Another man?' And as I thought it through, it became clear that I had a very rare situation. The rocks in his head fit the holes in mine. Together we really are a remarkable combination of sensibilities and awarenesses. We are harmonious again; we bring great strength to each other and each other's work. George and I are best friends. There is no one hundred percent. The ninety percent we have is rather remarkable."

Who works? How much does he or she make? How is the money spent?

As with Betsy and George, the answers to these questions affect the marriage only in terms of how both partners *feel* about the situation. What's right is what is acceptable:

NORENE PECK: I love being a homemaker. Ever since I was a little girl I dreamed of having my own beautiful home and family, and that's exactly what I have. I hated working nine to five in an office. I was tired while I was working, and had no energy to do anything else except on weekends. I always had the "Sunday-night blues" anticipating work on Mondays.

ROSE KOVAC: I'm not the kind of woman who can sit around the house all day doing nothing, or having lunch with the ladies. My children are now old enough to manage without me until dinnertime, and I find that I have more energy and accomplish more with a busy schedule that I did before.

One woman is enervated by work, the other energized by it. Does this have anything to do with generational attitudes toward careers for women? Not a thing, in this case. Rose is a dozen years older than the "traditional" Norene. It's entirely a matter of what two different people find personally rewarding. What about their husbands' feelings, though?

BRAD PECK: There is a nice feeling of security knowing my family is waiting for me when I get home. I guess we're old-fashioned, but we like it that way. It's not that I don't believe married women should be working; for those who want to that's fine. It's also good to know that Norene has the background to be able to go back to work anytime she wants to. I know I'll never need her help financially, but someday she might change her mind about working, and whatever she decided to do would be okay with me.

STEPHEN KOVAC: I think I would have felt badly about Rose's job if she was forced to do it to help out, instead of working to feel productive and better about herself. I have no idea what she does with her money, nor do I care, but I do notice a new cinnabar vase in the living room, or a sexy silk dress for the reunion. She did pay for her own car, a new Honda Civic, which gave our eldest son, George, the pleasure of owning her old Datsun.

While their wives' feelings about working are completely opposite, Brad and Stephen exhibit a similar and very common attitude on this subject. It's important to both of them to feel that they are the *real* breadwinners. It's fine for their wives to work if they want to, but—and it's a pretty big but—they can feel truly good about it only on the condition that it isn't economically necessary. When it is necessary, the situation can change drastically.

Brendan and Sally Dunn, both thirty-nine, have been married for thirteen years and have a twelve-year-old son. He creates neon lighting for clubs and boutiques and she is a successful stockbroker. They met at a meditation class and were married—at Sally's insistence—in a Buddhist ceremony and honeymooned in India. Both have waist-length hair, and both enjoy going to rock clubs and concerts several times a week, often with their son, Sean.

In the first years of their marriage, Brendan was making very good money. He could indulge his passion for electronic equipment and she could occasionally travel to India. Although Sally has an Ivy League degree, her employment history was haphazard. She'd been a waitress at a vegetarian restaurant, an assistant at encounter groups, and was involved in antipoverty programs—all before her son was born.

"Brendan worked very hard and brought home the money, and I stayed home, very happily. I chanted and played the tambora with my friends. I volunteered at the Buddhist center and took Sean playing in the park. Brendan was always the boss, and I'd have to ask him for money, but I didn't mind."

Brendan worked then at a very "loose" organization, and the boss and employees often partied together well into the night, sometimes with Sean sleeping on Brendan's lap. One night, after a lot of tension and drinking, Brendan and his boss "almost tore each other apart" in the lounge of a rock club, and he was out of his long-time job. Until then, it had never occurred to Sally that they had virtually no savings.

"We went from eating out every evening to Spaghetti-O's— overnight," she recalls. "'Oh, God,' I thought, 'we're all going to starve.' Brendan became very sullen and withdrawn. He ignored Sean and he was mean to me. I felt very alone and I'd sit with my head in my arms and just cry my eyes out every day and dream I was someplace else."

"I was brought up in a very patriarchal home," says Brendan, "and I was used to controlling the family. I was also very attached to my freedom—you know, having a good time and a fair amount of spending money. I felt trapped and bored, and I didn't care who else was miserable."

Sally lost interest in sex and spent her time crying or seeking refuge at the Buddhist center. Sean, who shares his father's introverted, sullen tendencies, began having problems at school. "I just couldn't do anything," Sally says. "I couldn't handle my life or either of my guys. I shivered with fear—really trembling."

Unable to find work, Brendan borrowed from his father and "almost had an affair—but the girl wasn't that interested."

In desperation, Sally finally got a secretarial job at a major brokerage firm. She put her long hair up and borrowed a friend's clothes. Although things remained tense at home and Brendan grew even more frustrated, Sally's employers soon recognized her high intelligence and potential energy. Coming from an educated, conservative family, Sally found herself feeling more and more comfortable in a Wall Street environment. "I really got into all this investment stuff and found a way to see the bright side of my new life. And I hadn't been so challenged since school, and that was a high." Sally needed to feel good at work, because it was still difficult at home. "I'd come back from the office exhausted and find two sulking, demanding boys. I had to cook every night and straighten up the apartment. I'd find Sean staring at his train set and Brendan wouldn't look up from his book."

But her job eventually seemed to galvanize Brendan. While Sally was attending a broker training program, he got together with a friend and started a new lighting business, with additional help from his father. "For a while," he says, "there was still no money, but I wasn't as restless at home. I worked long hours and just came home to sleep. But now I slept with Sally cuddled under my arm. It was coming back to us."

Even though Brendan is successful again, Sally doesn't think about giving up her job. Brendan is still head of the house and doesn't do much to help out at home, but as a birthday present last year he hired a part time housekeeper so that Sally could be at peace with her dual role of stockbroker/homemaker. While Brendan is proud of her, it doesn't matter much to him whether she works or not. He isn't friendly with her Wall Street pals or much interested in the Dow Jones, but he loves Sally's being more "up." "We're back to fun," says Brendan. "She's changed her clothes and manages to get along with all those stuffy people, but we're still ourselves—people who go out and make a party and pick up the check. When I want to have a giggle at Sally's expense—like after I hear her speaking some funny language about stocks and bonds—I remember that she got into this to keep the family going, and I haven't forgotten how hard it was for her. So now she enjoys it—that's hardly a crime. I get a kick out of seeing her in her uniform and carrying all those important papers in her briefcase." Brendan smiles. "I even bought the briefcase for her."

DOUG ELLIS: Like most families with a business we have a closer involvement with how each dollar comes in and how it goes out, but we look at money as a convenience and not a goal in itself. By that I mean we don't worship it or save it all for a rainy day or worry about it constantly. We try to enjoy what we have and still provide for our future, the kids' education, and retirement.

NANCY ELLIS: Doug is more relaxed about money problems than I am. I'm the one who does both the business and the family bookkeeping, and I guess I worry more about the future. I make sure our insurance premiums are paid up, that our savings and bonds are secure, and that we have enough money for those extras like family vacations and renovations to the house.

For Karen and Bill Spofford, the future is full of ifs and whens. Married for eleven years, Karen is a department manager for a big Chicago publishing company, while Bill is a comedy writer and performer. In Chicago, Bill was making a respectable living writing, appearing in commercials, and doing some stand-up comedy at local clubs. But three years ago he moved to Los Angeles, while Karen remained in Chicago, and they are together far less than they would like.

"I had to give myself the chance to really make it in comedy the way I think I can," says Bill. "If I didn't try it, I couldn't live with myself, and I think eventually Karen couldn't live with me. I had to find out if I would be successful at what I love."

Karen and Bill discussed his move to Los Angeles for several months, knowing it would mean long separations since she was determined to stay in Chicago. "I started here right out of college as a secretary in the publishing company. I'm still at the same company, but now I'm head of my department. I worked hard to become an executive, and I'm respected around town for what I do. I have a certain standard of living here, and I can't just give up everything I worked so hard to achieve for something that's still iffy. It's not that I don't want to be with him, but we had a difficult decision to make. I felt we needed some sort of security. I have it through my job, and I really feel this is a blanket of security that covers us both."

Money is obviously not the chief concern to Bill. "I need a roof over my head and a sandwich in my stomach. It's the work that turns me on now, but I don't know if that'll be my feeling next year or next week."

"Bill does live more hand-to-mouth. I have some savings and I've bought a few stocks. I'd like to buy a home someday. Right now we don't even have any life insurance, except for a small company policy. But I'm used to a certain way of living. I have a nice place to live, I wear good clothes. If we had more money, the main thing would be that we could visit more."

"I think Karen expects more than I do. The house, the vacations, are something she plans on, and we'll have to have them someday. I wouldn't be in California if I didn't think I'd make it."

"When Bill first left he was just full of optimism, but I felt more like it was the end of the world. Now, when he leaves, I adjust and he just starts bawling. It's tough out there for him."

Bill has had some success in California, but the breakthrough hasn't come. "My partners and I have done some independent comedy films—we produce, direct, and write. We've had hard times getting post-production money, although there has been interest. But I feel in my gut that it'll happen."

"I've offered them some money, but Bill won't take it."

"I did take her old car when she got the new one. But Karen has made enough sacrifices already. Hell, her whole life, every day, is a sacrifice. I'm not proud. If I were sleeping in the streets, I'd take her money—but probably just to get a bus home."

"I think he'd feel like a louse if he left me here in Chicago and then asked for support. He not only does have too much pride, but he's also too considerate."

"Someday, we'll probably be rich people with seven kids, an accountant, a tax lawyer, and a stock portfolio we couldn't lift."

"It was understood that it was going to take time. He said, 'I'm going,' and I said, 'I'm not going,' but there was never a feeling that this might be the end of the marriage. There's a lifelong commitment to each other."

"There's no getting around the hurt that this situation produces. She's my wife and I ache for her. But I don't expect her to leave everything she's worked for because I'm trying to do my own thing. Maybe sometime in the future she can apply her skills out in California, but I can't demand that. In the meantime I'm giving this a couple of more years. I wouldn't do this if I thought it was some sort of pipe dream. There's been so much positive response that it's only a question of sticking it out."

"It's a puzzle to both of us. I can't give him a time limit. I know we're going to live together eventually, but I don't know where or when it's going to happen."

"This marriage is strong because we've survived all this, and when we are together, there's something warmer, more physically exciting, all those things other couples don't necessarily have. We're hanging in there, but the trade-off is rough, I admit."

Is Bill and Karen's marriage really such a good one, or is he taking advantage of Karen? Isn't she being forced to live a lonely life for the sake of an adolescent kind of dream that Bill has? "I wouldn't put up with it," a lot of women would say.

Well, a lot of women wouldn't, of course. But that doesn't mean that something is wrong with the marriage because she does. She believes in Bill and she believes in their marriage. To deny him the opportunity to try to prove himself, she suggests, would be far more damaging to the marriage than the enforced separation is. Some may see her as a victim, but it seems clear that she doesn't see herself that way.

And it isn't really fair to charge Bill with taking advantage of her. She's not supporting him, after all. Let's remember all those women —everybody knows one—who worked to put their husbands through law or medical school only to be left in the lurch once their husbands had their degrees in hand. That's not the kind of thing that's going on here. It may not be according to the rulebook, but both Karen and Bill feel a commitment to one another that goes beyond conventional assumptions.

The way money is handled is only one of many "rules" the ten-year marriage of Judy Gehrke and Louis Rodriguez has broken. They're one of those couples you wouldn't have expected to get together in the first place, and you'd certainly have your doubts about their making it last. They're very different people from utterly different backgrounds. Significantly, though, both those backgrounds are atypical to begin with.

Judy grew up in the Midwest, the oldest of five children, and the only girl. Self-described as "headstrong," she was the first member of her family to go to college. Her initial ambition was to become a doctor, since she was very gifted in math and science. But during her first year and a half at Northwestern, she took Russian as a scientific language and ending up majoring in it. She eventually took a doctorate at Harvard and became an interpreter. That may sound very conservative, but there was another side to her also. She calls herself a "Woodstock kid," and she was active in the antiwar movement and did a lot of design work even as she pursued her degrees. She turned away from medicine because of the other students pursuing that goal. As she puts it, "They squirreled themselves away in labs and didn't even know what season it was." Judy Gehrke was nothing if not open to the world around her.

Louis was born in Puerto Rico, but from age three to ten he lived in a Catholic orphanage in New York—his parents had separated and his mother had tuberculosis. Life in the orphanage, far from being bleak, widened Louis's horizons. The children were of many nationalities, and he was exposed to a much wider variety of experiences than would likely have been the case had he grown up in a Puerto Rican community. "I loved it," Louis says flatly. "Everything was taken care of. You put down what you wanted for Christmas and you got it. We went to rodeos, the Howdy Doody show. I was a cub scout, went camping, fishing. It was wonderful."

When he was ten, his mother was well enough to have him live with her again, and he returned to Puerto Rico. But he felt cut off in some way from the Spanish culture, and dropped out of school in the eleventh grade. He wanted to be a painter, an artist, but when he and Judy met, he was the doorman at her apartment building. He was not thinking of the future, just painting and playing chess in his free hours, living alone. He had been the doorman for three years before he and Judy reached the point where, as Louis puts it, "we acknowledged that we could talk."

"I thought he was a creep," Judy says with a grin. "I was traveling for my work, and was hardly home, and when I was home I was very lonely, and desperate for the company of some male. On my job, all I was meeting were married men, and my friends were in the suburbs. One night I met an old friend for drinks, and he was very nice, but just a friend. I got a bit drunk, and when I got home, Louis and I got to talking—longer than the usual 'Where's my dry cleaning?' We talked for about two hours."

"It was bizarre for me. I'd known her for three years but could never think of enough to say to fill five minutes."

Louis wanted to see her again and called her on the house phone to ask her to dinner. She was busy, and he thought it was a brush-off. But a few days later she asked him to lunch. "I felt he was different; instead of reading the racing form like the other doormen, he was always reading a chess book or *The New York Times*. We went to lunch. And a week later he moved in with me."

Louis quit his job as doorman, since that would have made for a very awkward situation. It was an intense relationship, and not only sexually. "Because he was out of work and I was starting a design company," Judy explains, "we were together all the time. Always together. Louis worked for me. It was a housewares business, and ultimately we felt this would solidify our connection and that Louis would run the whole shipping department."

Was Judy supporting him?

"No, she was not. I was on unemployment, and from day one I always supported myself."

"But the company was not making it. I was very scared."

"If I bought a pizza for sixty-five cents, she would yell, 'You know we can't afford it.'"

"I used to get angry because he didn't take responsibility; but he shouldn't have, if it was not his obligation. That business failure was my first, and I had to confront it. But it was a bad time. He's right, I would yell and scream. But he managed to handle me through that period. He knew I was not going to make it, and instead of trying to force that awareness into me before I could accept it, he gently and reassuringly waited for me to confirm the reality of the situation."

Having survived the hurdle of Judy's business failure, they got married, "for us, society, our friends," as Louis puts it. Friends, however, had been another obstacle, at least in terms of their acceptance of Louis. In our society how much money you make and what you do for a living are the measure of worth for many people. Would Judy's very educated friends accept Louis? Or would they judge him on what he did instead of who he was as a person?

Judy explains, "I had sort of set up a series of social situations with my friends to see if I could handle it. He passed! But some of my friends could not contend with what he actually did, working as a housepainter and handyman. So they categorized him as a contractor in real estate."

"They were unable to accept a lowly housepainter. But I didn't feel insecure about myself."

Judy set up the social situations to see if *she* could handle it, and "*he* passed!" The implication here is that Judy wanted to see if she could handle an anticipated rejection of Louis by her friends. The fact that he passed was clearly his doing, and no doubt had a lot to do with his self-acceptance and security.

Did Judy feel that she had a diamond in the rough, and think that once they were married she would educate him?

"I encouraged him to try to do other things, because I felt that what he did was really too demanding physically. But he really didn't want to go back to school."

They are planning to have a child, and Louis has that all figured out. "We both know that she has to continue to work. Judy could not just be a housewife. I would not mind taking over most of the household duties and caring for our child. My work will allow me the time to do it. I work five hours a day. I can work somewhat and still be home rather than having a strange person care for our child."

The relationship has progressed to a point beyond doubts. Judy says, "He has to hang around, or my IRA and Keogh plan will be all messed up, plus the house is in his name."

"So we have to get along," says Louis. "Besides, we have a lot of fun together."

"He's a practical joker. And I love to hear his stories about the homes of the people he works for."

"One woman had pictures of Norman Mailer all over her house. I remarked that she must like him a lot. She said, 'I do, I am his mother!'"

"And I like to talk to him about the content of my work. He loves to listen because, in this comfortable way, he loves to learn."

"We've left something out. I love her very much. She makes me very happy. I love Judy."

"He is extremely supportive. If I come home from a bad day, he is there. Not that he always takes my side, but he is so willing to listen. I need him so. We bring so much to each other."

It is frequently outsiders who create many of the problems for partners from "different worlds," Judy feels. "People who follow the rules are often jealous of those who don't and who make it nevertheless," she says.

We bring so much to each other. Isn't that what it is all about? One of the reasons we have so many *bad* marriages is that too much attention is paid to the externals of the situation. People of certain classes or educational backgrounds, or colors, or religions, or income levels aren't *supposed* to marry each other. It doesn't look right. Family and friends will disapprove. Of course, discrepancies in background can cause problems. Nobody's going to deny that. When the externals all match up like drapes and slipcovers, we say, "They're made for each other." But we're forgetting that "We bring so much to each other" is a much more important matter. Judy and Louis went into marriage with their eyes open to the problems, and certain that they were good for each other.

Another couple who have broken the rules, in a quite different way, are Marilyn and Rod Gist. Married for eleven years, they have two young children. Marilyn is an account executive with an advertising agency in downtown Miami. Rod, who used to be in advertising also, is now a freelance writer working at home so that he can care for their children.

Rod says that this role reversal was never a matter of purposeful decision, that it just happened naturally for them. "Soon after we were married I quit the agency and started writing at home. I was never a nine-to-five guy and hated having to dress in the three-piece uniform and report to an office. I felt my creativity was stifled, and I was tired and listless all the time."

"I, on the other hand, loved the office," Marilyn says. "I need the discipline and the routine to be productive. If I couldn't go to work every day, I'd never get dressed at all. I tried working at home when I was pregnant, and hated it. I could hardly wait to get back to the office."

"I knew Marilyn hated housework, while I found it very soothing. I do a lot of thinking while I work around the house. We do have a cleaning woman come in once a week, so it's easy for me to keep the house up between times."

"Once I had Dawn, our oldest, I felt very guilty about wanting to go back to work right away. Both our mothers were horrified that I did, and our friends thought we were crazy. They thought Rod was lazy and didn't want to support us, even though his freelance writing did, and still does, bring in half our income. They said I was a bad mother for wanting to leave the children—with their own father! At first I went back on a part-time basis. I hurried home every evening expecting to find chaos. Instead I found everything in better shape than when I left."

"It wasn't easy when they were younger to get much writing done. I'd have to wait till nap time, and sometimes I was so tired I would take my nap when they did. Once I got organized and they were in kindergarten I had a schedule worked out perfectly." Even so, Rod does admit that there were times when he regretted the decision to be a house husband. "But the feeling didn't last. There were times when everything went wrong and the frustration was enormous. The kind of day when the washing machine broke down, the dinner burnt, and the kids were cranky from sunup till sundown. But the alternative of going to the office was worse to think about. And I tried not to lose my temper or my sense of humor."

"There were many days," Marilyn adds, "when my boss was nasty, the client was irritating, and I hated my work. But then I'd come home and hear about what Rod had been through, and I knew I couldn't handle that. We talked about both going to work and hiring a housekeeper, but the children are too young. We both felt uncomfortable with that. Maybe when they are older. Just because we have a different arrangement doesn't mean I'm not just as interested in my children and their problems as Rod is, regardless of what people think. I try to make time for pediatrician's appointments, PTA meetings, the dentist. We do much of that together."

"One thing about being a house husband is that you never have to come home after a tough day at the office and listen to a nagging wife. I think I have a greater understanding of my wife, and she of me."

"We do take a lot of ribbing because of the way we run our lives, but we're happy. Last Christmas, Rod got a subscription to *Family Circle* and I received one to *California Business*! I really respect the fact that Rod has allowed me to pursue the career I've always wanted without hassle in spite of what other people think of it. I think that takes a real man, someone strong, whose ego isn't threatened."

"I respect her paycheck. . . . Just kidding!"

Jack and Sylvia Roseman have been married for thirty-seven years and have two daughters in their early thirties. Sylvia is an administrative assistant and Jack works for a large trucking company outside Chicago.

What do you do with your paycheck, Jack?

JACK: I fold it in half and bring it home. After that I don't know what happens.

Do you write out checks or pay bills?

JACK: Nothing. I get an allowance that I spend on lunch or going out or gas.

SYLVIA: I put Jack's checks in the bank to cover our monthly expenses and we use mine to live on. Our money is equally mine and his.

Would it upset you if Sylvia earned more than you?

JACK: I'd be happy.

You never argue about money?

JACK: Never. I give it to her and she spends it. It's as simple as that.

SYLVIA: About twenty years ago we had a problem. Jack had a job that didn't pay much and he couldn't get a raise. I didn't believe he was really asking for one.

JACK: I'd ask for a raise and the boss would say, "See me next week." Next week he'd say, "See me the end of the week." Every day Sylvia would say, "Did you ask him?" And I'd quote him verbatim. "See me the end of the week . . . see me next week." It went on for months like that.

SYLVIA: That was the only time in our marriage that I didn't believe him. It was definitely the worst time for us.

Did you consider divorce?

SYLVIA: No, but there was a strain. If we ever would've divorced, it would have been then.

How did things get better?

JACK: Eventually, I got a raise.

And Jack laughs.

"I thought I married an incredibly brilliant man with incredibly bad luck," says Erica Marlowe. "We had a lot of financial problems, and when I started helping out at the office I saw that Ross was making dumb mistakes that screwed us out of the money we did make. I thought, 'I married a stupid man.' I was attracted by his brilliance, and this realization made me sick."

Ross had just started his graphics business in New York City when he and Erica were married fourteen years ago. They had a daughter a year after the marriage, and it was another four years before Erica decided to try to work with Ross at the company. Even though she had almost no working experience, she quickly understood that Ross wasn't handling the financial side of the business right. "I saw Ross's weaknesses for the first time. We fought like cats and dogs about prices he quoted or whether to get the newest or some cheap equipment."

"I still don't see anything wrong with the way I did business," Ross says. "Erica knew I'd never be the corporate type. I think my problem was being overwhelmed with work. All the details, all the paperwork, all the crap from people. Then, when Erica came on strong, I wasn't ready for it. She became very assertive and very ambitious. I thought she was happy staying home with the baby."

"I thought so, too," says Erica. "I went to work because Ross needed help. Then I realized that I *needed* to get away from the TV set and the mothers in the playground. I'd always felt Ross was so much smarter than me, and I discovered there were areas where he couldn't cut it but I could."

"Eventually Erica took over all the sales and negotiations. She took my work around to people and set prices. Whenever I get involved in those areas, we still argue, so I only do it if there's no other way."

Their business took a sharp turn upward. "Ross was really a free-spirited creative type. Financial issues and bullshit with clients always bored him. He was best alone at his desk creating, and when I was able to really relieve him of the rest, things took off. I couldn't believe how hard-nosed I could be with corporate types, but I psyched myself into it. I thought of our daughter's tuition and the mortgage and all the things I wanted and deserved, and I went after it. If I got one rejection, I'd get on the phone again and shoot for the moon."

"I'll admit I was threatened by Erica's balls—wow, did they ever come out of nowhere. But now we have enough money for a car. We go out and travel more, and there's still something left over. And even though we've taken on more work, I've been able to hire some people and do the things I got into this business for."

"Being able to handle people and business has changed my entire life," Erica says. "I stand up to repairmen and snotty waiters. I think a big shot is lucky to get my call. When we were married, we were kids, and new boots and a bottle of sangria were all we wanted. Now I feel like we're grown-ups who can handle grown-up problems."

Alan Landsburg and Linda Otto also work together. They are both producers for a film company that Alan owns. He is fifty-two and was married before; for Linda, forty-five, it is a first marriage, now in its twelfth year.

Before she met Alan, Linda had a casting company in New York. "I cast all Neil Simon's plays, everything on Broadway for Joe Papp, and I did a lot of television. After we married, I kept my casting company, because it was so lucrative. But the more I was around Alan and his work, the more I realized not only that I wanted to produce, but that I could. We'd been married for a couple of years when Alan gave me my first chance—a movie called *Torn Between Two Lovers.*"

Asked if Alan was her mentor, Linda replies simply, "Yeah. He taught me and my partner. We knew what we knew, but not what Alan knew. He was our mentor and our boss, and my husband. There was never any real problem working with him. He's still my boss."

Alan does not see himself, however, as a traditional male, the dominant partner. "My mother and father worked together. Work at home was always shared by all of us. Now at work I treat Linda's films the same way I treat anyone else's. We just have more to share when we're at home. If she doesn't like what I suggest, she won't do it."

"On a professional level, I've always acted like a producer, not his wife."

"The nice thing," Alan says, "is that she was a professional before I met her. She had matured and knew what she was doing. A mentor, maybe, but I don't see myself as a teacher. It was a matter of what my responsibility was to her, which was to give her the equipment to do the job she could do."

They are affectionate with one another at work, but only when it is appropriate. "When Linda's just starting a film and establishing a family of people working with her, I may hold back. If I come over and give her a kiss and a hug it can take away from the status she needs on the set."

Many men in Alan's position *would* give her that hug on the set—they'd be sure to because it would send a subtle message that they were really in control. Linda is the kind of person who might even want him to give her that hug, and to hell with how it looks, but she also understands that it is to her benefit that he refrains from doing it. There's a mutual understanding of the issues here that is a sign of a mature marriage.

Linda and Alan need a strong marital relationship, because both admit that they're workaholics. "Everything I'm doing," Linda says, "has been something I've dreamed of doing all my life and I haven't been able to turn anything down. I can't keep up this pace, because I don't feel it's good for me. I've got to take a rest for a while."

Can you shut off the work, or does it get in the way of your sexual relations?

Alan says, "For me, there's a lot of stress on either side, and it gets impossible to unwind."

"We just sort of hold onto each other," says Linda, "and think will we ever do it again. But no matter how excruciating the stress is, I never felt any loss of affection. When things are bad, sometimes even five or six times a day, I'll go into his office and just put my head on his lap."

"I'm perpetually overextended," Alan says.

Then why do so much?

"The reason for assuming more and more possible work is the fear of being without work," Alan says, even though he is a wealthy man.

Thomas Muller, thirty-eight, and Elizabeth Hanson, thirty-seven, have been married for ten years. Both are vice presidents—she of a public relations firm and he of a major brokerage company. They live in a luxurious co-op complex near New York's financial district. They also own a home in Connecticut and drive a green Jaguar. They are part of a growing breed of workaholic couples. Thomas often works until one in the morning. And while Elizabeth works only until seven or eight at night, she takes classes or attends business-related functions most evenings.

She calls him Thomas, and he calls her Kiddo.

ELIZABETH: We lived together for three years before we got married. I was afraid that as his wife there would be different expectations and that he would try to limit my activities or direct them more toward the home.

THOMAS: I'd been proposing to her for three years, so while we were on vacation I told her that if she didn't marry me, I'd break it off. It took her a couple of weeks to think it over.

ELIZABETH: We'd always had a very stormy relationship—we still do. We're both tough cookies with tempers and there is always one of us screaming at the door while the other is screaming on the way to the elevator.

THOMAS: We broke up a few times. But we always got back together as soon as we cooled off, usually in very romantic ways in nice restaurants.

ELIZABETH: Usually after eleven. But we're people who don't need much sleep. We will the energy.

THOMAS: Except when it comes to housework.

ELIZABETH: Someone comes in a couple of times a week to do the major stuff and to clean up our messes. Thomas is a very meticulous man in many ways, very picky. We look like the ultimate professionals, all put together and tailored. People are shocked when they come over and see eight or nine pizza boxes stacked outside the kitchen door. I push dirt under things and forget about it. I couldn't really live with a man who was always after me to straighten up. I throw things around and I live in disarray. My office looks the same, even after I fix it up.

THOMAS: Who needs to come home at night and have someone chasing after you with a vacuum cleaner? Our checkbooks and all that are in very good order. Housekeeping is the area in which we don't keep up, and the only time it bothers us is when we can't find something.

ELIZABETH: We spend an enormous amount on restaurants. We don't see friends often, but when we do, Thomas loves to grab the check. Otherwise, he's into real estate and investments. I like antiques and Oriental rugs. We love the things we've been able to acquire. Would I work this hard just for the satisfaction of it? No.

THOMAS: A lot of our friends go to great pains to contribute exactly fifty-fifty to the dime. But I think that's going too far. I trust Kiddo, and if she really wants my money, she'll have to divorce me.

ELIZABETH: We have separate checking accounts and bonds and things, but we keep a savings account together. We don't keep a strict accounting of who pays for what, although we try to keep it balanced. I don't know why. Maybe we think we've worked so hard, if one of us wants to blow it, let them do it with their own money. I think knowing we have money the other doesn't touch gives us a sense of security.

THOMAS: I don't think that diminishes our trust or our marriage. I think it's a safety net for both of us. But nothing is rigid. When you lead lives like ours, you have to play it by ear a lot.

ELIZABETH: He'll call me at the office and suggest that we do something or other. If I can, we do it, if not, we do it another time. Unless it's important, we don't plan ahead. I guess that's why we don't see friends much, and we rarely go to the theater. We're spontaneous people, and that's hard enough when it's just two of us involved.

THOMAS: There's little enough time to be alone together.

ELIZABETH: We spend a couple of hours together one or two nights a week, and sometimes a whole weekend. We don't need to spend endless hours together in order to feel connected. But when he was sleeping at the office I had to put an end to it before it became a routine. We are not one person because we're married, but we're two people who are supposed to have a life together. I'd never ask him to work normal hours. That would put a burden on me I don't want. We give each other freedom by not needing each other all the time. That doesn't mean there aren't moments when we miss each other a whole lot.

THOMAS: I think our lifestyles mesh very well. I love my Kiddo, and we've fulfilled many of our goals. We certainly don't think of ourselves as robots who are always on. But maybe other people think that.

Kari Clark, wife of television host and producer Dick Clark, worked for her husband for ten years before their marriage; they lived together for six of those years. After the marriage she went right on serving as his personal assistant.

Being married, what happens with the work situation—what is your position here, who are you?

"I am still working in the same way. I prefer to continue to say this is Kari, Dick's secretary. Otherwise, it just complicates it too much. I work as an employee in the company. During the working day, whatever he says goes. I do give my opinions, but I do not feel uncomfortable if he does not agree. I don't work as an equal. He is my boss, but when the day is over, we are then equal."

What happens about money?

"Well, he's a multimillionaire. I said *he*, because I don't think we are. I still get my regular paycheck—that's *my* money, and I like that. I have my car, I need my things. I buy whatever I want on our charges. We never discuss money. The accountant pays all the bills. Dick might go out and indulge himself with a purchase of a Rolls and a Bentley at the same time—he is into classic cars—that's fine with me, whatever he wants to do with his money."

Work and money means something quite different to you and me than to people like Harry and Leona Helmsley. But then, most of us don't run an empire worth over five billion dollars. Leona runs several hotels with an iron hand and is a strong influence on her husband. Yet she girlishly states that, "The only power I want is the approval of Harry that I've done a good job." Despite her own achievements, including winning prestigious awards like Realty Woman of the Year, Leona cherishes only one—"my marriage license."

After her first marriage ended in divorce, it didn't take long for Leona to achieve success in real estate. "I became the best broker in the city," she says proudly. "I was the talk of the real estate industry. Harry said, 'Whoever she is—get her!' I walked into his office and looked for a woman's picture, and there wasn't one. He asked me to join his firm and I told him he couldn't afford me. I did think he was a good-looking guy, but I didn't think of pursuing him."

Harry had been married for thirty-three years when he convinced Leona to work for him. The relationship took a personal turn, Harry explains, "partly because my relationship with my wife deteriorated and I wondered what to do with my life."

"I liked him," Leona admits, "but he was my boss, he was married, and he was a Quaker. What else did I need? My job was the most important thing in my life, and I wouldn't jeopardize that. Harry had to make the first move."

The first move was made and "one thing led to another," Harry says. "We both love to dance. Leona is a terrific dancer. And we enjoyed talking."

"You're a good kisser," Leona reminds him playfully.

"When you have flint and steel," Harry says with a smile, "you're going to have sparks."

Leona says they have grown closer over the thirteen years of their marriage. "Today we're one person, but we weren't when we married. We got along well and enjoyed each other, but it wasn't like it is today."

Leona puts as much work into her marriage as she does her hotels, like The Palace, over which she reigns as "Queen." "I deliver his food while he sits in front of the TV," says one of America's richest and most powerful women. "It makes me happy to see him happy. I love him, and money's the least of it."

Leona maintains that Harry's approval was always her top priority. "It was always my motivation. When we got married, I stopped working for a while. Then he came home and asked me about carpeting that he was replacing at the Park Lane Hotel and how he could save money on it. I told him not to do it cheaply, and the people who suggested it quit. I felt responsible. Gradually, I took over three hotels."

"Night and day we're thinking about the same things," says Harry. "Many couples have nothing to say to each other."

But Leona works because Harry supports her career. "I have no power. If he didn't want me to work, I wouldn't do it for a second. Harry's secure and knows I love him."

"I should've retired long ago," Harry says, "but Leona keeps me young—to the point that I've organized my business life on the basis that I'm going to last forever."

"You bet you are, darling," coos Leona, "unless I go first. Then I'll call over to tell you a secret, and the secret is, you're going, too."

How's that for a gal who doesn't think she has any real power?

A lot of people can't help being suspicious when someone like Leona Helmsley says, "Money's the least of it." Yeah, sure. But clearly there is far more than just money involved in her relationship with her husband. And on the other hand, there are people for whom money as money is far more important than it is to Leona Helmsley. Take Jeanne and Howard, a California couple who are both millionaires in their own right. They live in a forty-room mansion, own a stable of horses, a Learjet (which Jeanne will not use because she is afraid of flying), five classic cars, including a custom-made limousine (Jeanne does not drive and has a chauffeur), and also have seven people on their permanent staff.

There are moments when Jeanne and Howard seem straight out of a Jackie Collins novel. Can Jeanne really be the daughter of middle-class schoolteachers? Well, she won a beauty contest, a traditional route to Los Angeles. She wanted to be a movie star, but then she met Howard. He grew up in a small Texas town where he just happened to discover oil on his parents' modest property. Another American dream. They have two children, whom they are afraid of spoiling. But they are not reluctant to spoil themselves.

Jeanne is close to forty, beautiful enough to have been photographed for *Vogue* by Scavullo. She is the consummate collector, specializing in furniture, jewelry, and Chinese antiquities. "Collecting the pieces I have surrounded myself with gives me a sense of power I can't explain," says Jeanne. "It's that power which is the aphrodisiac. Finding an authentic Fabergé egg is like sexual fulfillment."

Howard, who collects only oil wells and money, is all for his wife's hobby. "What makes her happy makes me happy. I get a kick out of her excitement every time she picks up a piece of sculpture or a painting she's been dreaming of owning. She acts like a kid in a candy store, and I love it. At first I was the one to buy for her, but now she is so skillful at buying and selling she has her own accounts, funds, resources—she doesn't need my money."

Jeanne would like to have a museum for her collection. "I'd like to share the beauty I have found with the world. I want my name to be remembered in the art world. That's my dream. Most of all I would like to repay Howard in some way for what he has given me. The security, the freedom, the understanding that allowed me to pursue my own interests, not to mention the money he gave me to get started with. I don't think there is another man in the world who could cope with me. I'm very aware of that."

"I don't think there's anything I want that I don't have," Howard says. "Last weekend we attended a charity affair for the Music Center. Jeanne wore a spectacular gown and a diamond and emerald choker with matching earrings. When we walked into that room every head, male and female, turned to stare. I knew I was the luckiest man in the world."

Jeanne and Howard understand one another perfectly, and clearly belong together. A good marriage is not necessarily founded on values that we would admire or emulate. People must make a good marriage out of who they are, not what other people may think of them.

Nevertheless, there is more than one way to lead the life of the very rich.

Elbert and Lauresteen Hatchett have been married for twenty-three years and have three children. Their house in Bloomfield Hills, a Detroit suburb, has a mere twenty-four rooms, but the pool area "is three stories high—from the basement to beyond the second-floor bedrooms," Elbert describes with obvious pride. "There are twin waterfalls in it which cascade down from a topside Jacuzzi, and it also has guest dressing rooms, sauna, TV viewing room, poolside bar, and a playroom with a billiard table and pinball machines, an electric organ, and a full set of drums. We often invite several hundred guests for a splash party or a tennis tournament. A hundred and fifty spectators can be seated around the court and there are TV taping facilities."

Anyone making assumptions about the kind of people the Hatchetts are from this description would likely be way off base. The Hatchetts have special views about the meaning of money and success. To begin with, they are black. This should not in itself be a surprise—the number of black millionaires in this country is constantly increasing, not just among entertainers and sports figures, but also in professions that were once entirely a white province. Elbert is an attorney with a lucrative negligence and criminal law practice. Before their marriage, Lauresteen, also a college graduate, was a singer and music teacher; she continued to teach, basically supporting the family, in the first years of their married life.

About eighty percent of Elbert's law clients are white, and of those who are black, many are unable to pay their fees. "That's okay," Elbert says. "I grew up with people of the same sort, and I know how tough things can be. I think it's only right for me to give my time and talent to the community. I have been very fortunate," he says with emphasis.

Both Elbert and Lauresteen are active in civil rights work and a variety of charitable causes. "We hold benefits at our home," Lauresteen explains. "For instance, we raised money for a hospital in Detroit, to help children of all races. Other benefits have been to help black colleges keep going. We've had groups of teenagers over from the inner city for day-long outings. We also sponser T-Ball teams—that's a sort of pre-softball team for young kids. And I recently sang at an NAACP banquet. Really, whatever we can do, we will."

Elbert believes that having money has changed their lives in ways that go much beyond their house or the vacation ranch they own. "You can really be a better person, in terms of helping other people. We accept our responsibility. We have no guilt, because we're always giving back."

"Elbert has a very giving nature. Many people talk about doing things, but Elbert puts it into action. And our marriage has been enhanced by it, a lot. It's a coming together, an understanding. A lot of people go to Elbert's office and ask if he can help them, and he often can. But it's the projects we get involved in together that mean the most. They definitely bring us closer."

When she married, the wife, eighteen years younger than her husband, had not minded giving up her career as an actress. "I wasn't unhappy about no longer going around and beating on doors," she says. "What I was unhappy about in the first three or four years of our marriage was not having something to replace it with. I was painting, writing, doing a lot of reading, but I was in limbo."

One night her husband came home from work and said, "I don't make you happy, do I?"

"I was sort of shocked," she recalls. "I said, 'It isn't you, it's me.' It took *him* to tell *me* that I was unhappy."

Her husband says now, "I really thought she didn't love me anymore."

It was time for finding something more than just being a wife. "I didn't want to be like those women who were living through their husbands and had lost themselves. At parties, I gravitated towards the men's conversations. They were so much more interesting. I knew I needed something. I decided to go to UCLA to study Russian. He asked why I wasn't taking a language he knew, and I told him that Russian and Chinese were the two most important foreign languages in the world and that international relations was the area that I wanted to go into. He was almost crushed that I'd be speaking a language he wouldn't understand. He thought, 'Why my wife?'"

"I had a difficult time coping with that," he says. "I wasn't afraid of losing control. I was afraid I'd lose her because being my wife wasn't enough. That's what comes with ego," he admits. "My worry was how much we were going to drift apart while she was searching for her needs. I'd already fulfilled most of my needs."

The words spoken by this couple—and the problems that lie behind those words—are hardly uncommon. But the husband in this case is the movie and television star Lorne Greene, and at the point when he realized that his wife Nancy was unhappy, his television show *Bonanza* was, as Lorne puts it, "Hot as a pistol." He was at the height of his success. Of course, he had fulfilled most of his needs. It was difficult for him to understand why being Mrs. Lorne Greene wasn't enough for Nancy. For a man of his generation—he was seventy—it was wounding that Nancy wasn't satisfied. You can still hear the hurt, even after twenty-four years of marriage.

Fortunately, Lorne was big enough to recognize that his ego was getting in the way of understanding, and cared deeply enough about

Nancy's happiness to let her go after what she wanted. In the years since, she has become involved in public affairs on several levels—as a consultant on civil defense for various organizations and think tanks as well as for the late Hubert Humphrey, as publisher of an East-West relations newsletter, and as a founder of the Los Angeles branch of the National Women's Political Caucus.

Nancy's success gave Lorne some pause at times. "I was in the news business for fourteen years and I used to feel I was the expert," he notes.

"Now I'm the expert, and he doesn't like that sometimes."

"It used to bother me," Lorne admits, "but now I admire her ability. She's really phenomenal at all these meetings."

Even so, he still sometimes asks, "Why do you have to go now?"

"Intellectually he understands," Nancy says, "but he can retrogress momentarily emotionally before he gets control of it."

Nancy's career has changed their lives in a number of ways. "We used to have a lot of parties before Nancy got involved in all this. But you can take just so many show business parties, I discovered. Now we have many more friends from different walks of life. Nancy's work has made our lives more interesting. But now we live in a household where we can get seventy, maybe eighty calls a day. I'll ask Nancy to look after something and she'll tell me to do it because she has to go to the office. So a recent trip we made to China alone was so lovely."

"Until that trip we didn't realize how much other people invaded us, made demands on us," Nancy adds. "While we were driving home from the airport we decided not to let anyone ruin it for us."

"We need to have some time for ourselves. For instance, we went to Berlin for a few days because of Nancy's work. Then we went to Geneva for a couple of days just to relax by ourselves. We made the compromise."

Made the compromise. Initially, it was Lorne's to make, allowing Nancy to pursue her own interests. But now that she is a success on her own terms, she has begun to recognize that it's also important for her to compromise, to see to it that they have a private married life away from the demands of both their careers. It's time for her to give back some of the time Lorne "allowed" her to take for herself.

"I would love her doting on me and the kids, but I don't need that. I need her to be fulfilled and happy. As I need that for myself.

We are a very good couple because we both want the best for each other."

Lorne Greene died on September 11, 1987, at the age of seventy-two from severe respiratory failure following his admission and stay in the hospital for cancer.

On November 17, 1987, I had the following conversation with Nancy Greene on the telephone:

MARILYN: When did you find out how sick Lorne was?

NANCY: The last six months were all tests, etc., and he was not getting better. I did not leave him at all during this period, and I knew that when he entered the hospital, that if he was not out in five days, then he wouldn't make it. My psychic sense was very keen during this whole period. The doctors were finally turning to me for some of the answers. I made three typed pages of questions that I wanted answered. I was trying very hard to save his life by getting straight answers to the medical issues.

To the end he was robust looking, his heart was strong, and he died of respiratory complications following surgery. He actually waited for me to get there before he died. He asked the nurse, "Is she on the way"—and he heard me coming down the hall. When I got there he became very peaceful and died within the next ten minutes.

So it was probably a blessing, rather than see him wither away and suffer and die from cancer.

I hope I gave him enough during this period. I was with him all the time, just let all my work go. He was more important to me than anything.

MARILYN: What has it been like since he died?

NANCY: Actually, I have been so busy there has been little time to mourn. There was a tremendous outpouring from friends. I really didn't expect it, but I needed it—it's later, when they are gone, that I will really confront it.

MARILYN: What now?

NANCY: I never lost anybody before Lorne—it's a devastating experience, even two to three months later. I found myself crying easily, and I wasn't one to cry at all before.

But, I do have my work and a very full life. My life was never dependent on Lorne. Getting back to it is what it is all about for me.

His voice was so marvelous—I miss hearing that voice—I miss seeing him around. He always looked so strong and robust.

It is still too hard for me to assess the effect. It is too soon. I just miss the quiet times we had together, because they were so rare.

We spent the whole last year together. We went on a cruise, and I sensed how dependent on me he was becoming. I only hope I gave him enough, and that he felt that I did. We were a very good couple.

"Any man married to a famous woman *must*—and I underline must—have his own identity and his own work."

So says Peter Greenough, husband of Beverly Sills, who has followed her spectacular singing career with the demanding job of running the New York City Opera.

"My first wife died, and I brought three very young stepchildren with me. We have two children from our marriage. They now range in age from thirty-eight to twenty-five. Beverly is a very strong and determined person. She adopted my children and has truly been their mother, raising them from early childhood as if they were her own.

"Some men in my position," he continues, "find their work in their wives' careers, managing them, facilitating things for them, always traveling with them. That is not for me. I want Beverly to have her own career, and I want to have mine. I want to have my own identity and her to have hers. I am fortunately a newspaper columnist, and I do not have to work in any set place or any set time. But I have always been able to care for Beverly and our family in the style that we live in now, and her working had nothing to do with changing or improving our lifestyle. Of course, there are special pleasures, but they are not crucial to the way we live. Beverly has often said that she would stop working if it made me uncomfortable. But she needs her career as much as I need mine. I would never ask that of her.

For Joey and Cindy Adams, life is a glorious adventure—with work and money an integral part of it. They love travel, exploring parts of the world most of us can't pronounce. They love the finer things in life, and they both have terrific careers that allow them to indulge in the globe-trotting lifestyle they thrive on. Joey has written a number of books, is a successful comedian, writes a joke column for the *New York Post*, and has worked closely with many politicians and world leaders, beginning with Fiorello LaGuardia. Cindy's celebrity column also appears in the *Post*, an outlet for her insider news and barbed wit. She is a serious writer, as well, and published a biography of the late Indonesian president Sukarno—just one of the world leaders whose confidante she had become.

Although she was a struggling singer and comedienne still in her teens and Joey was an established comic when they met, common interests brought them together. "The chemistry was right," explains Cindy. "We spoke the same language—we were both in show business, both middle-class New Yorkers who liked good clothes, good food, good living."

"And we also had humor," adds Joey.

Before Cindy blossomed into a talented writer, she enjoyed simply being Mrs. Joey Adams. "I gave up my career when we got married, mostly because I had no career to give up. But I was driven to do something. I had a ninety-nine percent average in high school, but I wasn't sure what my real talents were. Joey's lifestyle and career were very hot and, in the beginning, it was sufficient success for me. I suddenly got a mink coat and beautiful designer clothes and I lived on Fifth Avenue."

"We did everything with love and joy," says Joey. "We enjoyed the money, fame, and glory, but we never did it for those reasons. We've just loved being in this business together every second. She was my partner in everything. I wrote a book about her, *Cindy and I*, because I was so proud of her."

"The world was my stage during those first years," says Cindy. "He was the costume designer, the setting designer, and I was playing the role of rich and important lady and loving it."

That role had a reasonably long run—six or seven years—but then it was time for something else. "Joey was in Las Vegas appearing with Zsa Zsa Gabor, and I knew there was a great deal more I could do than just attend Joey's performances. So I went to the Columbia School of Journalism to learn how to write."

"I encouraged her to write the way she talks," says Joey. "She had such a good sense of humor. She was a great help to me when President Kennedy sent me on a world tour. She started off each show speaking the language—in Afghanistan, Cambodia, Laos. Then, when she met the leaders, Prince Sihanouk of Cambodia, President Sukarno, they all fell in love with her. She'd talk to a king the same way she'd talk to a headwaiter. They could let their hair down with Cindy. She was a great ambassador, not only for me, but for our country."

"I'd started writing professionally about that time. I began on a junky weekly interviewing Joey's celebrity friends. He allowed it because it was sort of amusing. He thought, 'Cindy's running around interviewing Frank Sinatra today. What fun.' Everybody laughed. Then I moved up to *TV Guide*. I had a 'screw you' mentality. I thought, 'So what if I blow this? I'll put on my sable and go to dinner.' It was partially stupidity. I was just being me, because I didn't know enough not to be, or how to be any other way. Joey didn't care if I blew it, either. I could say, 'Screw you,' because I had Joey's love."

"I watched her get better and better and kept getting more proud of her. I never thought I was the teacher and she was the pupil. I was learning also."

"We're even more devoted now. Our lives became more and more intertwined. I'm not sure if either of us could make it on our own now, because each of us is the instigator and the support system for the other."

"There's no professional jealousy, either. Cindy didn't want to work at the *New York Post*, because I was there and she thought it was my turf. The editors and publisher and I had to insist that she do her column there."

"Areas like that are sensitivities, not insecurities, and we're sensitive to each other's needs," Cindy says. "If we're at a party and it's more my people, I'll make sure that Joey's circulating enough, and he does the same for me."

"Even though I have nothing to do with Cindy's column, I think of it as our column. The same with my joke column. If I have to speak at a dinner, she'll stay up all night to go over the lines. Everything's a partnership. I take care of the money, but she wouldn't have to ask me for anything. She's got a good deal—everything she earns she keeps, and I pay the income tax on it. If she wants another coat, I'll give her six. She trusts me and never asks about money."

"If you have to ask every time you want a hat, you're out of your mind," says Cindy.

"We're just one in every single way," Joey says.

And that's the whole key to their marriage.

Kenny Rogers has had eleven platinum records—more than any other solo male singing star. That means a great deal of money to spend. How it gets spent is something that occasionally causes his wife Marianne, who was herself a star of *Hee Haw* until the birth of their child Christopher, to put her foot down. She recalls the purchase for fourteen million dollars of the Dino DeLaurentis estate in Los Angeles. She had been against buying it, and it had turned out to be a mistake. "But Kenny loves remodeling and reconstruction," she says. "One of our strongest confrontations—over nine years we have only had about five arguments—was one of his remodeling jobs. He gets very carried away. And a mirrored stairwell in the barn was the straw that broke the camel's back. I was in tears. He finally said, 'What hurts most is that you're right.'"

Marianne doesn't feel they are hooked on the money for its own sake, although she says, "I know I often yearn for a simpler existence. I can do without an awful lot of what we have. We had wonderful times when Kenny was in debt and I helped him out."

Partially as a reaction to their wealth, Marianne became deeply involved in charity work, not only making donations but also a great many personal appearances as well, and doing vast amounts of behind-the-scenes detail work. "I'm up early in the morning and then working until late at night doing what has to be done. Stacks of paperwork for charities that I involved myself with before Christopher was born. When he arrived, gifts came from all over, and I felt I had to respond personally to every one because of the individual involvement of the people. I thought I would have a nervous breakdown. Now I'm pulling back from all kinds of activities so I can concentrate on Christopher."

Kenny himself worries about Marianne's enormous involvement in charity work. "If you ask me, what Marianne needs more than anything else in the world is a real hobby. She has gotten caught up in these charities. They can be a vacuum that pulls you in and absorbs you. And Marianne with her guilt feels obligated to do what is asked. I want to help her do what she enjoys without guilt. Charities are just as happy with money as they are with personal services."

Kenny feels that Marianne doesn't rise to her full potential. "She has tremendous talents. In so many areas. I have always encouraged her to go out and do things. But I think she feels guilty about enjoying herself. She is a wonderful painter. I'll bet she never mentioned that to you."

In spite of some stress, the marriage is nevertheless based on very strong grounds. "I have been up and down," Kenny says, "and I realize that this is all temporary. I never needed the degree of success that I got. The truth is, one of the happiest moments in my life was when Marianne and I first met and I had nothing. I was borrowing money from her to pay my child-support payments. If I had met her with this pace going, we might never have had the chance to lay the foundation we have."

Kenny readily admits that his sense of security about their relationship evolved in part from the fact that Marianne committed herself to him when he had nothing. "That is why I never feel threatened. I also feel that I have something to offer her that no one else can. Whenever I articulate this it sounds wrong—but I feel it. What I have to offer Marianne is that I genuinely care about her. I never want her to be hurt or upset. I will protect her against anything I can."

That does not mean controlling her, however. Her self-growth is also deeply important to him. "There's a phrase I love," says Kenny Rogers. "A man of quality is never threatened by a woman of equality. I encourage her for her. I think marriage is worth working at. It is not easy. I have heard many say that if you have a good marriage, you don't have to work at it. I think that is garbage. It requires constant attention. Our arguments have strengthened our marriage. We learned from each one. My need to love is much more important than my need for success. But this realization came before the success did. That is what makes it so important. I knew when I met Marianne and fell in love with her that my relationship with her and the joy I felt were far more important than the success I had been after all my life. Who could have anticipated this, anyway? I had been running for the wrong goal. With Marianne, I am truly happy."

For us, marriage meant children.
—*Maxine Rosenblum*

I can't see myself at this time accommodating
myself to the structure of a child's life.
—*Mel Erlich*

Children: What is a family?

The role of children in a successful marriage is as complex as our society. There are those who continue to believe, as their parents did before them, that children are the main reason for marriage and therefore should be its primary focus. Some couples even see children as the ultimate and most lasting bond between them. But there are others who feel that children represent not a bond but bondage— an obstacle to personal freedom and a threat to the marriage. In today's world, each of these points of view is socially sanctioned and, providing both partners agree, either can be a component of a good marriage. Although a happy marriage is certainly a prerequisite for raising children, a good marriage does not require the presence of children to be happy itself.

Indeed, it is widely accepted among marriage counselors that many people, from all backgrounds and at all economic levels, are not well suited to the role of parents. Fortunately, more people who would not make good parents are coming to recognize that fact, and seek other grounds on which to base their relationship. Most of the people you will meet here do have children, and they make it very clear that successful parenting can occur in many different situations. There is no single model or cluster of recommended models for good parenting. However, it should be noted that none of these couples had children to save a marriage. If there were problems in raising their children—and sometimes there were severe ones—these couples were not overwhelmed by them, nor did the problems cause them to regret having children. In fact, in the process of solving family difficulties, many of these couples were able to reassess, change, and strengthen the marital relationship itself.

Arlene and Malcolm Rose adore children. They've been married for seventeen years and have five children of their own, as well as an adopted Korean child who is now fifteen. Their ramshackle house in Redondo Beach, California, literally spills over with children. And they are considering adopting another one.

Although she looks twenty, with long brown hair, no makeup, and dressed in shorts and sneakers, Arlene is close to forty. She graduated from UCLA with a degree in anthropology and has a part-time job at United Airlines. Malcolm is a professor of English at UCLA; he's an attractive man in his early forties with a lopsided grin and a perpetual twinkle. Children love him; they crawl all over him, pull at his beard, and search his pockets. Both he and his house have the same rumpled good humor.

MARILYN: Don't all these children get on your nerves sometimes?

MALCOLM: Very rarely. They are a constant source of joy to me. Their curiosity is stimulating and fascinating. Of course, I'm not with them as much as Arlene is, but I always look forward to the time I spend with them.

MARILYN: What about you, Arlene, since you do spend more time with them?

ARLENE: Sometimes I get a little crazy, which is the reason I have a part-time job. I do need the company of adults, but if I'm away from the children for even a short time, I look forward to coming home.

MARILYN: Do you feel the children have mainly contributed to the success of the marriage?

MALCOLM: Definitely. I always wanted a large family. I come from one myself, although not quite *this* large. I think having a lot of children is both a challenge and a treat.

ARLENE: We never planned it this way. We thought three would be perfect, but once we had three, a few more seemed even better. It gets easier with practice. I don't think it's the answer for most people. I was an only child, and I always dreamed of this house and this family. I was lucky to find a man who wanted the same kind of life. Most men would be bonkers by now.

MARILYN: There must be a problem with privacy, though. I don't just mean sex, but simply being together as two people who love each other.

MALCOLM: That's why we make it a point to get away for a weekend alone once in a while. We take a cabin with a brook that flows right by. We just read, take long walks in the woods, and at night we light the fireplace and make passionate love. I think two of our children were conceived there.

MARILYN: So your private times end up creating less privacy!

ARLENE: Even so, it's about time for another trip. Actually, I don't think we will have any more of our own, but we will probably adopt some children who need a family. Paul, our Korean son, is just as precious to me as the rest. Giving birth to a healthy child is still a miracle. Every time I've counted ten tiny fingers and toes, I have been in awe of that miracle. It doesn't matter if the child is born to *you* or not.

MARILYN: More kids mean more expenses, though. I understand that you can save a lot in terms of hand-me-down clothes and things like that in large families. But what do you do about Christmas presents for this brood?

ARLENE: It costs us less for presents than most families with children—and we have more fun. We don't buy presents except for bikes and musical instruments. Everything else we make ourselves.

MALCOLM: We have a Santa's workshop over the garage. We

start early, around August or September. The boys work with me in the shop and the girls work with Arlene in the den. Sometimes we vary it.

MARILYN: Do you make things for each other?

MALCOLM: Oh, yes. And we also buy something.

ARLENE: Last year, Malcolm gave me one of the best presents I've ever had. All the children gathered around, and in the box was what appeared to be an ordinary rock about two inches long. The rock was split in half and inside was a perfect fossil of a coiled sea snail. It's hundreds of thousands of years old. It sits on my dressing table, and the children love to run their fingers over it when I open it for them. I'm glad they can appreciate a sense of history.

MALCOLM: Some people say to us, "How can you bring so many kids into this dangerous world?" Well, everybody is concerned about the future—whether there will *be* one. But that doesn't mean we should just stop living or having children. They are the hope of the world. Everybody's children are important to me. I've honestly tried to make the world a better place, and I can only hope my children will do the same.

I wonder if Malcolm and Arlene would consider adopting a deserving adult.

Susanne and Brian Henry create something of the same feeling. They have five children—the result of the fact that it is a second marriage for both of them. With divorce and remarriage a commonplace situation, many couples must deal with the melding of two sets of children into one family, and the Henrys have managed it with considerable aplomb.

Susanne is thirty-two, Brian forty-eight, and they have been married for twelve years. She holds an account executive position with a major airline, and he is an attorney. They met at a local fair in Oklahoma, where Susanne and her two-year-old daughter lived. Brian was vacationing with his three sons—then ages four, seven, and eight. They were married three months later and subsequently had a son of their own.

"It was a big change," Susanne says of becoming the mother of four at the age of twenty. "But our brood kept us so busy there really wasn't much time to think about it. We were very much in love. We were both used to hard work, and we felt it would work out—and we were right! We both loved the idea of a big family—not that I anticipated having it so soon. But I did feel it was exciting and a big challenge."

"We had problems, sure," Brian says, "but we just coped with them. We thought of ourselves as very lucky to have found each other. We felt like soul mates right away, and we wanted to share everything. The difficulties, which were more like day-to-day nuisances, were often a real pain in the ass. But that's just part of life. They will always be there, in one form or another."

Susanne says that the biggest problem was that the house was too small. "Until our oldest, Kevin, left for college, share was the only arrangement the kids understood. We always let them have their friends over, and often I really wanted to find a place to hide."

"Space and, of course, privacy," Brian agrees, "have always been a problem. We would often meet for lunch so we could be alone to talk."

The lack of privacy, Susanne admits, smiling, affected their sex life. "Especially for me. Brian was used to having a bunch of kids around, but I was always worried there'd be a knock on the door. Finally, Brian decided to hold a family meeting about needing our own space, privacy, and the importance of respecting that need. After the discussion, we put a large Do Not Disturb sign on our bedroom door when appropriate."

"The funny thing was," Brian adds, "that all the kids demanded one. Even though they all shared rooms, they'd put the sign up over their beds, which meant, 'Leave me alone, I'm in my space.'"

Meetings became a regular part of the family regimen. "It was the only way to create any order and discipline," Brian says. "Each kid had so many issues to discuss; we had to establish a code of behavior. Generally, I dealt with discipline."

"Everyone had a list of chores. In the morning, Brian and I went to work, the older kids to school, and my mother or a part-time housekeeper helped with the younger ones."

"Basically," Brian says, "we've tried to teach the kids to make decisions for themselves. They all get allowances—not the same amount, but in proportion to their ages. Allowances are for personal extras like junk food, records, things they do with their friends. We provide the necessities. What we do with conflicts is simply use common sense—we talk it over and negotiate."

"When we moved to this house we all worked on it. All the children are very handy. We did our own painting, blacktopped the roads, put in details like wood beams on the ceiling. As a result," Susanne says, "we all love this house dearly, and I know it is a home the kids will want to return to when they're in college or wherever they go. It's been difficult at times—and still is—but underneath it all, we work hard, love each other, and share the problems and the good times."

"I think our kids know that they come from a home that has a strong commitment," Brian adds. "They feel the love and attachment here. They may have been treated rough at times, but they all know how to take care of themselves and each other. That may be the most important contribution a parent can make to a kid."

Both the Roses and the Henrys are realistic couples. They wanted large families, but they fully acknowledged to themselves and to one another that having children implies hard work and sacrifice. That acknowledgment is crucial even for couples who have far more money than either the Roses or the Henrys; people who think merely in terms of financial sacrifice are fooling themselves. Time, energy, and the needs of the self must also be sacrificed in the raising of happy children. Couples must be truly committed to making parenthood a very significant phase of their lives over a period of twenty years or more, and that requires a strong fundamental relationship within the marriage. Too many people have children before they are ready, or simply because they think they should have children, that it's the "done thing."

Fortunately, an increasing number of people have the sense to realize that they would be better off waiting. That is the case with Jeffrey Goidel, a clinical psychologist, and Harlene Cooper, a fashion designer. Both thirty-one, they have been married for ten years and live on Long Island.

Jeffrey and Harlene want children, but not until they reach their mid-thirties. They discussed the question—as all couples should—before they were married. "There was a real rap session," Harlene says. "He wanted one and I wanted two. So we settled on one and a half."

Many marriage counselors would agree with their reasons for waiting. Harlene says that they want to enjoy their freedom thoroughly now—so that they will be mature enough to accept a child without reservations. Jeffrey also feels it's essential to develop their careers to the point that they will be able to provide a child with proper care instead of having three people struggling on one income.

"We also feel," Jeffrey says, "that when the time comes, the responsibility for the care of the baby will be fully shared. Harlene's schedule isn't flexible. But I hope by then to be established enough so I'll have more flexibility myself. I think a lot of people in our generation suffered from not really having two parents. I remember when I was in first grade I was a pumpkin in a play. My mother and aunts came to see me, but my father was working. Well, I want to see my kid as a pumpkin."

This is not, as Jeffrey sees it, a matter of giving up his career. "If Harlene doesn't get home until late afternoon, I can see my patients at night. The main point is, it's going to be my kid, too. I don't see why it should all be her responsibility. Besides, she makes more money than I do. She's *got* to work!"

Ray Kerns is in many ways the kind of father Jeffrey Goidel looks forward to being. Ray's wife June says, "Ray was a better mother than I was. He's a very meticulous person. When Dennis was a baby we lived in a very small apartment and had no room for a washing machine. Every night Ray took Dennis's dirty clothes and hand-washed them in the sink. One thing I love about Ray is that nothing is too good for his children. We scrimp on our own clothes and entertainment, but we give the kids the best. He is also a big believer in family togetherness. Even if he goes to get the car fixed, he wants all of us to come."

Ironically, Ray is a man who thought he'd probably never get married. He was thirty-six and had been living with June, then twenty-seven, for a year when she suggested they get married or forget about it. It is a very good marriage, but it means hard work for both Ray and June. Ray has a job with the government, and June is an editorial assistant. She has always worked, except for brief periods when Dennis and his sister Samantha, six years younger, were born. For some time when Dennis was young, she was a Tupperware dealer, which gave her more flexible hours. But she was then made a manager and, in terms of hours spent working, it became a full-time job. With both parents working, it has meant taking advantage of every child-care possibility.

June took her current nine-to-five job when Dennis was nine and Samantha was three. "I paid the mother of Dennis's best friend to take care of him after school. Samantha went into full-time day care. Fortunately, I have been very active in the day-care center. It was a cooperative nursery, and to keep costs low we had to have bingo nights, fairs, garage sales, all kinds of things to raise money. Being so involved kept me abreast of what was happening at the center."

Dennis is now fourteen and Samantha eight. But even with both kids in school, the daily logistics are complex. There's another day-care center one block from Samantha's school. "I take her there at seven forty-five," Ray explains. "Then I have to run back to make my bus to work. About an hour later, they take her to school. Then at three they pick her up."

"I work about an hour's drive away so I can't pick her up when they close at six. Neither can Ray. So, it's Dennis's job. He started doing it when he was twelve."

"A couple of years before that," Ray adds, "Dennis got involved in Little League and other activities and didn't want a babysitter any more. In some ways he resents having to pick up his sister by six. But it's taught him a sense of responsibility. He also works now delivering newspapers."

"As a concerned working mother, I made the rule that he must call me when he gets home. If he doesn't, I get very upset, and he knows it when I walk in the door."

Even with such a hectic schedule, the Kernses are very involved with their children's activities. When Samantha was having reading problems at school, June, who had been attending night school, quit to give her daughter extra help. "For six months we worked together, and Samantha loved every moment of it. Even now, before she goes to sleep every night, we get into bed together and read. It's a very special time. I tried to give each of the children a special time, but Dennis is older now and doesn't need it. He's got his friends and interests. Actually, when he used to have special time with me, he'd ask Samantha to join us."

"Most people waste time," says Ray. "Many of Dennis's friends have mothers who don't work and their children don't get any attention. Their parents don't take them places or do things with them the way we do. I mean, why have children in the first place?"

Many parents talk about quality time. It's one of the great rationalizations of our two-career world. But when Ray Kerns says it, you believe him. Both he and June clearly put great effort into raising their children. Ask June how she gets everything accomplished and she replies, "If I had to sit and think about it, I'd go crazy. On weekends, we're always doing something as a family. We go roller-skating, apple-picking—we're a family of doers. I need to keep moving; it gives me a solid feeling of accomplishment."

The kind of life the Kernses live, however, is definitely not for some couples. Take Pat and Marcy Marks, for example, who have been married for sixteen years. He comes from an affluent San Francisco family and has two brothers; she is one of four children born into a middle-class Los Angeles family. Pat, a very successful lawyer, and Marcy, a travel writer and gourmet cook, have been around the world several times. They maintain apartments in London and New York and have a beach house in Malibu. They're vital, career-oriented people enjoying life in their middle forties.

Did you ever consider having children?

PAT: No. We made the decision before we were married that we would not. For a lot of reasons that are right for us. We just have too many interests and enjoy too many activities to give a child the proper attention and time. I think if you're going to bring a child into the world, you owe them a degree of dedication and time that we are not prepared to give.

MARCY: Telling children that you love them is just not good enough. I have many friends with careers who are also involved in various causes and interests. They spend very little time with their children. They rationalize with that "quality time" cop-out. That's bullshit! In their formative years, children need to have their parents around—especially their mothers. They don't need a five-minute bedtime story and a hug as their parents get ready to go out on the town. I knew I wouldn't be able to give more than that—and it's not enough, by far. It would be terribly unfair to burden a child with me for a mother or Pat for a father. People like us who do have children feel guilty most of the time. They attack each other out of guilt, and it creates a miserable family life. It's not for me!"

So you don't think a woman needs children to feel fulfilled?

MARCY: I don't believe that for a minute. I certainly don't need children to feel fulfilled. In fact, though I love my husband very much, I don't believe that our love is what makes me feel fulfilled, either. I'm happy I have Pat, but I create my own sense of fulfillment. If that sounds strange, it may be, but it's honest.

Mel and Eleanor Erlich are professional people, both with master's degrees. Both were only children and had somewhat isolated childhoods. They were friends for two years before becoming romantically involved. Married for a dozen years, Mel is forty-five and Eleanor is thirty-eight.

MARILYN: As your life goes on, do you think that it becomes less likely that you will have children?

MEL: Yes, it may be too much of a gamble. We must deal with it, or the chance will pass us by.

ELEANOR: We have talked about it, but I have never had that great maternal desire. We have a lot of fun as it is. We are very playful.

MARILYN: Playful in what way?

ELEANOR: Around this apartment there are lots of characters with names and personalities—stuffed animals, flowerpots, throw pillows. They have adventures. Mel is very likely to tell me a twenty-minute story about someone who does not exist.

MEL: These creatures not only have names, they have lives and do things in the apartment when we are not here.

MARILYN: I get it. You're both nuts!

MEL: Exactly.

ELEANOR: There is a rich fun side to this relationship. We enjoy all sorts of pursuits, and run around the city a lot. And we're both very involved with our careers. I just don't know if I am willing to give it up and make the sacrifices necessary to having children.

MARILYN: Do these "characters" who live here cause any problems?

MEL: They function mainly at the whimsy of the live people, so they are not a problem.

MARILYN: Are they a substitute for children?

MEL: Perhaps. Grown-ups have to play, too.

ELEANOR: Because we are playful, I think we would make terrific parents. I'm really torn, though. I like the way we are living. Our financial life is so comfortable for us.

MARILYN: What about adoption at a later time?

MEL: There are so many children without parents, that seems a right thing to do. But I can't see myself accommodating myself to the structure of a child's life at this time.

ELEANOR: It would be too much of a major revamping.

Couples who feel complete without children can seem "odd" to people for whom children are an important aspect of marriage. But then, people without children sometimes look at the problems other couples have with their kids and count themselves lucky to be out of it. And certainly it is true that couples who have children just because that's the "normal" way often discover that those children can exacerbate any problems that exist within the marriage. Gwen and Harold Simpson are just such a couple. Married for twenty-four years, they have three grown children. The youngest, a son of seventeen, attends a private school for problem children. They also have a daughter in graduate school and a son finishing college. Gwen had just finished college herself and was teaching when she met Harold, a veterinarian, and moved from her home in Philadelphia to Detroit.

They had their first child a year after marrying, which was not what Gwen had wanted. "It was very difficult for me, because I was not really ready to give up my teaching career. At first, I was very unhappy. Then we had two more. And I was the dominant one in raising them. I was always the disciplinarian. The result was that I had three very angry children. I was the bad guy all the time—in fact, many times, Harold would side with the kids. Instead of acting like a parent, he became one of the kids. I was the only adult parent in the family."

Gwen was pushed into this role. Harold admits marrying her for her strength. "When we first met, I really admired how together she was. I always felt at loose ends, disorganized and not really sure of what I wanted. Gwen's strength was her biggest attraction. But I also wanted a woman to be there for me, to be at home and have time for me. I wanted her there physically and emotionally for me. I also wanted children and a real family life."

Harold also now recognizes that his relationship with his children became more important than Gwen. "I wasn't aware of that, but looking back, I guess it was true. I loved having children, and they became very important to me. I felt that I had to sort of protect them from Gwen. I didn't want to fight with them all the time the way she did. All you get are hostile feelings and no love. So I gave in to them a lot."

Gwen is aware of how tough she was with the children. "I was very compulsive, and the wimpier Harold got, the tougher I would get. I was very angry. I didn't like the role that was forced on me, but I couldn't find any way out. I would set limits, and then he would say, 'I don't think they have to come home so early.' The kids knew instinctively to ask me first and after I said no, they would go to him and he'd say yes. His decision would ultimately win out, because there were four against one. I'd just get tired and drop it."

This situation had the inevitable impact on Gwen's relationship with her husband. "I was resentful all the time. I didn't respect him as a man or a parent. That's where all our problems centered—on the kids. For a person with my sense of discipline and high standards of behavior, nothing could have been worse than losing respect for him."

The problem was compounded by the fact that Harold needed his children's love more than their respect. "So, I lost the respect of both my kids and my wife. The kids came to me because I was an easy touch. They didn't respect me at all. But with Gwen, I always knew, no matter what, there was a deep feeling of love underneath all our problems. We could always come back together emotionally, because I had a genuine desire to change and work things out."

Gwen and Harold got therapeutic help with the children. "But we were also very aware that somehow we would have to deal with this dominant/passive struggle that went on between us," Gwen says. "We always knew that once we got the anger out of the way, a feeling of love would surface. We do know, profoundly, that this relationship is very good and we can always reach down and find it again."

All three children became confused and insecure as a result of the struggle that was going on in Gwen's and Harold's relationship, but it affected their youngest son most deeply. "He began to get into trouble with drugs, stealing. He was unable to function at school," Gwen says. "He really needed a strong father figure. We were very lucky to find an excellent special school. It's very structured and closely involves the parents in therapy with the child. The school's philosophy makes a lot of sense—the child's emotional growth can't be accomplished without involving the parents and siblings and changing the home environment. After a year at this school, he's off drugs and he's taking care of himself physically. He's beginning to open up to us emotionally. We feel there's been a lot of progress."

Becoming involved in their son's therapy has in fact helped the whole family, Gwen feels. "As a whole, we're all much closer. The other children are open and express their feelings, and we're able to work on problems that are bothering them together. As for Harold and I, we now recognize that we have different expectations, as most people do, and we have a real desire to work things out together."

"Gwen and I have a united front now, and the kids are so much happier. They feel more secure and they have respect for both of us. I think we'll give it another twenty-five years, and if it still doesn't work, then I'm leaving."

TOBY (MRS. ITZHAK) PERLMAN: We're raising our children the way we were raised. I lived in a pressure cooker in some ways, but the pressure was different than in most Jewish households, where the first pressure is academic. As in "or you're dead." My parents didn't feel that way. And we don't feel that way about our children. We want them to do their best, but they don't have to be *the* best. I tell them, "Listen, if you think you're hearing me tell you to be *the* best, you're not hearing me right. Just *try* your best." My daughter came home with a forty the other day and I said, "How wonderful, you knew forty percent of things." On the other hand, I have one son who's a lazy bum, and I don't have much respect for that.

Married for twenty-five years, Lillian and Terrence Mullins have two daughters, Barbara, twenty-four, who lives in California, and Shawna, seventeen, who lives with her parents near Philadelphia. Shawna's musician boyfriend, Kevin, also lives with them. Lillian, forty-three, was forced to take over Terrence's real estate business after several strokes and heart attacks forced him to retire. Terrence is now only forty-five.

Although both the Mullins daughters have become rebellious,

they have done so in quite different ways. "Barbara was pretty straight until she graduated from college," Terrence explains. "Her entire outlook changed when she got involved with the antinuke groups. You know, the wine and cheese and pot set. Then she took off for California."

Lillian says that it was different for Shawna. "She was twelve when Terrence became ill, and I started spending all my time caring for him. She was on her own all the time. She really had a very traumatic home life. Terrence was very demanding. When he had his first stroke, it was really hell for her."

"She didn't have much of a father, even when she was little," Terrence admits. "I was immersed in my own business, and so was Lillian, later."

"Whatever Shawna did that I didn't like I sort of ignored because I didn't have time to deal with her. I love my children, and I didn't want to lose them. I should have said to Terrence, 'Look, we have a nurse and you're not alone. Give me time to be a person and a mother.' But I didn't, and it was Shawna who suffered."

Terrence shakes his head. "Shawna was always strong-willed and knew what she wanted. But I realize now that the weird way she dressed and acted up with her motorcycle friends and musicians was probably a plea for attention. I really demanded an awful lot from her. She had to exercise my legs, go to the store, help around the house. She always cooked and ate by herself."

Lillian thinks Shawna chose Kevin as a boyfriend because she needed a father and a strong male figure. "Kevin was strong, even though he's only a few years older. He gave her the compassion and attention she needed, and Terrence was just a frail man she had to take care of. And I was either attending to him or on the phone or going to real estate school. The way she got attention from me was to continuously make demands. She wanted the best clothes and all sorts of material things. It was her way of getting my love, and I gave the things to her to make up for the love and attention I couldn't provide. When she met Kevin, he was playing with a group at a local rock concert. He was friends with some of the boys in the neighborhood. She met him during a terrible two-week period when Terrence had another stroke and my father was dying. I was a total mental case. She was only fourteen. I first thought that Kevin was just one of the local boys that hung around. I didn't know that he was sleeping in my garage. When I found out that he didn't have a home, I guess I felt very sorry for him."

Terrence nods. "He was only seventeen and had no home. He begged us to let him sleep in the basement. If I were stronger, I'd forbid it. I'm much more straitlaced than Lillian, and I object strongly."

"Many people think we're kooks," Lillian says with a shrug. "I know the neighbors find it highly objectionable, but that's their problem."

Lillian and Terrence argued some about whether to allow Kevin to move into the basement, but Terrence was "in no shape to make a fuss at the time," as he puts it. Lillian decided to go along with the situation, partially out of sympathy for Kevin and partially out of the recognition that it was the only way to maintain any parental control over Shawna. "I didn't feel threatened at first that Shawna might run off with him. But about two years ago, she and I had a terrible fight and I slapped her real hard. It made me realize what I was turning into. It stopped me dead. I realized that I only had two choices. Either I lose my daughter and not know where she is or what's happening to her, or I could ease back into exercising some gentle control. I always thought that with time she'd outgrow him."

"I never thought he was good enough for Shawna," Terrence says.

"Kevin asked if he could have his band rehearse here. I wanted to have Shawna close by, and I liked the music. They do make noise and the neighbors complain—they've called the police a few times. I felt it was my house and they could go to hell."

Lillian says that there have been a few problems with drugs, but just pot. "I'd go down and say, 'Okay, pot smokers out!'"

"My sister and brother-in-law said I should throw Kevin out and if Shawna wants to leave to let her go," Terrence says. "But it was our house and our decision."

It's clear that while Terrence doesn't approve himself, he is willing to back up his wife regardless of what others say. And he's willing to admit that it has been less of a problem than he had expected. "I get treated with respect. The kids always say please and thank you. But they're distant."

"They appreciate our giving them a place to congregate. When the house needed painting, they all volunteered. They threw a barbecue for us. They helped put in the swimming pool."

"Once in a while," Terrence adds, "they'll vacuum, clean the windows, put up storm windows."

Although Terrence admits this somewhat grudgingly, he is coping. He respects his wife's strength and goes along with her, perhaps in part because she actually seems to enjoy the situation. "I think I'm a mother image for all of them," Lillian says, "but I don't interfere. Some of them have said to me that they wish they could talk to their own mothers the way they do to me. I just try to understand them. And I still have my daughter home with me. That's what matters most."

While Lillian and Terrence have persevered and found a unique solution to a difficult problem, their trials—like those of Gwen and Harold—would perhaps give prospective parents some pause. But people who want children are not usually swayed by object lessons in reality. Regardless of the obstacles, they feel that their lives are not complete without a child.

For Terry and Jim Englisis, the obstacle was a medical one. Married for fifteen years, they are both in their mid-thirties. Terry works as an executive secretary and Jim is a construction worker.

Terry was two years behind Jim in high school and her older brother was a good friend of Jim's. "I always knew I'd marry him," Terry says. "That was how I planned on living my life. I have a pretty good job now, and I was thrilled when I got my promotion. It's important. But it wasn't what I dreamed of. Maybe it's unusual for these times, but I talked to my girlfriends about being Mrs. Jim Englisis—and having a houseful of babies." But within a year after their marriage, they realized that there was a problem about conceiving a child. "We started trying maybe six months after we were married," Terry says. "Every month—nothing."

"We both went to doctors," Jim says. "Lots of doctors."

It turned out that Terry would not be able to have a child of her own. "I cried a lot for a while, but Jim was really good with me. When he said he could live with it and we'd have a wonderful life, I believed him."

"It didn't come as a shock to me," Jim says. "I was prepared mentally. I tried to hide my feelings, because no one could have felt worse about it than Terry. I never thought, 'I'll get a divorce and marry someone else because she can't have my kid.' But I was hurting. I told Terry we could adopt in a while."

They waited seven years before adopting, however. "It didn't end our lives. We didn't sit around sad all the time."

"We were happy. We'd accepted our lives," Terry says.

"But we always felt a little less than complete."

They both vividly remember the joy when they got their son Mike. "He was a really tiny thing," Jim recalls. "When he was a couple of days old we got a call and they said he was all ours. The shock almost blew me out of my seat. I was never so happy."

"We'd had a lot of suffering over the years, but it was like it all went away at once. We were floating. The day we got the news, Jim's mother came over and we put our arms around each other and cried."

Having a child was not easy financially, however. "We'd just bought a house," Terry says, "and the debts, the furniture needs— everything was tremendous. There was no way we could do without my income at that point. So I took my vacation time, and then my mother took over. I got up every morning and had to just tear myself away from Mike. But I wasn't crying about it. I had a son, and I knew he was being taken care of by someone we trusted and who loved him."

"I felt Terry hadn't turned out so bad," Jim says with a grin, "so it was okay for her mother to be with little Mike."

When a couple waits a long time for a child, one of two things is likely to happen—they may be better parents, or they may spoil the child. How did that work for Terry and Jim?

"The instinct was there to give him everything he wanted," Jim says. "Not just from us but from thirty people who'd pick him up and kiss him."

"By the time he was three weeks old he had enough toys to last until he's a teenager. It's good that we have a big basement."

"But the good thing was that we had more maturity by this time. We even read some of the books that I would've thought were a crock when I was younger. So is he spoiled?" Jim says. "Not in this family. We knew he needed to stay on this earth and not in the clouds."

They discussed at length when they should tell Mike he was adopted. "Our parents wanted us to hold off on telling him, but we thought he should know from us before someone told him. We explained it to him when he was five, and I think he understood it," Terry says.

"He's a real happy kid," Jim says. "And you know something? He looks more and more like me all the time."

The career of Smokey Robinson has survived doo wop, the British Invasion, acid rock, heavy metal, disco, and New Wave, and he is still turning out top-ten hits. His marriage to his wife Claudette is still another success story—they have been married twenty-eight years, unusual in the music business.

They were married when he was nineteen and she was seventeen. She was working as a secretary at a YMCA, making more money than he was, but he had a new job with the singer Berry Gordy and wanted Claudette to go on the road with him. Within two years, Smokey's song "Shop Around" had become Gordy's first million-seller and led to Smokey's forming his own group, the legendary Miracles. Claudette also sang with the group, and she continued to record with her husband for seventeen years. But after nine years she stopped traveling with him.

"I'd had five miscarriages. We thought about adopting, but the doctors kept saying, 'You're still very young.' So it was always 'Maybe next time.' But some of my pregnancies lasted into the sixth month. Once it was twin girls, and their breathing was already under development."

So you made the decision to focus on having a child?

"Yes. I had to stay in bed for nine months."

Was that the most difficult part, or being separated from Smokey?

"I missed Smokey. And I was used to traveling, performing, to companionship of the group. But Smokey's family kept me occupied."

And the doctors were right. You had a son.

"He's eighteen now. My daughter is sixteen. I'd wanted at least four. But I tutor children, too. I'd wanted to become a teacher before I married Smokey. We've lived in California for a long time now, but a day in my life is not Hollywood. Up at seven, get the kids off to school, do my tutoring. I am very home and family oriented. Working with Smokey was wonderful. But we have more than I ever dreamed. I feel very blessed."

Stu and Judith Goldblum also wanted a houseful of kids. In their case, a medical problem of a different sort—and its psychological impact on Judith—have created some tension between the couple.

In their mid-thirties, Stu and Judith have been married for eleven years. Stu is a copywriter for a cable TV station in Boston, and Judith is a housewife. When Judith became pregnant, they were both ecstatic. But a difficult pregnancy was followed by a premature birth, and their daughter was born with little chance for survival.

"She had everything from congenital heart failure to a collapsed lung," Judith recounts. "Her esophagus wasn't connected properly, so she couldn't swallow. They had to do microsurgery on her. She only had the slimmest chance of making it."

A trauma of this kind puts enormous strain on a marriage. Stu describes it vividly. "According to doctors and social workers we spoke to, most marriages couldn't survive such an ordeal. But we're both very strong people. The strain for me was in trying to keep my job and pay the bills while I worried every minute about whether my child would live or die. Judith kept vigil every day at the hospital. We were thoroughly exhausted all the time, but we hung in. I felt incredible strength in Judith, which gave me courage. And we loved the baby very much. It was that combination—our strength and our love for her, plus the miracle of surgery—that brought our daughter through. That's what the doctors told us."

Judith adds, "She could have ended up being a vegetable or retarded for life. Thank God we have a beautiful, healthy child— more intelligent than we ever dreamed possible. We're just thrilled she's alive and here with us."

The survival of such a child, especially an only child, can make her the emotional focal point of the marriage. When their daughter was a baby, Stu and Judith always had one ear cocked for the slightest cough. "As they get older," Stu says, "it's hard for any child to give up that special closeness and comfort. She still wants to sleep with us, and it's hard to say no."

Judith finds this somewhat disconcerting. "But I'm still very closely involved with her well-being. When she's sick, I'd rather have her in our bed. We know she's basically healthy now, but it's hard to forget how fragile she was. We let her get away with a lot of special privileges we wouldn't otherwise. I think we both worry much more than average parents, but she's not really all that spoiled, considering."

Stu is the disciplinarian, and he says that if he were home more, he wouldn't spoil her as much. "But I'm very involved with my job, and there are just so many hours in the day. I try to communicate with her as much as possible to let her know I care a lot. I'm very physical with her, and kiss and hug her even when she annoys the hell out of me. I'm like those lions you see with cubs jumping all over them. Even if they're annoyed, they tolerate it."

"Stu would love to have more children," Judith says. "Doreen is intrigued by babies and wants to have a brother or sister. After all the spoiling, I don't know how she'd react to the competition. But the truth is, I'm afraid to have more. I don't think I could go through an ordeal like that again."

"My wanting to have more children really hasn't been such a big problem, but it is a sore spot between us. Judith knows how I feel, but she's very practical and doesn't believe in adoption. I'm very romantic about the subject of family, and I'd love to have a house filled with kids. I might have to hold down five or six jobs, but it would be worth it to me. As a kid, I was always envious of friends who had seven or eight brothers and sisters."

Does Stu believe that children is what marriage is all about?

"No, but they're very important—because they create a real family. Otherwise, you just have a marriage."

The Goldblums nearly lost their child, and that changed the plans Stu had for their marriage. Karen and Jackson North, married twenty-eight years, did lose a son a dozen years ago. The boy was thirteen, killed in a car driven by an older teenager, who lived. Never did the Norths need to draw more on the strength of their marriage.

JACKSON: At first we both retreated into ourselves to mourn. For one year I walked around like a zombie. I couldn't look at other kids his age playing in the park or walking home from school. I kept expecting to see him turn the corner any minute—like it had all been some kind of horrible mistake. It took a while to reach out to Karen and share our grief. But in the end we were able to accept each other's support. It bound us to each other, and there was mutual comfort in the sharing.

KAREN: I think I had a small nervous breakdown when it happened. I was heavily sedated most of the time. I remember I turned the days around and slept most of the day and was awake most of the night. I could not be consoled by anyone, not by my other children, my parents, my friends, or my husband. It was a nightmare. I wrote hate letters to the boy who was driving the car, but I never mailed them. I curled up into a ball and couldn't stand to be touched. My skin hurt, I couldn't swallow food, I was a complete mess. One day I woke up from some nightmare and Jackson was holding me and telling me it would be all right. Finally, I was able to cry and let it all out. I thought I'd never be able to stop. It was a catharsis.

JACKSON: It's been ten years, but every year on the anniversary of David's death we turn to each other. Karen cries and I hold her and say all the words of comfort I can think of, and I hope it eases the pain somewhat. Thank God our other children are healthy and happy, and we expect a grandchild in the spring, but I don't believe parents ever get over the loss of a child.

KAREN: Without Jackson's love and support, I'm not sure that I would have had the strength to go on living.

The world knows Robert Bell as "Kool"—the driving force behind the rock group Kool and the Gang, whose upbeat, positive hits include "Fresh" and "Celebrate," and whose good works encourage kids to stay off drugs and in school. At home, Kool is Robert to his wife of seventeen years, Sakinah. They met while in the eighth grade and married at age nineteen. Unlike many marriages between young people, this one has thrived, and while the Bells have two teenage sons, in many ways they look and seem like a couple of kids in love.

Robert came from a less than affluent family that was large and loving despite the fact that his parents were separated. Sakinah, whose big family was and is extremely close, married Robert because they wanted to live together and she knew her strict father wouldn't tolerate that without marriage. For the first couple of years Sakinah traveled with Robert and felt like part of the band. But soon there was a son, Mohammed. "I thought he was a doll," says Sakinah, "but he grew up so fast. Having a lot of sisters, I had no problem with babysitters. If there was someplace I wanted to go, I could dump him off with one of them. So it was like having a kid but not having a kid. I thought he would remain a baby. Eventually I realized that someday he was going to be a grown person and that he was going to be with us for a while. When Hakim was born two years later, I realized the babysitters had to stop and I had to be there."

Robert says, "And I realized that to a certain degree I couldn't fulfill my obligations as a father, being on the road a lot."

"I accepted that this was the situation," Sakinah says. "I'd just have to do the best I could. I was both mother and father, and then when Robert returned home it was like a separate life. Without him I had to take leadership and do everything. When he was home the kids would go to him and give him his parenthood back. I wanted them to get to know Robert and also let them know they had to ask Dad for certain things."

"I was starting to become more involved with the business side of my work, and that took up more time I could otherwise have spent with the kids," Robert admits.

"I think our kids were raised the way Robert was. They had no father around, but they had so many relatives that it really didn't dawn on them that they missed him until he came back and there'd be a big celebration. When they were just toddlers it was easy. I had to sacrifice a social life, but I just felt it was my duty as a parent to do the best I could do with them. I could've had someone come in to take care of them, but I wanted to raise them myself."

Luckily for Sakinah, Robert—unlike many successful men— allowed her to be her own person. "He never applied any pressure in terms of how the kids should be raised, and I appreciated that. It gave me a sense of independence and helped me maintain my sanity. And when the children were older, I went back to school. I think Robert's a wonderful husband, because he gives me space and he doesn't question much. There's a trust there."

"I knew she was handling things fine, and I had my own problems outside," says Robert.

"He was and is the backbone of the group, and I didn't want to add extra pressure. Now I have my own shop in New York and I design clothes for the group and for other people. It's something I've always wanted to do. Robert was very supportive."

She does sometimes wish Robert were around more. "Not so much for me as for the kids. They're getting older and their values seem to be changing. They have so much, and I'm concerned about their being spoiled. But there's just so much a mother can do with boys. A father needs to take on a different role, give them someone to talk to. Kids today have so much experience—too much too soon. And as parents we have to instill the morals we were brought up with, things like respect for their elders. But it's rough. They're competing with their peers, and they have to deal with peer pressure. Plus they have the pressure of having a famous father, and other children gravitate toward them for that reason. They have so much to deal with, and I'm just trying to keep them balanced. They know they can get whatever it is they want, but sometimes I make them work for it."

Ironically, while it's difficult for Robert to spend as much time as he'd like with his own children, he is very involved in helping other kids. "I take a lot of pride in my project It's Kool to Stay in School." The project is based on giving students with perfect attendance records at selected schools tickets to Kool and The Gang concerts. "We want to develop the project in other areas, including scholarships," Robert says.

He is also involved in efforts to help develop areas of West Africa, creating jobs for the adults and providing better education for the children. While he recognizes that all these endeavors take time away from his own children, he makes an effort to inform his kids what he is doing and why, in the hope that they will one day want to become involved in these or similar projects themselves. "The force behind me," he says, "is to see that the family is secure—your immediate family, and the rest of your family, including friends and people you work with, and then the universal family. I believe that much was given to me and so much is expected of me. I think we all have a duty in life, and my duty is to help when I can."

Most parents hope, to one degree or another, that their children will grow up to share their values. Couples in a good marriage may feel that what has worked for them ought to work for their children. But there are those wise people who recognize that as the world changes, so do the elements of a good marriage, and understand that their own model may not be adequate to ensure their children's future happiness. Carole Cooper and Richard Leibner, married for twenty-three years, raise some of these concerns.

Carole is her husband's partner in N.S. Bienstock. They are superagents, representing such clients as Dan Rather, Diane Sawyer, Mike Wallace, Morley Safer, and Ed Bradley. At the time of their marriage, Richard was an accountant and Carole produced commercials. He soon joined N.S. Bienstock, whereas she gave up her career for several years to raise their two sons, now aged twenty and seventeen.

They have definitely passed on their own values to their two sons. Carole notes that their older son has been dating one girl since he was eighteen. "He just spent five weeks in L.A., separated from her except for one weekend. He went to parties but not on dates. He has a monogamous attitude because of us."

Another example the couple have set is that of equality. Even before the women's movement, Richard helped out around the house and otherwise treated Carole as an equal. "I knew Carole would've been a major executive in the advertising industry if she hadn't stopped working after the kids were born." He recalls with amusement an exchange he and Carole had after they had been married about seven years, when she was beginning to get restless at home. They were looking through their wedding album and noticed how few of the couples in their age group were still married. "I said to Carole, 'These divorces are so ugly—they're beating the kids up. If we ever get divorced, I don't think we'd do that.' And Carole said, 'No sweat—we'd cut a deal in a minute. We both came into the marriage with very little difference in money. I want half whatever we're worth and no alimony.' I said, 'You're kidding!' And she said, 'There's one hook. You're a very, very good father and you have a profession. I gave up my career, and if we split there's not going to be a situation where I'm holding down a lower-paying job and I'm taking care of two kids on a marginal amount of money while you're out getting laid every night with a different woman. So, you'll get possession of the kids and I'll go out every night and party.'"

The actual possibility of divorce is so remote that the kids were taken aback when the couple came home arguing two nights in a row. Says Richard, "On this second night one of the kids was downstairs with us, and then he disappeared and we continued to talk the thing through. Ten minutes later both kids came down and Adam said, 'I don't know what's going on with you two.' And Jonathan said, 'But I'm going with you and Adam's going with Mommy.' It was said with a sense of humor, but it was their way of saying they didn't like what they were seeing."

Now that the boys are older, their parents see less of them. "They used to spend most weekends with us at our beach house on Fire Island," says Carole. "Now they're there once in a while. I think they do it thinking, 'Mom will like it if we come out.'"

"I want them to be independent," Richard says. "I want them to be able to cut it on their own. I don't want to have to be responsible for them, and I don't want them to have to come to dinner because Wednesday night is the night to come to dinner. When they develop their own relationships, when they want to see me is when I'll want to see them. I will put no demands on them. Still, they ticked me off the other night. They were going to see The Grateful Dead, and I've never seen the Dead in concert. I like rock music, and I asked if I could go with them. They said, 'No. You'll inhibit us at a Dead concert. You can't go.' I said, 'You S.O.B.'s.' We speak very honestly and openly with one another."

"Richard and I have friends who say they can't bear the thought of their youngest child going away to college, and Richard and I looked at each other and said at the same time, 'We can't wait.' That has nothing to do with not loving them. Like all parents, you worry sometimes."

What worries her most is that the boys may have developed an unrealistic picture of how life is for most people. "It's a lot to live up to," she says. "A successful mother. A successful father. We've been married twenty-three years and we love each other and we have money and we have houses. It doesn't always work for the positive, as far as the children are concerned. It's an awful lot for a kid to accomplish. You can't know for sure. All you can do is hope."

Good Morning America weather forecaster Spencer Christian and his wife Diane have been married for seventeen years and live with their two children in New Jersey. Diane is a part-time travel agent.

SPENCER: Our kids know that we both came from modest

beginnings and that growing up in Virginia, with segregation, I had a lot of obstacles to overcome in order to become a success. Diane and I discussed how not to bring up spoiled little preppies. We had a lot of discussions with the kids on what sound values and unsound values are, and I guess somewhere along the way they must have picked up some positive things. They're courteous and they don't expect people to treat them differently because their dad is on *Good Morning America.*

DIANE: They had a Spencer Christian Day in Richmond, Virginia, and it was a whirlwind. I looked around and saw my daughter just surrounded by little girls, signing autographs. She finds it wonderful that her father's a star, but she's not spoiled by it. Another time, we were standing in line at a movie theater and the manager asked us to just come in. We said, "Oh no, we'll just wait in line." But he insisted, and it was either come in or make a scene. So we went in. Spencer hates that. When we got home we discussed it, and the kids thought it was awful that that happened. They said, "Why don't people treat everyone just like people no matter who they are?"

How do you instill that attitude in them?

DIANE: Our son is twelve and he gets a five-dollar allowance. Our daughter is nine and gets three dollars. They even said, "Maybe we ought to do something for this." One sets the table at night and the other clears it. They're responsible for keeping up their rooms. At one point we had a woman come in to clean, and I told them it was not her job to pick things up for them and that she was instructed to put anything on the floor into the trash. So the night before she came they would busily straighten up.

So it's your example, by not having live-in help or a flamboyant lifestyle?

SPENCER: I guess that's right. They go to a nice private school, where a lot of the kids get dropped off by limousine and they go to fancy camps. For so many kids there's no relationship between the kids and their parents. They learn about what money can buy, but not about relationships and having to work for something. I want my kids to learn the value of work and appreciate everything they earn, with the emphasis on the word *earn.* By not having live-in help we can at least give some sense of what we are trying to convey.

Do you spend a lot of time with your kids?

SPENCER: When the kids were very young I worked the kind of schedule that allowed me to spend a lot of time with them during the daytime hours. I was home a lot in the mornings to do the feedings and the bathing and all the sorts of things most daddies don't do—most of them probably don't want to—but I enjoyed doing that because I always wanted to be a full participant as a parent. I wanted so much to do everything that I was envious I couldn't breastfeed. But I gave baths, changed diapers, and gave large blocks of time so Diane could get out of the house. Even now, when Diane goes on travel-agent junkets, I'll take time off to spend with the kids for a week or two. Those are wonderful times—my little private time to be with my kids so they can get to know me better.

DIANE: Spencer likes to do everything with the children. We had a chance to go to Europe, and he wanted to take them, but I thought they were too young. Spencer didn't want to go without them, but he said, "If you want to go, go ahead," so I went with a girlfriend. When he announced that on the air, he got all kinds of calls saying, "Are you nuts to let your wife go to Europe alone? Now my wife wants to go." Spencer wasn't amused—to begin with, the word *let* upset him.

Did he survive your being away?

DIANE: The house was a wreck when I got home. He said, "How do you expect me to take care of the kids *and* the kitchen?" When I said, "I have no problem," he laughed because he realized what he'd said.

What kind of outings do you have with the children?

SPENCER: We play sports all the time. We take them to dinner at fine restaurants, we take them to shows, we expose them to cultural things. We enjoy going to dinner with our kids more than with most adults we know. It's a very special time to be together and for us to open up and treat them like adults. We want to hear what's on their minds, how they feel about the world.

How do they feel? Have you talked to them about drugs?

SPENCER: Jason asked me about them. I explained to him that in the generation I grew up in, we were exposed to things we now think are harmful but in those days we thought were okay to try. I hope because my warnings come from experience that he'll take them more seriously.

Do you think they're developing a positive attitude toward marriage from your example?

DIANE: I think they are. Spencer and I have talked about how they perceive our marriage. They see us argue once in a while; it wouldn't be normal if they didn't. But they also see a lot of hugging and kissing. We're not embarrassed by that, and the kids will say, "They're at it again," and leave the room.

Married for fifty years, Marylou and Bill Sanford lead a busy, contented retired life. They are very wealthy, but they have a very strong sense of family continuity, of the interaction between one generation and the next.

Bill is a classic American success story. "I came from a very poor, lower-middle-class family. My father was a factory worker, and we were six kids. My mother knew how to stretch a dollar. To this day I can't stand the smell of lamb stew—that was our Sunday-night supper special. But all the time I was growing up I knew I would make it out of that slum. By the time I was eighteen, I was working in the local haberdashery, managing the store. My parents were disappointed, because they'd wanted me to go to college, but they couldn't do anything to help me financially. By the time I was thirty I was a partner in that store and ready to buy another."

Bill says that his parents never really comprehended the kind of money he eventually started making. In fact, his father's attitude about money helped shape the way Bill treated his own sons. "I offered to buy my parents a house in a better neighborhood, but there was no way they would leave their old friends. The only thing that they allowed me to do for them was send my father back to school. It was his dream to graduate from college, and he spent years getting his degree. That gave him more pleasure than any material gift I could have made, and recognizing that helped me sort out my own priorities in life, as well. I saw to it that our sons learned to take money seriously at an early age. They were given allowances, but if they needed extra money they had to work for it, even though we could well afford to give them much more."

Marylou says, "We started a college fund for each of them when they were born. We wanted to make sure they had the finest education we could give them."

"When they graduated, each boy was given a lump sum as a start in whatever business they chose, with the firm understanding that this was the *only* money they would receive from us, unless, of course, there was a health emergency and *only* if there was a health emergency. Thank God there never has been."

"Many of our friends thought that was wrong of us," Marylou says. "They felt that since we did have so much money, the boys should receive it."

"It was and still is my belief," Bill insists, "that inherited money would have deprived my sons of all ambition and drive. I've seen that sort of thing happen to too many sons of wealthy men."

But if Bill and Marylou held back on the money, they were lavish with their love. "Bill and I were always very affectionate with the children and with each other," Marylou says. "We expressed our love freely in front of the children, and I believe that helped give them a feeling of security and—even more important—encouraged them to show warmth and love in a physical way in their own marriages."

"Even as teenagers," Bill says, "our boys were never embarrassed being hugged by their parents. Some people think that isn't manly, but my boys are pretty tough guys and they still understand the power of a good bear hug."

I ask Bill how he treats his grandchildren, given his strictness in bringing up his sons to value a dollar.

Bill laughs. "Those kids are spoiled rotten, and I'm having a marvelous time doing it. Of course, my daughters-in-law may bar me from their homes if I show up with any more expensive presents. I don't understand—doesn't every three-year-old need a two-wheeler racing bike and a computer?"

Marylou shakes her head. "He turns it all into a joke, but their mothers are right. Giving elaborate gifts to children before they can appreciate them takes the thrill out of wanting something and working to get it later on. Bill is breaking his own rules. The women in this family are going on strike if he doesn't listen to reason."

Bill looks roguishly innocent. "I'm just trying to get all my pleasures in before I die, and seeing them open my presents is tops on my list."

Bill's behavior is perhaps a privilege of grandparents. But grandparents can also sometimes find themselves saddled with unexpected responsibilities. That is what happened to Ginny and Henry Mancini, who have been married for thirty-seven years. Henry is the enormously successful composer of such songs as "Days of Wine and Roses," "Moon River," and hundreds of others—winning three Oscars and countless Emmys along the way. But, in other respects, life hasn't always been easy for them. To begin with, Ginny, a beautiful and elegant woman, came from a very tough background.

"My childhood was just about as bad as it could get. My parents fought all the time, and my biggest joy was to save up ten cents and go to the movies, where I could lose myself in those romantic images. That was the only time I ever saw gentleness and affection between people."

Ginny's parents divorced, which was probably just as well for her. "My father was an insecure Irishman who beat my mother. She had a Mexican heritage and was wild-tempered also. I was the only child, and I went to live with my grandmother. I got my strength and my sense of values from her."

She was young when she married Henry Mancini, and they had three children quite quickly—and not much money. "It was a horrible time. Instead of having a second child, I had twins. I was very sick during both pregnancies. Sometimes I prayed to die. We had no money to hire help, and it was really hard handling three diaper-age children at the same time. Without Henry's help and cooperation, I never would have made it. I often collapsed under all the responsibilities, but he was always there to pick up the pieces."

Success came for Henry, but that wasn't the end of the problems. "Our kids were teenagers during the sixties, and that was a terrible time also. Henry would be out of town and I'd have to bail my son out of jail. I can't tell you how much marijuana I flushed down the toilet. They've settled down now, particularly my daughters, but my son had a child with a woman he wasn't married to. The woman lives in Chicago, and we're raising the child."

Initially, Ginny was very angry and resentful about having to take on this new burden at this time of her life. "We had this delicious freedom and a new house that we built to entertain in and have guests stay at. Nevertheless, without even discussing it, Henry and I both knew we had to do it. I called a family meeting and told everyone what I needed to help me deal with the situation. Actually, the crisis brought Henry and I much closer together. We have a way of uniting under pressure so that we have very few split decisions. When I was going through this terrible time with our grandchild, I announced that I was going to Europe for a month with a girlfriend, and Henry had no objections. I really needed it, and it cleared my head. Since I've been back, it's been a joy. Having a baby in the house brings a freshness to our lives. We can be outrageous. We can be silly. We're like young marrieds again."

And so we come full circle. A grandmother becomes a mother again. But Ginny's initial feelings of anger at being thrust back into the role of mother to an infant were instinctive. She felt that seasons of marriage were being violated. It takes a very special person to rise above nature's program and the sense that there is a time for everything, that feelings, expectations, and reactions should and do change over the years.

But the seasons are not engraved in stone. Nature intended people to begin to have children in their twenties. Yet many couples elect to have children a decade or more later. This does not in any way preclude them from being excellent parents. Indeed, the wait may often allow them to achieve a maturity and financial stability that makes them better parents.

Children can enhance a marriage; clearly many of the couples we have met here would not be nearly as happy without them. But it is also profoundly evident that being a parent requires a refocusing of the marriage relationship as a whole. And while some couples have a natural affinity for child-raising, for many others it is vital that the marriage be a strong one to begin with if it is to sustain the test of parenthood.

I told Terrence, "Either she goes or I go. If you
want a wife, you'd better tell your mother."
—*Lillian Mullins*

I was afraid of how attracted she was to this
particular friend. I was never afraid of losing
her to a penis. It was the brain I was worried
about.
—*Henry Bendak*

In-laws and friends: Barriers and connections

"If we'd let her, she would have destroyed our marriage."

Who's being talked about? A mother-in-law? That may be the obvious conclusion, but it could also be a friend of either the husband or wife. In-laws and friends both bring a strong outside influence to bear on any marriage, and how the couple respond to that influence often reveals a great deal about the strength or weakness of the relationship.

In-laws, mothers and fathers, can and do break up marriages all the time. People who see their children as extensions of themselves instead of as individuals in their own right, people insecure enough to view a child's spouse as direct competition for the affection of that child, and even people who are really trying to help but managing only to get in the way—the sins of in-laws are legion.

105

But let's not forget friends. They can be just as jealous, meddlesome, and disapproving as any parent. Especially in the early years of a marriage they can cause serious problems. For like a parent, they've known you a lot longer than your new spouse. They have their rights—and they are often all too eager to exercise them.

Both in-laws and friends can also, of course, be loyal, supportive, and helpful in myriad ways. Their understanding can bolster a marriage; their advice can be invaluable. Let's begin, therefore, on a positive note, with the words of a man who feels that his eventual success as an art dealer owes a great deal to his in-laws.

SIMON LIBERMAN: "My father was a pattern cutter, and his main interest was sports. There was a cultural background in the family— my grandfather had been an opera singer and my mother had studied music. But there was no chance for me to get a formal education. My father died when I was sixteen, and I had to quit school and go to work doing anything I could—delivering groceries, soda jerking, dog walking."

Joan was already your girlfriend then. Did the fact that she came from a well-to-do family and would be going on to college cause problems?

SIMON: No, I was never threatened by any of that. I was more than a boyfriend. I was almost like a part of that family. Her father never made me feel I was any less than they were. And I would do Joan's homework along with her. She literally educated me. She took the Bronx out of the boy. She saw things in me that I didn't and apparently so did her father. He came from a poor Lower East Side background, and I think he saw a lot of himself in my raw potential and ambition. I wanted to know about business, and he was there to help me. He had a high-class gift shop, and I learned so much just by watching him conduct his business. I think he admired my constant need to learn. But not only did I learn from him, I was attached to this whole very cultured family. I just grabbed on to all their knowledge. Because I wasn't educated, I worked harder. Joan's father respected that. He would talk to me like an equal, asking my opinions and making me feel like somebody. I was never treated as if I wasn't good enough for his daughter. It was always accepted that one day we'd get married. We were so in love and couldn't stand to be apart.

How long did it take you to get out of the delivery boy stage?

SIMON: One day a lighting fixture salesman my future father-in-law dealt with said he was planning to give up a certain line. I knew the line and I knew the people. I went to them to apply for the job. They asked if I had experience. I didn't, and they said it was necessary. So I suggested that while they were looking for someone with experience they put me to work temporarily. I was still seventeen when I started and I was there for three years. I went from $35,000 to $125,000 in billings, so I was making money by the time I got married. Then I was drafted. But once I got back from the army I built things up to the point that I had my own factory making high-level copies of Tiffany lamps, and then I became one of the top dealers in Tiffany glass and other Art Deco antiques.

Could you have made it without Joan and her family?

SIMON: I was always highly motivated. But they gave me the confidence I needed—and, more important, the education. I couldn't have gotten more from a college degree. My father-in-law really extended himself for me. I was very lucky to have this man to give me support after my father died—not just in a business sense, but emotionally, too. I think I would've made it anyway, but having him and Joan in my corner really assured my success. I never had the chance to doubt myself, because they believed in me.

There were a lot of people who *didn't* believe in the marriage of Marlene and David Barnaby, including both sets of parents. David was a horse trainer from Wyoming and Marlene was from a prominent horse-breeding family in Colorado. That sounds like a good match, aside from the fact that Marlene's family was considerably wealthier. But that wasn't the problem. David, now thirty-nine, is black, while Marlene, twenty-eight, is white.

They met at various horse shows and knew each other for several years as friends and fellow professionals. Their decision to buy and train a horse together was the beginning of a closer relationship that eventually led to love and marriage.

"Soon after I began working with Marlene in our breeding business, I knew we were a perfect couple and I was determined for us to marry, no matter what our parents thought."

"I was not as strong as David," Marlene says. "My mother's effect on me was considerable. But David's was stronger. I went through a great deal of ambivalence. It was so strange—I was not really aware of David's color before we became lovers and thought about marrying."

David's parents weren't happy about it, either, and David and Marlene looked for ways to defuse the situation. They felt that a very specific financial plan would help to quell the fears of their in-laws. "David insisted that he sign a prenuptial agreement keeping him from receiving any of my inheritance. We established separate credit ratings and also set up separate checking accounts in addition to the joint account we shared through the business."

"We also decided to draw up wills to cover our other assets," David continues. "We intended to keep the financial side of our marriage very businesslike. We each kept the assets we brought to the marriage separate and treated our business as if we were partners, not spouses."

Neither of them felt that this arrangement diluted their strong emotional ties. "On the contrary," David says. "Getting past that, understanding why it was necessary, made us feel much more deeply connected. Also, we realized that although we were doing much of this for special reasons, it would be good for the kind of relationship we wanted."

"I had been raised to be very independent when it came to managing money—I'd been involved with my father's business since I was a teenager. I like feeling independent financially. I also like the feeling of building a life and a business with David. I have both."

Now married for fourteen years, they have two children—Candice, twelve, and Jason, ten. The birth of the children helped to bring both sets of in-laws around, as it often does. At that point the natural linkage of professional interests began to assert itself. "My dad," Marlene relates, "asked me if we wanted to form a partnership involving a new home he was getting. We agreed, and this enhanced our family ties as well as the business. My mother traveled with us to horse shows, and she was a tremendous help to me with the children. I was able to concentrate on the pressures of showing horses knowing my mother and not some strange babysitter was with the children."

"My father also got into the act," David says. "He is a fine trainer and has always been my role model. Marlene's father and my dad hit it off, and he now takes some of our horses to his place in Wyoming to do the initial training. My mother is not well, and isn't able to join us when we travel, but we frequently send the children to vacation at the Wyoming ranch, and Grandma Barnaby's cooking is the high point of the trip."

"We decided to marry really assuming that we would be faced with our parents' hostility permanently," Marlene says. "Not expecting to have a close family relationship, I think the fact that we do is the most important aspect of our lives today. David has two brothers, I have an older sister, and they all have children. Come the holidays, it is really exciting to experience the love and warmth and connection between all these relatives."

"I value that, too," David says. "But for me the deep sense of commitment and love that exists between the two of us is the most precious thing."

Married for eleven years, Alan and Joan Miller have two girls, eight and six. Originally from Minnesota, they moved to California five years ago when Alan's father opened a restaurant in the San Fernando Valley and the whole family decided to relocate. Alan is an only child, adored by his parents. His mother has constantly interfered in their lives, and it has required a good deal of toughness on Joan's part, and some fresh understanding on Alan's, to deal with the problem.

"When the girls were babies," Joan says, "my mother-in-law used to call us night and day concerned about the children. She was especially concerned about their eating habits, and she would question me about exactly what each child ate. I mean, she wanted *details*, how many mouthfuls of what. Amy, my oldest, was a poor eater, and each time I had to describe her eating habits to my mother-in-law it made me tense and anxious, which was transmitted in turn to the child. It took a good pediatrician to put a stop to that. He told me to hang up if my mother-in-law called and asked me to give her a full report on carrots and peas. She got the picture."

"The situation is getting better day by day," Alan says. "Therapy has really helped me. I had to be able to deal with the guilt of saying no to my mother. I've come to realize that she is basically a negative person, although she does mean well. I've talked to my dad about it, but his solution is to tune her out when she gets that way."

"A perfect example of her negativity happened last month. Alan and I spent a much-needed weekend in Las Vegas alone. When we got back, the first thing my mother-in-law asked was, 'How much did you lose?' It never occurred to her to ask if we had a good time. She's just a pessimist, and it hurts me to have to deal with her."

While many husbands would try to ignore the situation—as Alan's own father does—Alan has taken steps on his own to correct matters. "I've started working out a secret code with my mother. Every time she starts interfering or being negative about our family, I wink at her and give her a thumbs-down signal. She's trying very hard to catch herself, and she is aware, so maybe it's not too late for her to learn. She knows what the consequences could be if she doesn't."

One of the consequences could be having her son and daughter-in-law move away. Although Alan has his own business, he has been thinking about changing jobs. "I've been working on a mobile park development in Palmdale on weekends. Two friends of mine bought it, and we've been going up every weekend to help out. It started as an excuse to get the whole family away for the weekend. I worry about the kids' spending too much time with their grandmother—I don't want them to become spoiled. The guys have been paying our expenses plus something, and I've been considering either working for them or buying into the project."

Joan is all for the idea. "I wouldn't mind living up there. The girls love the country, everything is less expensive, and we'd be away from my mother-in-law's influence."

Joan, a former elementary school teacher, would also like to go back to work once the children are a little older, and she would feel comfortable about leaving them with a babysitter or at a day-care center. Her mother-in-law is, of course, very against that prospect, which only makes Joan more determined.

Much as Joan resents her mother-in-law's interference, it has not caused serious problems in her relationship with Alan, because he sympathizes with her point of view and tries to remedy the problems—even if it sometimes takes him a while. "When we were first married," Joan recalls, "my mother-in-law felt that Alan should continue to send her a check every week, as he had done when he was single. I resented that, since I was working at the time. We needed new furniture, a car, basics that we were trying to save for. And I felt that in a way it was my money that was going to her. Besides that, her husband was supporting her. I saw no reason for sending that check, even if the amount was small."

"I agreed with Joan," Alan says, "but at first I couldn't bring myself to hurt my mother's feelings. She was used to buying a few things, presents for the family, things she didn't want to ask my father for, and I had always helped her out. It was extremely hard for me to explain to her how Joan felt, but I did and she was surprisingly understanding."

For Terrence Mullins, taking sides against his mother was almost impossible. We've already heard about the difficulties he and his wife Lillian encountered with their daughter Shawna and her live-in boyfriend. Years before, when their older daughter Barbara was only five and Shawna had not yet been born, the Mullinses had gone through a troubled period of another kind when Terrence's mother moved in with them.

"She lived with us after my father died," Terrence recalls, "and Lillian felt she took over the household."

"She paid fifteen dollars a week room and board, but she'd tell me what curtains to buy, what food, how to do this and do that. And she was hardly pulling her weight. She didn't want to babysit Barbara. So even when she was there, the neighbor's daughter came in. The girl was uncomfortable about it. Barbara would get up with nightmares—she thought things were crawling all over her. But my mother-in-law would leave it completely to the babysitter to handle. She'd only take over in a real emergency, like the time we were going to a wedding and the sitter canceled out at the last minute."

"I'd go to the movies with my mother, and Lillian didn't like that either."

"I stayed home with Barbara. One of my mother-in-law's friends told me that when Terrence took his mother out she behaved as though she was with a boyfriend. She held his hand, put her head on his shoulder. After the movie, they'd go for ice cream."

"I was torn between my wife and my mother," Terrence admits.

"Lillian's not the argumentative type, but we did have discussions about it. Then finally they had a huge fight and my mother went next door to a friend's house."

"I said that I wouldn't tolerate it anymore. I told Terrence, 'Either she goes or I go. If you want a wife you'd better tell your mother.' Terrence told me, 'This is my *mother*.' But I was tired of it. When I was with him, he'd occasionally argue with her, but not strongly. I didn't know whether she wanted her son to leave with her or what. That fight with her was the first time I said what I thought of her. And believe me, she never minced words."

"At the time, my mother was going with a man. Lillian told her she should marry him, and my mother said Lillian was trying to get rid of her. But she did get married shortly after. Thank God."

Luis and Maria Lopez were both born in Mexico, but were raised and educated in Los Angeles. Married for fifteen years, with two sons, aged nine and thirteen, they met in high school and became sweethearts. She worked as a cashier in a local Mexican restaurant, taking time off to have her two children. She still works there on a part-time basis. Although she never went to college, she is extremely well read, knowledgeable about her Mexican heritage, and fluently bilingual. She earns about seven thousand dollars a year.

Luis makes about twenty thousand from the clothing business he owns in the neighborhood. A graduate of Los Angeles City College, he is still a registered alien and owns property in Mexico City left to him by his father. He is thinking of becoming a citizen, because he wants to run for local office. His widowed mother lives with the family.

They don't mind the extra expense of having Luis's mother with them at all. "The Mexican diet was designed for large families," Luis says, "rice, beans, cheaper cuts of meat, tortillas. If you can feed five you can feed seven, and so on."

Nor does Maria have any qualms about the situation. "I don't feel any competition. In fact, the more help I can get, the better. If prepared properly, Mexican food is very laborious, so the more hands working in the kitchen, the easier it is for me. Unfortunately, I don't have any daughters. My sister has two girls, and even the little one is learning to make tortillas at seven. So my mother-in-law is a big help."

Both have a special attitude about older people. Luis notes that there are very few retirement homes in Mexico. "We are taught to respect our elders, and old folks homes are not the way to treat older people. My father used to say, 'They didn't put me out of the house when I was a child, helpless and unable to contribute to the family. So now when they are older, it is time to pay them back by taking the same kind of care of them.'"

Maria agrees. "Respect for our elders is so important to Mexicans. I was raised on a ranch until I was seven and we came to the United States. But I still remember that in my mother's house everyone stood at attention when my grandfather walked into a room. Adults put out their cigarettes and didn't speak until my grandfather spoke to them. Children were not excused to go to bed until my grandfather made the sign of the cross, blessed them, and gave permission."

The Lopezes are not that strict with their own children. They recognize the need to become anglicized—at least up to a point. But respect for their elders remains great; Luis's mother is seen not as intruding into their life, but as a natural part of it.

HE: My parents always had polite dinner parties, and I was drilled on how to behave like a gentleman. The guests would all sit around the dining room with plastic smiles making polite conversation. Then, inevitably, someone would ask me to play the piano and my mother would straighten my bow tie. After I finished playing Mozart or something, I had to bow to them and there'd be this tiny applause. When I got older, I finally rebelled. I tried something that rocked a little and I jumped up and down like Jerry Lee Lewis and no one asked me to play again.

SHE: At least they didn't lock you up. When my parents entertained, they were always afraid I'd embarrass them—come down wearing the wrong clothes or say something radical or foul-mouthed. I don't know what they thought, but I had to stay in my room and every hour or so my mother would bring me a soda or whatever I needed so I wouldn't have to go out where people would see me.

This is Richard and Wendy Willis, in their early thirties and married for eleven years. She is a dog groomer and he's a graphic artist. Both are free spirits from conservative families. They met when their respective parents dragged them both to a formal party. Richard didn't want to go; Wendy was so shocked to be asked she didn't even resist. During the party, Wendy stepped out onto the terrace to light up a joint and found Richard, who had the same idea. They shared the joint, their feelings about the party, and discovered that they were kindred spirits in a hostile environment. They have been together ever since—and so have their parents.

"When they come over," Richard says, "they try to come in a pack, so there's four of them and only two of us. Then they start in criticizing."

"They don't like our clothes, hairstyles, professions, friends, politics, or furniture," says Wendy. "You name it and they don't like it. The worst problem in a long time came when I got this frizzy perm. Richard's mother was beside herself about it because we have a family wedding coming up. 'Can't you get rid of it for the wedding? Cover it up somehow? You can't go like that!'"

"They all agree about how appalling we both are, so our own parents never come to our defense if the other set starts in putting us down. Wendy's mother will say, 'Why don't you have a child?' And my father will say, 'How can they have children when they're children themselves?' All our brothers and sisters are in what our parents would call 'respectable' professions or are terrific housewives and mothers, so we're all they've got to complain about."

"They still think we try to be different just to annoy them," Wendy adds. "They say 'nonconformist' in the same tone as 'communist' or 'child molester.' They ask why we can't be like everyone else, and we say it's because we're not like everyone else. We're not into money or what the Joneses are up to. We live day by day and do what feels good for us."

"The funny thing," Richard says, "is that because all four of them think there's something wrong with us, it's helped us to feel a lot better about ourselves. When Wendy and I were younger, and on our own against our parents, we'd sometimes think maybe there was something wrong with us. Now we know better. We are who we are, and as long as we approve of each other, it doesn't matter what they think."

"One day we got so fed up with being told that we had a compulsion to thumb our noses at society that we threw all four of them out."

"They never apologized," Richard adds. "They just called and came over a week later. They're never going to see our point of view. I can't say that they really like us, but they do love us. And in a way you could say that we don't have any in-law problems, because they're like four peas in a pod. We've just accepted the situation, and the battle goes on."

Parental disapproval of lifestyle has caused problems for Bill and Karen Spofford ever since Bill's decision—recounted in Chapter Two—to go to California to pursue his career as a comic while Karen stayed in Chicago.

"Neither Bill's nor my parents were happy about it," Karen says, "but mine were worse."

"Her parents have given her a hard time, and it's difficult because with me away she has to rely on them. They're very traditional Catholics and they think Karen should be home having babies. Her working is bad enough, but having an absentee husband is too much."

"We used to fight about it all the time, but now it's just an occasional jab. They're hurt and confused by our lifestyle. They keep it a secret from the rest of the relatives. They're embarrassed."

"It's like trying to explain rock and roll to your parents; they just don't get it. One night we sat down with Karen's parents and told them about my going west. The veins kind of popped out of her father's forehead, and her mother sat with her head way down. The next day her mother called crying, and we had to reassure her. I think she was afraid we'd have some kind of open marriage and was afraid that I was going on a lark. I guess she had visions of me smoking marijuana on the Sunset Strip and seeking female companionship."

What about Bill's parents? Karen says, "I've always liked them. I don't see them much, because they're back in St. Louis. Maybe once a year we get together. But we talk every few weeks, and they're supportive now. You go through a period of saying, 'It's our lives,' and yelling. But then things calm down. I think Bill's mother sometimes feels sorry for me because I don't have a child and I'm not getting any younger. Sometimes maybe she wonders, if I really wanted to have a child wouldn't I quit my job and go straighten Bill out. But it's not something that's put into words. We don't argue about it now."

Karen's parents, who live just outside Chicago, asked her if "I wanted to live with them so I could save money and not be lonely. But that would be like going back to childhood and make our marriage seem almost nonexistent. Our home is our home, even if I'm usually the only one living in it. They do invite me over a lot, and I like to go."

"I know not to call Karen on Sunday when the rates are low, because she's with her folks. I think it gives her a sense of being loved and nurtured that she needs. And she was brought up with a strong sense of commitment to family. That helps keep us going, too."

"My family does not believe in divorce—period. I think if they were less religious they'd have gotten me a lawyer and the phone numbers of a few eligible guys."

Bill smiles. "Therein lies the argument for devout in-laws."

Karen and Bill know the disapproval is still there, under the surface, but at least it is suppressed. Both sets of in-laws now keep their mouths shut. It took time, but Karen's and Bill's argument that it was their lives has at least brought about quietude if not full acceptance.

Time helps, but it can be a very long time. Susan Prince didn't speak to her in-laws for years. She and her husband Larry have been married for eleven years and have a seven-year-old son, Ted. He is a manager of a clothing store, and she is a nursery school teacher.

Larry has no problems with Susan's parents. "I get along with everyone, including my in-laws. They may think Susan could have found a better provider, but they never act that way toward me."

Susan's parents are very comfortable financially, and help out by paying for Ted's school and summer camp. Usually it is the well-off in-laws who cause the trouble, but in this case the situation is reversed.

"Larry's parents thought I was too aggressive. Actually, they thought I had a big mouth. And they were afraid that I was spoiled and would never be satisfied with what Larry could do financially. They always let him know that I spent too much on clothes for me and Ted."

"I have a few connections and I try to get some things wholesale, but it made my parents boil to see them all decked out."

"I'm not one to be quiet and go home and scream there. I told Larry's parents it was none of their business and to bug off, that simply."

Did Larry back her up?

"Yes, but in a quiet way. I broke off with them for years. Larry didn't, but I understood that."

"Ted and I went to visit my parents alone, and it was awkward. My parents bad-mouthed Susan, and I told them either to keep quiet or we'd stop coming."

"The worst thing that happened was one night when Larry went over there and they actually had some girl there to meet him. I couldn't believe their gall. Luckily, I didn't hear about this until much later."

How did Larry handle that situation?

"I ignored the girl. I put on the TV and pretended she wasn't there."

Susan says that it was mostly time that softened the situation. "Also, we had some problems with Ted's vision, and we started talking about it on the phone." A grandchild to the rescue, once again. "It's okay now," Susan says, "but we're not close. I guess they finally recognized that I wanted to be with Larry even if we didn't have much money. I was brought up to snap my fingers and I'd get whatever I wanted. I knew if I married Larry there'd be a struggle. I married him because I loved him, not because we'd be rich. I could've stayed home and had the luxuries. I'd rather have him than anyone, and I've never thought I made a mistake. A lot of my friends married lawyers and doctors and they're not happy. I am. Call it chemistry."

Call it grounds for marriage.

We're all our parents' children, but we are not their appendages. Life in general is a matter of becoming, not repeating—of learning who we are rather than echoing what our parents are. Parental disapproval or meddling cannot usually destroy a good marriage, although it can and often does contribute to the collapse of marriages that always were on shaky grounds.

Sometimes, though, an in-law can be the force that rescues a marriage from real trouble.

Carl and Willy (short for Wilhelmina, a name Willy feels only a reigning monarch can get away with) Burkhardt met when they were teenagers and have been married over twenty years. They are in their early forties and have two preteen children. Neither went to college, but Carl is a clever businessman and owns several garages in Denver. They live in the large home he grew up in, but have converted part of it into an apartment for his mother. Willy calls her Mama, and she is profoundly grateful to her.

Willy, a chic, slim woman, is wearing a T-shirt that says, "I survived my husband's mid-life crisis." The colors match the full-length fox coat that hangs in her closet. Both were birthday gifts from her husband. "He's always been too generous," says Willy, "and done everything in a big, dramatic way. He goes overboard and he spends money as fast as he makes it. That's what got us into trouble."

"Both of us like to have a good time," says Carl. "We used to go out and do the town almost every night, and we'd leave the kids with my mother."

"Carl was always picking up the check, so there was never a shortage of friends. Then Carl got bored with just closing the bars. Believe me, when he gets to feeling claustrophobic, the whole world becomes a trap. He wasn't interested in his family or his business, and he got completely different friends."

"I started drinking more," Carl admits, "and then I hooked up with some people who did coke. A guy who carries a lot of cash becomes popular very fast."

"He got drunk *and* stoned and suddenly he was a very pushy, abusive guy. If I looked at someone he'd call me a whore and push me a little. I didn't know him anymore and I didn't want to live with a stranger—especially one who was screwing around. But this didn't happen overnight. Carl didn't discuss this sudden rage of his. He seemed to feel if he went out more and got higher, everything would be okay. He'd treat me like dirt at night, then come home from work the next day with flowers or pick me up in a limo. He's a romantic that way, but after a while it stopped working. I'd yell at him, and he'd throw things around and I'd feel physically threatened, although I was more terrified mentally than physically."

Carl's mother began to take action. "She warned me," Carl remembers. "She said, 'You've erased twenty years of happiness. If you cut Willy off, you cut off everything you ever did in your life.' That made sense to me, but I was out of control."

"As tough as Mama was with Carl, that's how tender she was with me. I'd go crying to her at all hours and she'd comfort me, rocking me in her arms and telling me things would get better. I even slept with her a few times like a little girl. And she took the pressure off me by taking care of the kids. I called a lawyer a few times, but Mama convinced me to let things wait. I was ready to move in with my brother in New York, but she said, 'Where will your kids sleep?'"

"Willy slept through all the good stuff," Carl says. "Mama was on guard duty every night, staring out the window waiting for me. There was a cashier I used to see, and when Mama caught us she started cursing out the window, calling Ellen 'that horseface.' The girl never came back. She wasn't afraid of seeing the wife or kids, but Mama terrorized her."

The memory makes Carl and Willy laugh together.

"Mama told me," Willy continues, "that she didn't know if she had a son anymore, but she loved her daughter—meaning me."

"I tried to make things right with Willy a few times, but I always screwed it up. After a few days I'd get high, and things would be worse than before. My mother owns the house, and she was ready to throw me out. I couldn't stand to be cut off from my family completely, and at this point I didn't have much money."

"Carl always carried a really fat wad of cash, and it would go poof and disappear like magic at night. Mama would sneak into his wallet and take a couple of hundreds every chance she got. That's how we kept going."

"My business was going to hell like everything else, but not as fast. I was in bad shape, but something stopped me from hitting rock bottom. I decided to get help."

"Mama wasn't the type to believe in psychiatrists," says Willy, "but even so, she got the name of someone who handled a lot of drug cases. Still, we think what helped Carl the most was Mama yelling 'Grow up!' all the time. She wore him down."

"Once I seriously tried to get better, it was easy," Carl says. "I wasn't a longtime addict. I just wanted to break out—to 'stay with it' or whatever. I was still young. I enjoyed being with my wife, but these things get under your skin, this desire to go off. What saved me was that my family ties were so strong. I knew what I had, and I just had to wake up. I'm lucky Willy was with my mother instead of another man when I stopped dreaming."

When we speak of "the ties that bind" we usually think first of family ties. They may bind us together or tie us in knots, but they're always there. But friends can be just as important. For many people, in fact, friends exert an even greater influence than family. Who hasn't had a friend who was the "only person who really understands"? Such friends can be invaluable, helping us to grow, steadying us when we are falling apart, and allowing us to truly be ourselves. But such friends have also made a large emotional investment in us— we are important to their own equilibrium in ways we can't always fully understand. And when we pull back from the ties of such a friendship, investing our interest and our caring in new ways, a friend can turn into an enemy of our hopes.

It's not just in-laws who try to break up marriages. Friends do it, too, especially when the friends remain single themselves. That happened to Benjy and Jay Lenart. Now in their early forties and married for eleven years, they live near Los Angeles with their children, aged two and four.

Both were over thirty when they married, and Benjy in particular has bad memories of being single. "It was the pits for me," she says. "All my friends were miserable, too. Women who are alone too long get a hard edge to them from so many years of unhappiness. It wasn't that I had a lot of intense, unhappy relationships. It was more like a series of one-night stands that I tried to stretch into two nights, or three-date affairs that I tried to keep going for three weeks when they were already over."

"When I first met Benjy," Jay admits, "I was turned off by her cynicism. I think other men must've been, too. No matter what I said, I knew she was thinking, 'Oh, sure. Sure we'll go away for a weekend. . . . Sure we'll do something for New Year's. . . .' She didn't want to let herself believe. But I thought there was something softer underneath, worth holding on to. But that's more than I can say about some of her girlfriends. Some of them have been through the mill a few times and they're leathery on the outside—hard and kinky."

One of those friends was a girl named Priscilla, who caused trouble from the start. "When we started dating," Jay recalls, "a lot of Benjy's bar friends faded out of the picture, but Priscilla called every day and Benjy met her for lunch a couple of times a week. Benjy wanted to be with me, but Priscilla would ask, 'Why can't you come out with me tonight? What's he going to do to you?'"

"I'd gone out enough for ten lives, and I wanted to stay home," Benjy admits. "Do you know that I never saw *Mary Tyler Moore* or *The Odd Couple* until I got married? I came home to shower and pick up my messages. But for Priscilla, going out was a compulsion, and I knew where she was coming from. You have to understand the nature of these friendships. I didn't hang around with the girls who always had a few guys dangling or who were engaged. Priscilla and I met at a pickup place in Santa Monica called the Car House. Guys called it the Whore House and we called it Suds and Studs. We spent hours talking about why we were striking out or what guy stood us up or dumped us for no reason. Priscilla and I were attracted by each other's misery. I was allergic to women who were happy and actually expected a guy to call back."

"Thus I became topic number one for discussion," Jay says. "At first Benjy told Priscilla I was nothing special, but I was good to her. When Benjy really fell for me, Priscilla kept telling her she could do better."

"I married Jay anyway, but even after that I'd talk to Priscilla every time we had a fight. But mostly I was happy, and that didn't make Priscilla feel any better. I'm sure if the situations had been reversed I'd have been jealous of her happiness. When your friends get married you often feel betrayed in some way and some people don't handle those feelings graciously."

"Then a few years into the marriage Benjy and I went through a bad time," Jay recalls. "There were no kids yet, and we were living in two little rooms together. We just started bickering about everything."

"We fought about what cookies to get, whether his hair was too short, anything."

"Then the phone would ring and I'd hear Benjy talking in this code. 'Yes, business is bad this week, and I haven't had a really good order in two weeks.' That was Benjy telling Priscilla about our sex life."

"Guilty as charged," says Benjy.

"It was just a bad time. We knew we loved each other, but we were getting on each other's nerves. And it didn't help that I was always wondering what in God's name Priscilla was saying on the other end of the phone."

"Priscilla kept pushing me, saying I could do better than Jay. And I felt I had changed enough so that maybe I could find someone else. I knew in the back of my mind that the reason I'd changed was because of Jay's love. If I'd talked to my mother or sisters they probably would have reminded me of that. But I wanted sympathy, and Priscilla was on my side a hundred and ten percent and always pushing me to leave Jay."

"So Benjy decided to go stay with Priscilla for a while. She packed a little bag, taking all her valuables. Priscilla had eaten away at her trust and was giving her the lowdown on how wives got screwed by their ex-husbands and their lawyers. She got Benjy at a moment of weakness."

"When I got to Priscilla's I just wanted to have a few drinks and die. I didn't want to talk about it. So you can imagine how shocked I was when I saw three of her creepy friends from group therapy sitting there waiting for me. They knew everything—and who knows what awful things Priscilla had made up. This guy put his arm around me and started making jokes about Jay's beer belly and saying, 'It's hard today, but you're well rid of him.' Another guy squeezed my hand and asked, 'Did he beat you?' so I knew Priscilla had really been exaggerating. She'd finally overplayed her hand, and I thank God she did. I got up and left and ran home to Jay as fast as I could."

"We ignored each other all evening," says Jay. "Then I woke up about four in the morning and I slipped my leg under the blanket to get close to her. I gave her a little kiss on the cheek and she made half-conscious little affectionate groans and let me squeeze her finger. That's Benjy's weak spot—she loves to have a finger squeezed when she's half asleep."

"The next day we laughed a lot. We kidded around and called each other impossible and pointed blame in a playful way. And that was it. We started having fun again, and all the joy came back. Later, I told Jay about all Priscilla's sessions on the phone, and we got so we could joke about it. And I ended the relationship with Priscilla. It wasn't pleasant. There were a lot of weepy calls and then nasty ones. I feel sorry for Priscilla and all those people like her. I just don't think they have the ability to be happy. But I wasn't going to go down with them. I still have single friends and I confide in them on occasion, but we're drawn together by work, by humor, not by misery. I don't need that stuff anymore."

KAREN NORTH: You have to face it, a woman lawyer and a hardware store owner are an offbeat mix. It makes a lot of people nervous. We have a few very good friends, and since our work takes us into two separate worlds we both have a lot of acquaintances, but I wouldn't call them friends. We started narrowing down our circle some years ago when many of my so-called friends objected to the fact that my husband was not what they considered a "professional." That snobbish attitude disturbed me at first, but then I realized that it was provoked by jealous people who envied our relationship and this marriage.

JACKSON NORTH: That nonsense never bothered me, except that I don't like to see Karen hurt. I've met many people like that; most are empty and insecure, or they wouldn't feel the need to put other people down. Sometimes a customer comes into my store and takes it for granted that I'm beneath them. They're the ones who never look you in the eye and try to act superior because they're spending five bucks on a light bulb. Karen had one friend who used to call us up in the middle of the night if a fuse blew. Her husband was such a brilliant doctor, a "professional," but he didn't even know how to change a fuse. I just laughed.

Harry and Lu Bendak have been married for nineteen years and have two children. He owns a lumber store and she is a computer programmer. They are in their early forties.

"When we got married Lu was a gorgeous secretary and I was a nice guy with a weight problem who was building up a successful business and starting to smoke good cigars. I was the clever one and she was the cute one. Now she's both."

"Harry's getting cuter every year," Lu says as she gives his cheek an affectionate pinch.

They can joke about it now, but there were problems about Lu's development as a woman with her own successful career and her own business friends. It began ten years ago, after both children had started school. At first, Lu just took a part-time job, but within a few years it was full-time and Lu was designing computer systems for major companies—some of them out of town. Along the way she joined a health club, acquired a more stylish hairdo, a chic and costly wardrobe, and a more ambitious and sophisticated group of work friends.

"It's the classic story of realizing in my thirties how much I loved having a career and realizing what I was capable of. Harry was as happy about it as I was until I started working late and traveling. No one else we know has a wife who goes out of town on business—and I'm always traveling with men. These guys are more than coworkers. We spend a lot of time away together, and we've become very close on a personal level. We kid around and have a good time, but that's all. Harry never called to make sure I was in my room or that kind of paranoid stuff, he just gave me the third degree when I got home. I did have a good time and I did share things with one guy in particular that I didn't with Harry. Harry tried to make me feel guilty, but I just wouldn't accept that."

"I was afraid of how attracted she was to this particular friend. I was never afraid of losing her to a penis. It was the brain I worried about. All these slim, good-looking guys with three or four brains stuffed into their heads. I'm not a college graduate, and the kind of stuff Lu deals with is way over my head. When she described a project she was working on to me, it was like talking to the wall. So when we're with these guys she works with, my brain feels paralyzed. Her work is so important to her that I know she gets something from these men she can't get from me. It's not sex, but it's very exciting to her. And it got so I couldn't stand it when Lu went to a function or for a drink after work with these guys. I wasn't really clear about what upset me, but I knew it made me feel small."

"He needed help," says Lu. "He would confront me and I would fight back. 'What do you think goes on with these men?' And he wouldn't have an answer. He came at me in a pathetic way—it wasn't an anger that was feisty or strong. He'd never been pathetic before, and he had no reason to be now. I started pushing therapy on him, and he finally agreed. He had to realize that I couldn't avoid being with men. And I refused on principle to compromise my right to have them as friends."

The therapy worked. "I understood that I was my own worst enemy. The only problem was one I was making up in my own head. I had to recognize that my wife loves her work and these guys are part of it. But she doesn't love them, she loves me. I had this old idea that a husband and wife were supposed to be everything to each other. And that may still work for some people, but it wasn't true for Lu. She needs her work. But she also needs me. There isn't a conflict, if you look at it right."

"And now he has a very different attitude. For instance, we had a barbecue recently and all the people from my office came over. We started talking shop. . . ."

"As usual," Harry puts in lightly.

"As usual. But it didn't bother Harry. He was lying on a lounge chair listening to a ballgame with a big smile on his face."

"I feel comfortable just being myself now. And it's interesting, I get the feeling that her friends like me better that way. They feel more comfortable with me, too."

Cindy and Hank Lewis live in a suburb of Kansas City, on a tree-lined street of roomy but not really fancy houses built in the 1950s. Everybody has a big back yard, and almost everybody has children. The Lewises, married for eighteen years, have two teenagers, a boy and a girl.

"This neighborhood is like a big middle-class commune," says Cindy. "A lot of people here work for the same company, either the husband or the wife. Everybody knows everybody, and it's a very friendly atmosphere. We have special friends—one family next door and another in the next street—but people just generally get along. You wouldn't move here if you didn't want to see a lot of neighbors, have a lot of friends."

What do you mean by middle-class commune? You don't share expenses with other people, do you?

"Well, not mortgages or things like that," Hank says. "But we own a boat together with our next-door neighbors. Sometimes we use it together, sometimes separately. It's a sort of time-sharing proposition. Our friends in the next block have a swimming pool, and our kids are welcome over there anytime so long as they call first. Their kids are about the same age as ours."

Do you do something in return, or are they just open-house kind of people?

"They like to travel more than we do," says Cindy, "so we usually take their kids for a couple of weeks every summer while they go off on their own someplace. Nobody really keeps score on these things. You just do it."

Do you all just drop in on one another a lot, or is it like the swimming pool situation—call first?

"There's a fair amount of dropping in during the weekends," Cindy says, "but you usually know if other people are having guests or are going to be busy on some project. There's a lot of calling back and forth. If somebody is going to the farmer's market, for instance, they'll call and say, 'Can I pick up anything for you?' That kind of thing. But a lot of things are planned. Barbecues or poker nights. We rotate it around."

It all sounds a little like a television ad. Perfect America.

Hank grins. "Yes, we've been accused of that before. And I suppose it is kind of corny in a way. I'm sure a lot of people couldn't stand it. But we love it."

"In fact, about three years ago Hank was offered another job, in Chicago. It would have meant another ten thousand a year, but we looked into it pretty carefully and it seemed as though most of the extra money would be eaten up by higher expenses. And we really didn't want to leave here. I think we all would have been pretty unhappy about it."

"Partially, we were thinking about the kids. But it's more than that. We really care about our friends here, and I don't think it's all that easy to make really good friends in a big city."

Does anybody around here ever get divorced?

"Of course," says Cindy. "I mean, this isn't a fantasy or something. People have problems. But if there is a divorce, the people usually move away."

How does this way of living affect your marriage? Or isn't that an issue?

"Oh, I think it is an issue," Hank says. "The only bad time we ever had was a dozen years ago when we lived in Dallas for three years. We had an apartment in a high rise and we didn't know many people. We felt kind of hemmed in, and we started getting on each other's nerves. It wasn't a kind of life we were happy with. We'd quarrel about the dumbest things. Cindy finally said she thought we needed to get out of there, and I agreed with her. We're very gregarious people, and I think it's important for us to have a lot of friends around. It makes us more relaxed with each other."

"It's funny," Cindy says. "I have a sister ten years older than I am, and she's just the opposite from me. You can hardly pry her and her husband apart for ten minutes, and they really resist social gatherings. We don't really get along. I guess it might have something to do with her being an only child for ten years and then having me show up. I was not appreciated. She didn't want to have much to do with me, and my parents were very busy, so I took the route of making a lot of friends."

What about you, Hank? Does your upbringing have anything to do with this need for friends?

"I was one of five children. I'm sure that explains it."

And what you have here is kind of an extended family.

"You got it," agrees Hank.

For some couples, having friends does mean seeing people regularly, as often as several times a week, telephoning back and forth, or dropping by unannounced. But other people find that confining and even tiresome in the long run. Married twenty-two years, Jim and Denise Amato are both high school teachers outside New York City—she in foreign languages, he in history. They don't have nearly as many friends in New York as they used to, and that's fine by them, because they have friends all over the world.

They skimp on other things so that they can travel abroad every summer, and they've made friends wherever they've gone—there are photographs of them all over their modest home.

"Most people don't understand our lifestyle, or maybe they're a little jealous of it," Denise says. "I guess we are bored more easily than most people. Friends here have a subtle way of getting across the point that you're some kind of kook if you pick up and go instead of fixing up the house and hosting pot-luck cookouts. But they don't really come out and say it, so eventually it gets to the point that there's no serious communication going on at all. And you wonder—is a true friend someone you go out to eat with once a week and make small talk, or is it someone you see once a year, or even once every two or three years, but whom you feel extremely alive and totally yourself with?"

When they began traveling extensively, Jim and Denise were just two teachers on vacation, but they quickly began "accumulating friends," as they call it. "We soon found," Jim says, "that we were receiving more Christmas cards from overseas than from friends in the U.S. The cards would say 'Come back to Italy next year,' or 'Visit us soon,' or 'Come see the new baby.' And they meant it. We have beautiful friendships with these people. Part of it is that since we don't see them often, it's a very intense experience when we do. There's never this chitchat about bosses and crabgrass. We see what is new and we know when it's time to leave. There's an incredible warmth and depth of feeling in these friendships. They really open up their hearts to us and make us part of the family. It's an adventure."

"Jim and I are more doers than dreamers. My father always talked about people he knew in France during the Second World War. He would speak about them with such love and say, 'I really ought to go back and see them,' but he never did. We do."

"People tell us we're missing something because we have no children," Jim says. "But they're missing something by not having all our experiences. And so far as kids go, we have a lot of longtime friends abroad and we've watched their kids grow up. We've always had a terrific rapport with them. I think they sense that we're young at heart. It was Uncle Jim and Aunt Denise in whatever language. And now we often have one of those kids staying with us for a while when they come to America to vacation or study. You can't have it all, but I think we come pretty close."

"When we travel, we always take records and T-shirts, things like that for the kids. It's nice to be thought of as authorities on what's hip in America. We love our friends and their children dearly, and we wouldn't trade our lives for anyone's."

But there are also people who travel all over the world and find the forming and maintaining of friendships difficult. Stars of the entertainment world have a special problem when it comes to friends—or, really, two separate problems. Robert Bell of Kool and the Gang echoes the statements of many celebrities, from Smokey and Claudette Robinson to Kenny and Marianne Rogers:

"It's difficult for us in terms of having friends. We're not always that good at knowing who likes us for ourselves and who wants to hang out with Kool. I gravitate toward friendships with music people, because we have so much in common and the understanding is there. But it is very difficult to maintain a normal social life with people like Lionel Ritchie or the Jacksons or Sugar Ray Leonard. When I'm around they're not around. It's very hard to get together when we're all traveling all the time."

And he adds, "Even though we don't socialize with friends that much, I've got my family, and my wife's family. My sister is really my best friend. She's always been there, and she knows me so well. For me, nothing is so precious as family."

The public often feels that celebrities are being hypocritical when they complain about their lack of privacy or the difficulty of leading a normal life. But there is a cost—and friendship can be a part of that cost.

There are celebrities who don't agree that it's a problem for them to maintain friendships, though—like Cindy and Joey Adams. During their thirty years together they have cultivated a large circle of good friends. "Many are celebrities, simply because of the areas we've moved in. Our friendship with Ruth and Milton Berle and with the Henny Youngmans began in the first years of our marriage. More recently we've become very good friends with Anthony Quinn and his wife, Deborah Raffin and her husband, and Tovah and Ernest Borgnine."

"You've never had a problem with people trying to become friends in order to use you in some way?" I ask.

"After thirty years, your antennae get very sharp, and if people are there for the wrong reason you can sense it. And you back away."

"Do you have friends who aren't celebrities?"

"I have several close girlfriends from even before I married Joey, and we have remained close." But then, like Robert Bell, Cindy gets back to family. "My mother is still my very closest friend," she says. "She's a very important presence in my life."

JASON: We just don't have time for unnecessary friends. We both work sixty- to seventy-hour weeks. There are certainly people we have dinner with occasionally, and there are people we keep in touch with regularly, but mostly by phone. And we see people at our health clubs. But we don't really have many friends of the kind you keep up with because you were bosom buddies in college.

Are you saying you only have useful friends?

CAROLE: Well, that makes us sound kind of cold and hard, but I suppose it is true. I guess you might call them "networking friends." They're people who can help you get things done. It's a two-way street, of course. We put them in touch with people who can do things for them, and they return the favor. You have to understand, we don't keep up with people *just* because they're useful. We like them, too.

JASON: Most of them. Let's be honest.

But it's not a matter of sentiment? Or just good times?

CAROLE: No. Jason has two sisters and I have a brother. We save the sentiment for the family. A lot of friendships are really hypocritical anyway. People think that having a lot of "best" friends shows what a good person you are. I don't buy that. People who need a lot of emotionally involved friends are usually pretty insecure. We don't need that kind of emotional support system. For emotional support we can turn to one another.

Neither of you have friends you confide in about personal things? Nobody you could call up and say, "I'm mad at Carole," or "Jason is driving me crazy"?

CAROLE: If Jason is driving me crazy, which rarely happens, I tell Jason.

JASON: She sure does. I don't like that kind of thing anyway, ratting on your husband or wife to friends. I don't want to hear it from people, and I certainly wouldn't do it myself.

CAROLE: What it comes down to is that Jason and I are one another's best friend. When that's true, you don't need somebody else's shoulder to cry on.

Don and Rachel Barton recently moved to North Carolina after more than twenty years in New York City. They met seventeen years ago when both were working at a summer theater in New England, Don as an actor and Rachel as the assistant set designer. They started living together the following winter and married five years after that. Don is now teaching college courses in acting and directing, while

Rachel has just had her first children's book, which she both wrote and illustrated, accepted for publication. Both are very glad to be out of New York for a number of reasons, not least because it has enabled them to get away from all the people they know.

"We had too many friends," Rachel says. "That happens to people who work in the theater. You work so closely with people in such an intense way, and you inevitably find yourself getting very involved in one another's lives. Of course, theater people are always going off somewhere else, and you lose touch. Friends fall away. But even so, there are an awful lot left. And it can be just exhausting trying to keep all those relationships alive."

"Both of us got so we resented it," Don says. "People constantly calling up, wanting to get together, inviting you to another party, or wanting you to come see them in something—some showcase Off Off Broadway. Rachel and I had both changed in the last few years. We wanted more time to ourselves. Rachel was working on her writing and on illustrations for other people's books, and I had begun teaching. I never expected to be a star. I don't have the right looks; I was really born a character actor. So we were trying to get ourselves going in new directions. But people wouldn't let us alone."

"It wasn't just all the invitations to do things, either. People would call up and want to talk for hours, all the gossip, everything they thought about everything they'd seen in the theater or the movies or on television. We'd gotten beyond that. We were plain tired of it, and we'd get irritated. Then friends would get huffy in return, and we'd feel guilty about it."

Don laughs. "We both hate answering machines. We'd always had a service to take professional calls for us. But we finally got a machine at home just to filter out the calls. We'd listen to see who it was, and if it was somebody we really wanted to talk to, we'd answer, but mostly we wouldn't. And sometimes we wouldn't call back, either. If they said later that they'd left a message, we'd say the machine screwed up. But some people saw through it, and you'd hear them saying, 'I know you're there, you bastards.' In a funny way, of course, but still it made us feel like shits."

"So when this opportunity came up for Don down here, we jumped at it. There was more to it than just getting out from under all our friends, of course. New York has gotten so incredibly expensive.

And it's changed; it's gotten as hard and cold and frenetic as people always said it was. But that wasn't true ten years ago. We loved it. But it's as though it has decided to live up to its reputation."

"It's just the damn yuppies," Don puts in. "Godawful generation."

"Anyway, we moved down here, and it's been a wonderful change for us. We've made friends here, of course, but because we were new we could establish rules about socializing that fit where we are in our lives now. We want time together now, we want to be a lot quieter. And the people here don't know what we were like a few years ago, so they just accept it."

"Curiously, moving down here has really saved some of our old friendships," Don says. "People we loved but were absolutely ready to strangle. Now we write wonderful letters back and forth and talk on the phone a couple of times a month, and it's just right. One of our most frenetic friends came down here for a weekend awhile back and we had a good time. It was a lot of fun. But it lasted just long enough. We have a long history with him, and we would be sad to see it end, but if we were still in New York I'm sure that would have happened. This way we can go on being friends, and we're glad about that."

"It is strange," says Rachel, "but sometimes I think the only way to save a friendship is by seeing less of someone you care about."

Having friends is as important to Gary Hewitt as it is to his wife Sandy—even though he has no friends, to speak of. It's his wife's friends who are important to him. This seeming contradiction is central to their relationship. For Gary and Sandy have very different interests.

"I'm a sports nut," Sandy says. "Gary may watch tennis on TV twice a year. I'm also addicted to public affairs shows, and I curse at the TV set all the time. I scream at Kurt Waldheim or George Bush while Gary is in the kitchen or painting upstairs."

"We have nothing in common except each other," Gary agrees matter-of-factly. "Art is the only real thing for me except Sandy and my family. I don't see the point in watching the same people on television and hearing the same bullshit year after year."

Gary likes to stay close at home, where his studio is located, painting or playing with his video camera or guitar. He has little patience for social activities. But Sandy, who works at a public relations firm, thrives on her network of special-interest friends and often plans lunch or after-work drinks as much as two weeks ahead.

"I have a kind of arrogant need for people to hear my opinions—and I've got plenty of them," says Sandy. "I have some friends at work who've interned for congressmen or worked on campaigns, and we go over the newspapers together every morning. We go to political lectures and hand out political literature on streetcorners. All my friends are Democrats, and we go hunting for Republicans to beat up—verbally, of course."

Gary comes back to the sports question. "One of Sandy's major disappointments is that she hasn't been able to convince me that a guy running down a field with a football is an art form. The way she yells at the TV set, our neighbors must think I'm beating her. She'll look miserable and I'll go to comfort her, only to find out that the Yankees blew a five-run lead. Oh boy, a serious crisis!"

Friends thus play a vital role in the marriage, because they give Sandy something that her husband cannot. She is so passionate about sports and politics that Gary's indifference could make her feel bored and resentful. "Gary's a loner—except with me," she says. "I'm his wife and painting is his mistress, and he's faithful to the two of us only. But I see things going on, like all the numbers going up on the board on election night, and I yearn to be part of it. I need people to get excited about that with me. Gary's got a few friends, but they just talk business. On a day-to-day basis, he doesn't get phone calls or chat about life with anyone but me."

"People often wonder what we do together and why we got married in the first place. But not the people who really know us. They realize I married her to save her from herself," Gary teases. "We have a crystal-clear love. I met her at a party and fell in love with her that minute. I enjoy listening to her carry on about things, and I'm turned on by her passionate feelings."

"Gary's feelings about his work are just as strong," Sandy adds. "So we're not really that different."

"When we met, Sandy was unhappy, and I sensed it. She's not the type who likes to be alone, and she thought men were worse than Nixon—I remember her saying that. What a project she was. It wasn't easy making her smile like she does now."

"I had a good job, lots of friends and activities. But I was twenty-seven and there had never been anyone special in my life, unique. Gary was so gentle, and he took me along, getting me to sit back and relax a little, to speak more softly. He was the only man who held me and whispered to me. He still does that all the time."

"It's true, we're very cuddly together."

"I shouldn't tell you this, but Gary creates beautiful murals on my behind. Then I do funny things near the mirror so I can see them."

"Sandy cares for a lot of people, and she needs a whole group of friends, but more than anything else she has to have someone to squeeze, someone who'll squeeze back. And that's me."

"I'll come home from a lecture on disarmament and I'll be all up and intellectually stimulated and feeling great. Whatever friend I went to the lecture with will have something to eat with us, and Gary will just sort of listen. Then we'll be alone and I'll see Gary's little smile and I'll whisper, "Give me a hug." We talk silly a lot. It's the end of the day, and I can actually feel my blood pressure go down. I've always had the friends and the heavy discussions, but I never had anyone else who loved me."

*The freedom I feel being able to ask for what I
want when I want it has helped me to grow
sexually. I don't even mind rejection—some
nights he feigns headaches.*
—Julia Martinson

*I started to have an affair—to prove some-
thing, prove I was still a man. I found out you
don't just go to bed with someone, you also
have your wife along. Emotionally, you have
three people in bed.*
—George Heath

Sex and fidelity: Paths to fulfillment

The frankness or reserve with which people talk about sex varies
considerably from marriage to marriage, but it appears to have far
more to do with background than with age. An urban couple in their
sixties, for example, were far more forthright that a rural couple in
their twenties. Surprisingly, many couples who had real sexual
problems were not reluctant to discuss them. Rather, they took pride
in revealing how they overcame the difficulties or made the marriage
work in spite of them. And, as might be expected, couples with
extensive experience in unconventional sexual experimentation were
delighted to discuss their adventures.

Sex can be very important to one couple and of minor conse-
quence to another, but the attitudes expressed always provide vital
clues to the relationship in general. Whatever sexual problems may

135

exist in a marriage, they are far less crucial than the desire and ability to make whatever adjustments are necessary to maintain the bond. The adjustment may be as basic as one partner learning to live with less sex than he or she would like, or as complex as fully sanctioned infidelity. But, as in all areas of married life, solutions with respect to sexuality are intensely personal and take on the character of the fundamental relationship.

"Our love is based on friendship, but sex is sex," says Kari Clark, wife of television producer and host Dick Clark. "Good, solid sex. Our sex life is separate from our love life, and that's how we like it. We're both very sexual, and that's always been extremely important. We're very affectionate. We touch each other a lot and hold hands, but as far as sex goes, it doesn't involve deep feelings; it's more like a porno movie. Sex was the basis for our attraction, and ten years later, it's still very intense. But as far as I'm concerned, that's not the same as love. It's not the kind of romantic love that often goes with sex. Affection, romance, work, sex—they all have separate feelings. To me, that's much more satisfying. Our work is all work, our love is all love, and our sex is all sex."

Kari Clark's attitude bears out the observation of psychotherapist James F. Walters: "In a love relationship, sex can deepen what is already there, but it can't create what isn't there." Walters goes on to say, "You can have an active sex life without intimacy, and you can have intimacy without sex."

For Jeanne and Howard, the millionaire couple, sex is of little importance. She is focused on her art collecting, he on his money-making, and although they express a deep need for one another, the bond is based on other things than sex. "Howard and I enjoy sex," says Jeanne, "but we've discovered that neither one of us has a particularly strong sex drive. During sex, my mind never turns off other things. I've never had a vaginal orgasm, and don't believe many women have. I rarely experience any passionate desire for sex."

"That's true," says Howard. "I was thirty-two when we married. Before that I had spent ten years screwing everything that walked, sat, or stood. I never stopped. Then one day I got bored. It was suddenly ridiculous trying to prove my manhood that way. The pressure to perform was crazy. I wanted to be comfortable with a woman—in and out of bed. Don't misunderstand, I still get horny, but not very often, and Jeanne more than satisfies my needs."

For other couples, sex is crucial to the bond. Jim and Nora are an interracial couple, both of whom work at well-paying jobs. Physical passion is usually a hallmark of young first marriages, but Jim is in his mid-forties, Nora in her mid-thirties, and both have been married before.

"I'd had black lovers before I met Jim," Nora says, "and some were terrific and some were terrible. It has nothing to do with the myth about black men being better in bed. I think that any men who feel confident and good about themselves and who like women can be great lovers. Jim is one of those special men. The sex with him is better than any I've ever had, because he knows what I need and gives it to me. I think I do the same for him. I like to feel that I'm equal in every way except in the bedroom. There he is in total command, and I like it that way. I like to feel that I can completely surrender."

"When we first met I asked her if she could have an orgasm without being touched, and she laughed. She's not laughing anymore."

"That's true. We are so in tune that sometimes he can lie next to me and just talk and I can contract my pelvic muscles until I reach orgasm."

Jim and Nora have only been married four years, and since it is common for sexual passion to wane somewhat after the first few years of marriage, they may have some adjusting to do down the line. After a time, for many couples, things change. Larry and Jane are both psychiatrists. Their work in the same field provides a very special bond. Married for six years, they are very committed to their careers and work long, hard hours. On the subject of sex, Larry says, "The feelings between us are deep and very strong. But sex comes and goes. Sometimes it is terrific and sometimes we're just too tired to enjoy it."

Jane's feelings are quite precise. "Passion often means living at the edge of a precipice all the time—it generates excitement, fights, breaking up, getting back together—and I don't want that anymore. I think you can still have real pleasure on a much more even keel. Sometimes I think about having that kind of romantic intensity, but I know that for me what we have is much more important. I don't want to pay the price for passion."

Larry adds, "I guess you're also alluding to the excitement, the mystery of a new relationship, where sex is at the center of things. But once that's past, I think you have to realize that sex needs a different approach. Yes, you work at it. You learn to create excitement. For me, it means that I will plan to give up doing two or three things so that at eleven at night I'm not too tired. Otherwise, sex has no real vitality. I will think about making love to Jane before I get home. I'll put on music she likes, change my clothes, prepare dinner, allow time for her to relax and for us to talk together—or maybe I'll just attack her when she walks in the door!"

For Larry and Jane, sex has become one of many components of their marriage. Certainly it is an important one, providing pleasure, excitement, and an ongoing bond. But it's more like the piano in a quintet, not a trumpet solo. This is true in most good marriages. People do get married for sex—although most marriage counselors would warn against it. But to make the marriage work over the long term, other bonds must be developed more fully.

Married for twelve years, Lester and Babs David have one child. She is a purchasing manager and he works for a government agency. They are in their mid-forties and met as volunteers for a political campaign.

"When I met Lester," says Babs, "I could tell he was crazy about me right away. He asked me questions like what kind of wedding I wanted, things no other guy would say. It's so uncool. A few days after we met, someone gave us VIP seats for a baseball game and we spent the day together. We found we had a lot to talk about. But Lester also said something about people working together who want to have an intimate relationship."

"She told me she wouldn't want to get involved with anyone she was working with—as we were, of course—and she thought if people really cared for one another they could wait. She handled it well, made it all hypothetical."

"There were several talks about it. I couldn't have been less interested in Lester romantically, but I enjoyed the friendship. We were together at the office six or seven nights a week, then we'd go for a burger or a movie if we had the energy. Lester always has the energy. And he always paid, which was unusual. He was a gentle-man—but a bald gentleman with baggy pants and platform shoes."

"I knew I wasn't her type, but it didn't stop me. I was never a ladies' man, but I hung in there. I wasn't interested in a quick sexual relationship. I was going to marry her."

"We got along so well that I continued to see him. We came from similar backgrounds and we talked about our feelings all the time. We both love ballet and boxing—how's that for a combination? There are a lot of nights I'd probably have gone out with my girlfriends, but Lester came up with great tickets to something. But I wasn't using him. He knew he wasn't for me."

"There *was* method to my madness. I had the feeling that in the back of her head she was thinking of me in a new light. We had a discussion about how men will think some women okay for dating, but marry another type. Babs said the same thing was true for women, and that solid things were most important in the long run. Boy, did that give me hope!"

"But I was still finding myself physically attracted to the slick six-footer in the good suit and styled hair. Lester had a nice face, but he wasn't an athlete, and it showed."

"Babs kids me that I was like a great old house that needed a lot of work. When we were just friends, I think she was a little embarrassed to be seen with me."

"He wasn't up to my standards."

"Yes, I knew she was taking great pains to let people know that we weren't involved in 'that way.'"

"I remember that part of me was falling in love with Lester, but another part of me couldn't imagine going to bed with him. Going to bed for the first few times requires intense physical attraction. After that, it's how you feel about a person that counts, and you don't even notice the looks."

"Finally she let me kiss her, and it progressed . . ."

"Slowly," Babs interrupts.

"Very slowly to the next level. And that was that. I knew it would happen, because I understood her so well, and she's a woman who loves being known. She felt all her old boyfriends were strangers."

"That's true. This is the only relationship I've ever had where I feel at all in charge. I never worried that he wouldn't call me or that he was with someone else. I had always been tense with other guys, wondering what they'd think, what I should say, what they wanted to do. I was never in control of how far a relationship would go."

"Babs always said that I thought of her as a virgin, so she became one. She still tells me she's a virgin and makes me coax her."

"Lucky for us, Lester is a sensitive, beautiful lover—a real woman-pleaser. He hadn't had experience with a lot of women, but it was the quality of his lovemaking. He'd slept with people he cared about and respected, so he felt that their satisfaction was worthwhile. But I did insist on doing him over—outside. I got him into sports and diet. I got him to get rid of his terrible clothes, and when I finally dragged him in for a new toupee—hallelujah!"

"I understand why she did this, and frankly I'm grateful for the results. Believe me, it's no fun going through life looking like a putz. I wasn't the Adonis she'd always wanted, but I didn't have to look like a nerd, either. I thought it behooved me to make myself into something in between."

"I think he's a nice-looking man now. Anyway, my mother always told me, 'You can put a man on a diet and change his clothes, but you can't change what is inside.' And Lester is terrific inside."

"Her mother," says Lester, "is a very intelligent woman."

The degree to which sexual attitudes are intertwined with other aspects of a marriage is evident in the experiences of Mike and Julia Martinson, who have been married twenty years and have a nineteen-year-old son. Both were born and raised in San Diego. Mike, forty-four, is an attractive man with an easy smile, salt-and-pepper hair, and a casual grace. An executive with Continental Airlines, he served in the Air Force and is a veteran of the Vietnam War. Julia, a natural blonde with classic beauty and style, graduated from Wellesley College. She has long been involved in social causes, including marching with Reverend Martin Luther King in Selma and working for the ERA. She is an attorney, with a female partner, and specializes in divorce; her clients are largely women from low-income families.

As might be expected, the veteran and the feminist had some rocky times together. When their son was born, Julia felt peculiarly isolated from other young mothers. She simply felt different and strange.

"I would go to the park with the baby and sit there with all the other mothers talking about formulas and bowel movements and the house they were going to buy on Long Island to get out of the city. I thought there was something wrong with me. I didn't want to talk about diaper rash, and I was so bored with my life the last thing I would do was move to the suburbs. I wanted to go back to work. Every time I put the baby down for a nap, I took one, too. I'd fall into a deep sleep and feel drugged when I awoke. I knew it was symptomatic of depression. I was always thinking, 'Is this all there is?' My whole life seemed predetermined, and I couldn't bear it. So I went into analysis."

Mike remembers this troubled period well. "It was an emotional roller coaster from then on. I didn't know how to deal with Julia's anger, resentment, depression, and mood swings. I could understand her wanting to go back to work, even though not many women did that at the time. But sharing the housework was a real problem for me. I couldn't accept it, and close friends started calling me henpecked. Even my mother thought it was too much. I had an affair, and when she found out about it, Julia had one, too. But gradually the emotional conflicts eased. I stopped being so defensive. The war in Vietnam was a critical issue between us. I wouldn't say I was a hawk, but I believed we were right to be there at the time, and Julia's stand for peace provided one helluva conflict. When I came home from Nam, I saw things quite differently. I was even able to admit to Julia that she was right. I started listening to her without building mental blocks."

"The war was definitely a turning point for us," Julia agrees. "When I joined the peace movement, I started meeting other women who felt just like I did. I got involved in the women's movement after the war was over, and it was a relief to find other people who could verbalize all the feelings of outrage at the injustice of our position. For the first time in my life I did not feel out of step . . . or that maybe I was crazy."

"Many of Julia's friends came to our house, and while I was not invited to participate in their discussions, I overheard enough to make me sympathetic. When my father died and I saw how helpless my mother really was, after so many years of being sheltered and protected by him, I began to understand how women felt. My mother could hardly function without my dad. I came to see her as a victim of 'protective custody.'"

"That helped Mike get over the idea that I only wanted dominance or power. Mike fought me all those years because he thought I wanted control over him. I didn't. I just wanted to feel equal. I think most men have trouble understanding that women don't want to control their men. They just want enough independence so that men do not completely control their destiny. Mike and I started out so polarized that it took us years to come together enough to seek a decent balance in our relationship."

"One unexpected outcome of all this was that Julia's strength and determination heightened our enjoyment of sex. She is completely free and uninhibited in sex, but what I like best is that she has no difficulty in initiating sex. That's very exciting to a man. Sometimes I go to bed tired or not in the mood, and then Julia will instigate sex and I'm suddenly wide awake!"

"I was one of those women who faked orgasm just to get sex over with and make my husband happy. One night I was so relaxed because I was completely sure I wouldn't have an orgasm that I finally had one. After that there was no stopping me. I wanted to experience everything. I became obsessed with sex and drove poor Mike crazy. Now we've reached a balance, and the freedom I feel being able to ask for what I want when I want it has helped me to grow sexually. I don't even mind rejection—some nights he feigns headaches. But it doesn't happen very often."

Sex is a mirror that always reflects truths about the basic relationship between two people. When there are unresolved tensions, sex suffers. When a relationship like Mike and Julia's blossoms in a new way, a fresh sexual awakening occurs. Even in the case of Kari and Dick Clark, who regard sex as simply sex, that compartmentalization reflects their attitudes about their lives in general.

Joe and Vicky are both in their late fifties and have been married for six years. Joe was married twice before and Vicky once; both have grown children and grandchildren. Joe is impotent.

Joe brings up that fact first, and Vicky is quick to put the matter in perspective. "We discussed this before we were married. I finally made Joe understand that to me it wasn't a major problem, because my own sex drive is pretty low. I like things the way they are. I feel relaxed, secure, and unthreatened."

"Actually, I've been able to reach orgasm recently," Joe says, "even though I never have a real erection. We practice oral sex, and Vicky has shown me how to satisfy her manually. I love touching her and kissing her, and I know she doesn't think less of me for not being able to actually penetrate. For the past two years I've been working with a therapist, but Vicky is the best therapist I could have."

Vicky says she could count on one hand the times she has been brought to orgasm by the men in her life. "I can and do masturbate with Joe, but not too often. I enjoy the physical relationship we have, and orgasm just isn't a big thing for me. Some nights after work we come home, have dinner, and then take a hot mineral bath together. We spread a large bath towel on the bed and rub each other down with warm baby oil. We play soft music and use candlelight, and I feel like all my muscles are relaxed and my bones have melted. I enjoy that sensation better than any orgasm I've ever had. I fall asleep in Joe's arms like a contented cat."

Joe smiles. "Because I care so much for Vicky, I enjoy the pleasure I give her more than I ever enjoyed the anticipation of an orgasm. The pressure to perform and the fear of failure are gone. I feel free and secure. The idea that we are able to talk about all this has lifted a tremendous burden that I've carried around for years."

Joe and Vicky's previous marriages have a major bearing on their sexual attitudes. Vicky got married in the 1950s and, as she puts it, "bought the American dream. I expected my husband to be the knight in shining armor who, with a can of Ajax, would clean everything up. I had all the wrong expectations, and when he turned out to be simply an ordinary man with his own insecurities, fears, and faults, I felt disappointed and cheated. I don't blame him now for the breakup of that marriage. We were both quite unprepared. I do blame my parents, teachers, and society in general for giving my generation such unrealistic expectations."

Joe says he wanted a marriage "like Ozzie and Harriet. I resented my wives for wanting careers and outside fulfillment. I wanted a hot meal on the table when I came home from work, and I couldn't relate to their frustrations. It took me five years of analysis to feel comfortable just with myself and finally with women. I'm glad my own kids are more sensitive at a young age than I was. When I hear them communicate with each other about subjects we didn't dare discuss in the old days, I know there's hope for the future."

Joe and Vicky had known each other for fourteen years when

they married and had often turned to each other for comfort and emotional support. "I could always talk to Joe about anything. I found that I could open up to him more easily than I could to my closest women friends. I was terrified of getting married again. The men I picked were always wrong for me, and I seemed to go from one bad affair to another. Joe remained the most constant, stable man in my life, even though we were never lovers. When he proposed marriage, it seemed completely natural and right. I wondered why I hadn't thought of it before."

"She didn't take long to say yes, and we didn't even bother to tell our families and friends. We just did it."

The tender lovemaking Joe and Vicky have achieved is not simply making the best of it; rather, it is a reflection of the many ways they truly cherish one another.

Married for twelve years, both in their early forties, Ruth and Fred Howard have a combined income of over one hundred thousand and own a condo apartment in Beverly Hills. Fred is a very successful antiques dealer; Ruth, a licensed electrician, is semiretired but still does consulting work for architects. She is a lesbian and he is gay.

Fred has known he was gay since childhood. Ruth initially became aware of her sexual orientation in high school, but didn't become an active lesbian until her late twenties. She and Fred had known one another for years when they were married, and were aware of one another's sexual orientation from the beginning. "We met at a party given by a mutual friend," Ruth recalls, "and became instant pals. We started referring business to each other and developed a mutual respect for one another's talent. Fred was the first person, male or female, that I could really confide in. I could talk to him about anything without fear of being laughed at or put down. It was wonderful to find one person I could trust completely."

"I felt the same way about Ruth," Fred says. "It was like finding a sister and a best friend without any of the usual rivalry or competition. We started going away for weekends and holidays together, and when we got back to the city we'd have to separate and would really miss one another. I'd never experienced a close relationship with a woman before, and really enjoyed it. After a trip to New York, where we spent two weeks together, we both felt very depressed going back to our apartments alone in L.A. I suggested we try living together, and we found this condo. We were married in Las Vegas two years later."

I asked if they had ever had sex together.

"We tried it, but it didn't work out," Ruth says. "Sometimes we sleep together in the same bed. Fred loves cuddling, so we do that. He's great on a cold night, but we both know that sex can't work for us. Even so, I think we're more intimate than most married couples. I don't need a man to stick his penis into me to know we're closely connected."

"Sometimes when we're in bed together I wish I were heterosexual, because I love Ruth so much. There isn't anything I wouldn't do for her. Once we even tried one of those rubber penis shafts that give you a false erection, but the sight was so funny we couldn't stop laughing."

"Sex is an important part of my life," Ruth says. "There have been times that I've met a woman I thought I could live with, but I do love Fred and I don't believe I could ever leave him for another woman. I need to be with a man, especially one who cares about me as I know Fred does. So many gay women have hang-ups—guilt and unreasonable jealousy. I don't want to deal with that. If I go out with a woman and spend a night or a weekend, I can hardly wait to get home afterward."

"Our gay friends generally agree that ours is a good, stable marriage. Some of our straight friends don't even suspect that we're gay, and if they do they don't mention it. It's important to us to be accepted in both worlds as a couple, and we seem to be able to make the best of both worlds."

While they have complete freedom to have sex with whomever they want, even so Ruth and Fred both have experienced jealousy. "There have been times when Ruth has gone out on a date and come back either very late or the next day, and I've felt tremendous resentment. I've rationalized it by saying that my anger stems from concern about her safety. However, when I calm down we talk it out, and I realize that my anger is a form of jealousy that isn't fair to either one of us."

"I've felt the same way, but instead of showing anger I simply withdraw and sulk, which is almost worse. We're trying to be more considerate of one another's feelings. I call if I think I'm going to be out late or overnight, and Fred does the same."

"It's interesting to note that as the years go by we seem to have fewer and fewer late dates. For me it could be the scare of AIDS, but I think my sex drive has diminished. My need for companionship is satisfied just by being with Ruth."

"Sometimes I think it's just too much trouble to go out with women I know I am just using. I'd rather stay home or have dinner out with Fred. We have so much to talk about and enjoy together that we never seem to have enough private time for ourselves."

Couples in good marriages deal with the issue of sex their own way rather than following the rules of sex manuals or the examples of other people. It's what works for the two individuals within the particular marriage. The same wide range of feelings and attitudes exists when it comes to the issue of fidelity.

Some couples have very strong prohibitions about infidelity. In the following dialogue, I talked to each partner separately. The answers were almost identical, even though one spouse did not know what the other said.

"I told him that if I ever caught him cheating, I'd kill him or leave him. There's no in between. If he has a one-night stand while he's away, I wish he wouldn't tell me. He said I'd be the first to know, because it would never happen."

And from the other: "I think we have a very simple understanding. If she were unfaithful to me, I'd kill her. She'd kill me, too. And I think we've both had enough experience and experimentation in our lives to realize what a terrific thing we have and not take any chances on it."

This is Neile and Al Toffel talking. Both are in their forties and both have children by previous marriages. In Neile's case, that marriage was to the late actor Steve McQueen. It lasted for fifteen very difficult years. Neile was aware that Steve had affairs, but says that she blocked a lot of things out. "Those affairs never really meant anything. He needed to feel that he was a superstar. There was never any 'other woman' as such. It was very hard for him to come home and work at keeping love alive when there was so much instant gratification available to him. When I finally had an affair, however, he couldn't forgive me."

Although she claims that McQueen's affairs didn't mean anything, the pain of that experience obviously influences her attitude toward fidelity in her present marriage. But, "best intentions" or not, temptation is always there. In fact, marriage expert Dr. Albert Ellis believes that the person who is occasionally tempted is more normal than the one who is not.

PAT MARKS: A few years ago I almost had an affair with a woman I was working with. We had a late meeting, and she was coming on strong. I had a few drinks and was feeling no pain. I walked her to her car in the rain. We stood there for a minute and she leaned over and kissed me. I felt nothing but the need to get out of there, and I did. When I got home, Marcy was standing on the deck watching the rain. She was wearing one of those transparent negligees, and there was an ice bucket with my favorite white wine. I looked at my wife and felt an overwhelming surge of love for her. We made love on the floor of the living room, and afterwards I told her what had almost happened.

MARCY MARKS: Waiting for Pat that night, I think I knew something was happening. When he walked in the door I also knew that everything was all right. He didn't have to tell me what happened in that parking lot; I just knew. The funny thing was that even if it had happened, it wouldn't have changed anything between us. If it happened again to either of us, it would not affect our relationship. We have so much more than sex between us.

One couple views infidelity as justification for homicide, while another claims it wouldn't matter. How any given couple will actually react, though, is something that can only be tested in the event itself. And a great many couples don't want to test it out, don't want to see if their marriage could withstand the strain.

Mary Ann Mobley and Gary Collins, both forty-eight, have been married eighteen years and have a daughter. Gary also has two children from a previous marriage. Both are actors. Gary is the host of a syndicated television talk show, and has been master of ceremonies for the Miss America Pageant the past few years. Mary Ann is herself a former Miss America.

They are an exceptionally good-looking couple, yet both tend to play down their physical attractiveness. "Vanity isn't considered an attractive quality in the South, where I grew up," Mary Ann says. "I was never told I was pretty. I never expected to become Miss America, and after I did, all the way down the runway I kept thinking that I wasn't pretty enough. I still have insecurities about my looks, but Gary's been a great help with that."

"When you have that attitude," Gary says, "it's something you never lose. As a boy I knew I was good-looking, and I think it made things too easy for me. Until college I got by on my looks and charm. Then, in college, there were so many bright, attractive people that I realized I needed more. It was a difficult time, and I left college after two years to find myself in the army."

Neither Mary Ann nor Gary believes that their good looks can substitute for other qualities, but they are both aware of how striking the other is, and that a lot of other people out there are likely to go after one or the other of them. Asked what she would feel if Gary had an affair, Mary Ann has the same response as Neile Toffel: "I'd kill him. It'd be such a strain on your marriage if every time your husband went to work you had to worry about an assignation with a beautiful young lady in a dressing room. There's nothing worse than living with a person and wondering."

"This has never been tested with us," Gary says, "and I hope it won't ever be. I think when you're married for the right reasons, the opportunity doesn't really seem to be there even when you're away from your partner. You get into trouble when something is lacking. One of the biggest problems in all areas of marriage is that people feel they're missing something, that something's out there that can't be taken advantage of. You have to make some kind of compromise. Being married is more important to me than not being married. There's a little part of me that thinks there's something out there, but it's so far outweighed by the pleasure I get out of this marriage that I have to say, 'I can't have that if I want this.' I'd be devastated if Mary Ann were unfaithful, but I can't say it'd be the end of the marriage. There's so much invested in it, I couldn't just walk away."

Mary Ann does think adultery would end the marriage. "But I

don't think it could happen that way, because Gary has such integrity, such high standards. I think he'd get out of the marriage first, just as I would. I trust him—not because I'm so terrific, but because he has a commitment to this marriage."

"Our daughter wouldn't allow us to separate," Gary says with a grin. "One day I brought home a book I had to look at for a spot on the show. It was called *What Every Child Should Know About Divorce*, and our daughter found it. The next day Mary Ann and I were arguing about something, and she came bounding in saying, 'Not you! Everybody else can get a divorce, but not you guys.'"

It happened soon after Jackie and Barbara Cooper's twenty-fifth wedding anniversary. "Jackie had made a big thing out of our anniversary," Barbara recalls. "He gave me an emerald ring and diamonds—and I don't care about that kind of thing. I think he was really trying to make our marriage work. But he was having a big affair at the time. Then he came home from a trip and said he was 'drowning,' and an hour later he was gone. I went into a complete state of shock. The kids were off on their own by then. I was looking terrific. I thought it was supposed to be our time."

When Jackie Cooper married Barbara over thirty years ago, he had already had a lifetime of experience, a career as a child star in the *Our Gang* comedies and films like the original version of *The Champ*, followed by two failed marriages and the beginnings of a new career as a director. One of the reasons he was attracted to Barbara was the consistency of her life. "There was a continuity that I'd never had, and it was very refreshing," says Jackie. "Barbara lived with her family and had very old friends. There was a lot of strength and tradition in these families, and since my mother died when I was nineteen I'd felt that nobody really gave a good goddamn about me."

For many years their marriage was extremely strong. "I didn't think about other women," Barbara says. "It's not that I thought he never screwed around. But if it entered my mind, it would leave just as fast. I had three little babies and his career to work on, and he was the fourth little baby. It was a lot to take care of. I wanted to make everything perfect for him because he'd had such a miserable life before I met him. And with him it was always, 'I love you, I love you, my Barbara, my Barbara.'"

And then the crash came. "He'd been a little more irritable," Barbara says, "but that was the only real sign. He told me later it was an age thing—a big mid-life crisis. Our friends couldn't believe what was happening. Some of the women tried to convince me to see a lawyer, start divorce proceedings. But I wasn't ready."

Barbara was wise to wait, because it became clear that Jackie wasn't faring very well without her. "If Jackie wanted money, he came to me. He lived on credit cards. And within a month, he was back. He asked if he could come over to see me. He looked insane—I was going to put him in a hospital. He wanted to come home, if I'd have him. The next night was New Year's Eve, and he didn't come over. I told him on the phone, 'If you want to come home, you do it right now. And stay. I can't live like this.' He came home, and he was deathly ill, physically sick."

Barbara nursed him back to health, which helped to restore the bond between them. And despite the awful feelings she had experienced at the time, looking back Barbara admits, "The separation was the best thing for us. I took stock of myself and I didn't take things for granted anymore. We moved into another house after Jackie came back. I'd sold our old house while he was away, without telling him. That was spiteful, but the new house was exciting. It was the first time we were really living alone, and we were like two kids. It's wonderful now, but it took a little over a year to feel this way. It doesn't happen that you get over a separation like that right away. But I really think the marriage has been strengthened."

"I don't think either of us has a better time or laughs more with anyone else than we do with each other," Jackie says. "There's a lot of pain in a marriage, but one or the other of us tried to do something about the pain."

"As Jackie often says, 'I hear more now.' We both do. We are facing each other. Last week, Jackie was in a lousy mood and we had an argument. I went out the next day, and before I left I said, 'Whatever's on your mind, by the time I come home we'll talk about it or you'll change your mood. You have all day to think about it, but I'm not going to argue about whether or not something's bothering you.' When I came home it was over, and that was that."

I ask Jackie what his feelings about fidelity are now.

"There are people who say 'My husband loves me and I love him, but we go our separate ways.' That's not a marriage. People should try to be faithful."

Despite some feminist leanings, Barbara knows that Jackie thinks the woman should try harder. "If I'd been the one to leave, he wouldn't have accepted and taken me back. But in a funny way I feel freer now. For instance, I love the racetrack, and now I go by myself. It's just a little bit of Barbara's new independence. And that came from having to take stock."

The many years Barbara Cooper spent putting out of her mind any thought that Jackie was being unfaithful made it all the more likely that she would be stunned when he finally walked out. Other couples protect themselves against such shocks by keeping more clearly in mind the potential for lapses in faithfulness.

Steve Allen, the celebrated comedian, musician, writer, and talk show host, and his actress wife Jayne Meadows, who have been married more than thirty years, are a case in point. I talked with them separately, questioning Steve first.

MARILYN: Do you find humor in everything—including sex?

STEVE: The word *play* relates to both sex and humor. There's a playfulness to sex that's one of nature's blessings.

MARILYN: So you have a good sexual relationship?

STEVE: I've been lucky in many ways. We've all read about impotence and premature ejaculation, but I've never run into it. I don't know what a sexual problem is. I can't claim credit for it, but I've been fortunate in that as in so many other things.

MARILYN: Has the sexual revolution had any effect on you?

STEVE: It's made no difference whatsoever to us. Jayne and I are interested in romance and poetry and candlelight and violin music.

MARILYN: How important is fidelity?

STEVE: I think if Jayne had an affair, I'd be furious, but I doubt if the marriage would break up over that. I suppose theoretically there could be situations—although they seem to me very unhealthy—where two people say, "I love you but I do intend to have other partners now and then," and the other person says, "No problem." That's nonsense! Infidelity is one of the major factors in all divorces or—even worse—the terrible state of unhappiness in some marriages that stay together. Since the home is the environment in which new life is nurtured, I believe every effort has to be made to keep the marriage straight.

And how does Jayne Meadows feel about the same subject?

MARILYN: Could you have extramarital experiences that wouldn't necessarily threaten your marriage?

JAYNE: I don't think there is such a thing.

MARILYN: Are you vulnerable to attractive men? You look very sexual.

JAYNE: I am not, but my mother also gave off sexuality, and she was very prim. But I am vulnerable. One very handsome young man came to see me with Buddy Hackett while Steve was out of town. He asked me to dance with him at a party later on, but I wouldn't. He was just my type. I'm the most vulnerable person who ever lived. Just like an alcoholic, I have to stay away from temptation. Fortunately, Steve and I are very attracted to each other to this day. Maybe it's because we both have wild imaginations. I don't think frequency is what's important. What's important is how good it is when it happens. I think people who have sex too often have a problem. I don't think people have to talk about sex or have it every day to be sexy. I think the opposite is true.

MARILYN: How do you react when an attractive man is after you?

JAYNE: Well, recently a very attractive man was attracted to me and I to him. He was very much like Steve, and I was troubled by it. I went back to my psychiatrist and asked, "What is this?" He said, "You can look, but don't touch. It keeps you young."

MARILYN: Does Steve know about these things?

JAYNE: We've discussed this, and I think he liked the fact that I told the man I wasn't interested. He's been very jealous at times, but I think he's so secure now that he doesn't get jealous.

MARILYN: Are you the jealous type?

JAYNE: I never was. The sex act is only part of sexuality. Sex is flirting, touching, seeing a movie together.

MARILYN: Do you still flirt with Steve?

JAYNE: Steve says I flirt with dogs, children, women, old people, and men. You can do anything you want if you don't lose your femininity.

MARILYN: How would you feel if you found out Steve had an affair?

JAYNE: It wouldn't wreck the marriage. An affair is an affair.

MARILYN: What if you had one?

JAYNE: Women are different. Milton Berle told me that he stopped having flirtations and affairs when he realized that women took them seriously and men didn't. I fall in love completely. Men don't. Men have affairs.

MARILYN: *Did* Steve ever have an affair?

JAYNE: I'm sure he did. I felt so sorry for the other woman. I befriended her, because she hated me so. She was so jealous.

MARILYN: How did you cope with that?

JAYNE: Best fun I ever had in my life. Outsmarting, outwitting. For instance, she came over one day and said, "You're so wonderful about analyzing dreams, and I don't understand this dream I had the other night." She was sitting in front of her mirror and told the mirror to tell her the truth. Whatever the mirror told her—she couldn't remember—she broke it and awakened in a rage. I didn't tell her this, but I knew it was a matter of "Mirror, mirror on the wall, who's the fairest of them all?" And the mirror said, "Jayne." So my advice to women is, forget the affair. Be smart and keep your mouth shut.

A woman of a different generation and background whose name is Valerie agrees. She and her husband Curtis are a middle-class black couple who have been married for ten years. Curtis is the only black man in his company, and although he is very successful at his computer programming job, he can never be entirely sure that his promotions are not a matter of "tokenism." Valerie is very supportive of her husband, especially his need for "alone time." She has no qualms about discussing the issue of fidelity in his presence.

"Friday night is Curtis's night out with the boys. Sometimes he comes home very late, and sometimes he doesn't come home at all."

She insists she is not concerned about those absentee nights, nor jealous. "What I don't know doesn't hurt me, and I understand the special kind of pressure Curtis is under on the job. He needs to let off steam badly. He needs his space and time away from the family. I think most men do, and wives would be smart to give men that space. I'm sure Curtis has had some little bit on the side. But when I see that look that comes from tremendous tension in his work, I don't begrudge any little distraction or relief he can find. Also, I really enjoy the nights I have free. Sometimes I go out with my girlfriends, sometimes there's a little partying. Curtis and I both like to party, but that doesn't always mean we have to do it together. The only thing I worry about is his bringing a disease home to me. You have to be careful these days. But as long as that doesn't happen, a little casual messing around once in a while wouldn't take anything away from me. Women put too much importance on sex. Messing around doesn't have anything to do with love between two people. In fact, it might make him appreciate me even more."

And what about Curtis? How would he feel about Valerie having affairs?

"I don't think she would. I don't know how I'd react if I found she was stepping out on me. I don't think about it. I like to believe that when she goes out with the ladies she has a good time, maybe a couple of drinks and some laughs."

Curtis says he would rate their marital sex life as "terrific." "Val turns me on the same as she did when we were younger. I like the way she looks, the way she dresses and the musky perfume she wears."

Valerie, returning the compliment, says, "Curtis is a fabulous lover. Sex with him is always exciting. We're always fooling around with each other. Sometimes I could be sitting at the sewing machine and he comes into the room and looks at me in a certain way and I get crazy. Seeing him get turned on turns me on."

When the permissiveness is genuine and not a defensive pose, infidelity doesn't seem to threaten strong marriages. Many object that women like Jayne Meadows or Valerie, however "reasonable" they sound, are buying into a double standard; it's okay for the man but not the woman. The argument on this point can be very heated, but the truth is that some women are really not threatened. They don't look the other way; they face infidelity fairly and honestly.

And in other marriages, it is the man who sanctions infidelity—sometimes very directly.

Viewed from the outside, Sarah and Robert appear to have an ideal marriage. They've been married for twenty-four years and have four children ranging in age from eighteen to twenty-three who live with them in a sprawling house outside San Francisco. There are four dogs, a constant stream of guests, and an atmosphere that is informal, warm, and open. They are co-owners of an exclusive clothing boutique, but at home sweat suits and sneakers are de rigueur.

They have what Robert terms a rather unusual relationship. "There are a lot of couples who agree in principle with what we've been doing for years," he maintains. "Sarah is the most important person in my life—along with the children, of course. But in the best of times my sex drive has never been high. I worked that problem out with my shrink and with Sarah, whom I never want to lose. We decided that it would be acceptable for her to have extramarital affairs. We don't feel that interferes in any way with our relationship or our marriage."

"It isn't something I flaunt in this town," Sarah notes. "I am discreet enough to be sure that my activities remain private. I don't want people gossiping or hurting Robert in any way. In fact, it's been years since I had a sexual liaison with any man in Los Angeles. But I do a lot of traveling for business, and there are times in New York or Europe where I do have a quick affair. I have never been emotionally involved with another man. That would be impossible. I love Robert and respect our marriage too much for that to happen. To me, sex is a physical need like hunger or thirst. The older I get, the easier it is to control that need. I really believe that Americans place too much emphasis on the sexual part of marriage. That's why there are so many divorces. I would have no qualms about giving up sex completely if Robert asked me to."

Would Sarah allow Robert the same latitude? "We have discussed that, and I would feel the same way. If there was another woman today who could give him what he needs, I would be happy and grateful."

"Where is it written," Robert asks, "that two people must have the same need and desire for sex in order to have a good relationship? Who says that people can't love each other with very little sex or no sex at all?" He poses these questions calmly and with little display of defensiveness.

But can love really be as strong in a marriage with little sex?

Sarah answers without hesitation. "I don't know about other people, but I can speak strongly for myself. Only last month, when I was on a buying trip in New York, I got a call from our eldest son telling me that Robert was very sick with bacterial dysentery and had been rushed to the hospital. I canceled my appoints and left on the next plane. I remember feeling physically ill and so nervous my hands shook as I packed. I didn't know how sick he was, but I knew I couldn't go on living without him. It was a nightmare. I left the hotel, and as the doorman was putting my bags into the cab, I noticed that the traffic noises seemed muffled and that my vision seemed dim. It was like I was retreating behind a wall of cotton. That feeling stayed with me during the flight across the country, the ride to the hospital, and the walk through the corridor until I got to his room and saw that he was all right. Only then did my sight and hearing seem to return to normal. So you can see why I feel that even couples with ideal sex lives couldn't possibly feel more love for each other than we do."

Sarah and Robert worked out their solution to a sexual problem after many years of marriage. Some couples, though, are forced to face unusual difficulties from the start. Nancy and Jeff have been married for eighteen years and have two children, a fourteen-year-old girl and a ten-year-old boy. Jeff has great rapport with his children, and the family spends a lot of time together on outdoor sports, like camping and hiking. He is a good father and a seemingly perfect husband—except that he is bisexual.

Nancy knew that Jeff was bisexual when she married him.

"We were very close friends," she says. "I met him while I was dating his brother, and when that broke up, Jeff and I continued to be friends. I was shocked when he told me. I just couldn't believe it. He was so masculine and sexy. I thought there was something wrong with me . . . falling in love with a man who liked other men."

"Nancy was the first person I confided in. At that time, I was confused about sex. She was my best friend and the only person I could talk to."

Nancy did not marry Jeff with the expectation of changing his sexual habits. "I knew better than that. We went to see a doctor, and we never deluded ourselves. It was something we had to live with— or not. Actually, I was the one to push for marriage, agreeing to accept the problem and adjust to it."

It does bother her to know that there are times when her husband sleeps with a man. "But at least we're honest. Plenty of men cheat on their wives, drink, gamble—whatever. This part of Jeff's sex life has nothing to do with our love for each other and doesn't affect our family life or the time we spend together."

"Nancy and the kids are the most important people in my life. I think I appreciate my family more than most men who, so often, take their wives and children for granted. The fact that Nancy is so understanding about my occasional lapses helps make them less and less important to me. I think I'm coming to a point where I may be able to cut out that part of my life."

And what if Jeff were to discover that Nancy was sleeping with other men?

"What can I say? I'd be hurt, but you know, people in glass houses and all that."

"At the beginning," Nancy says, "I did have a few affairs, which Jeff knows about. It wasn't any good; I'm just not interested in sex without love."

Nancy says that her husband is a good lover. "He's very sensual. He knows my body and he knows how to please me."

Asked about the element of fear, the venereal diseases or dangerous encounters that often result from casual sex, he admitted that he had always been afraid and always tried to be cautious. "I couldn't bear it if I brought some disease home to Nancy, so I have periodic checkups. Also, I would never do anything as foolish as going to gay bars or cruising the streets. I've met men through business or at parties or at my health club, men like me, who appear to be straight. But they have their antennae up, so we do find each other. You can tell pretty fast if the other person is as cautious and discreet as you are. You would be surprised how many men in a major city are double-gated. There are many married men who are in the same situation I am. They are just as concerned about their families, although most of their wives are not aware of the situation."

Nancy doesn't think that she would even consider leaving Jeff. "Not anymore. If that had been going to happen, it would have happened a long time ago. I cherish the part of Jeff I have. It's much more than most of my friends with faithful husbands have." She smiles. "And I know there's not going to be another woman."

Jeff's sexual activities do cause tensions, however, including the possibility of being recognized or exposed by a gay friend in public, either deliberately or accidentally. "That is a chance you take," Jeff says. "It almost happened a few weeks ago. Nancy and I attended an awards dinner for a client of mine. There was a man at the next table with whom I'd had sex, and he'd obviously had too much to drink. Everybody in the business knows he's gay. I recognized him immediately, and he gave me a broad wink. I pretended not to notice, but I was in a cold sweat."

Nancy continues the story. "I realized what was going on, but there wasn't anything I could do. We held hands under the table and hoped the guy would disappear. But he was drunk. I saw him get up and start to approach our table, so I got up to meet him. I started talking fast and led him to the other side of the room. Even in his drunken stupor he realized who I was and what he had almost done. He apologized and went back to his table. I think I would have killed him to protect Jeff."

Similarities between these two couples—Sarah and Robert, Jeff and Nancy—are striking. Sarah and Jeff are both determined to shield their spouses from any embarrassment or hurt. Both couples compare themselves to others who have more "normal" marriages and insist that their own union has a greater degree of genuine caring and mutual respect. Is this a defense mechanism? Apparently not. They do care deeply and are committed to their marriages to an extraordinary degree. Clearly, a successful marriage is not necessarily dependent upon that overprized sexual exclusivity that most couples believe is their divine right.

Sarah's and Jeff's marriages require a reinterpretation of the word *fidelity*. In a different way, that is also true of another marriage, that of Stan and Judy, who look and act like a typical suburban couple. In their middle thirties, married for thirteen years with three children, they are both attractive in a pleasant sort of way. Stan is in the garment business and Judy is a housewife. Nothing unusual— except for their Wednesday nights.

Stan explains. "I heard about it from a friend in the garment district. It's a Wednesday orgy for couples only. No men are allowed in without a woman. People are carefully screened. No drugs, no alcohol except white wine. It sounded interesting to me, and about three years ago I told Judy about it."

"I though he was out of his mind, but I was curious. I agreed to go, providing I didn't have to participate or take my clothes off if I didn't want to."

"So off we went. The couple who gave it have a split-level house on a small secluded hill. We were told to lock all our valuables in the trunk of the car and just carry our car keys in. I noticed a lot of expensive cars—Mercedes, Rolls, Cadillacs—parked on the street and in the driveway. There was a man greeting people at the front door and discreetly taking ten dollars from each male guest. Judy was very nervous by then."

"I was when we walked in, but then I saw fully dressed couples sitting around the living room eating hors d'oeuvres and drinking wine, and I relaxed. I thought it was a mistake. These people didn't look like my idea of orgy-goers. We met some very congenial people and chatted the way you do at any cocktail party. I noticed an Olympic-sized pool outside. It turned out to be heated to ninety degrees, and there were stacks of yellow bath towels everywhere in the house and out by the pool."

"After a while people left the room and returned wearing towels. That's when Judy panicked."

"I wanted to go home, but another couple suggested we go out to see the pool, and it was pleasant. I slipped out of my clothes and put on a towel like everybody else."

"Then we were taken on a tour of the house by another couple. Most rooms had two or three beds, and there were a few couples on them. We were taken into the main room, which was completely mirrored—walls, ceiling. In the center of the room was a large round mattress. The room was candlelit and there were pillows all along the side. We sat down on some pillows and watched a couple on the mattress making love."

Judy starts to laugh. "I wanted to leave in the middle, but I didn't know if that was polite, so we sat there for a while. I was not in the least turned on."

"I was, but I could see that Judy was uneasy, so we left."

"We had sex the minute we got home. The most amazing thing about it to me was that it was the most passionate, exciting night we'd ever had. I had intense, multiple orgasms, which I never had before."

"About a month later, Judy suggested we go to the orgy again.

During that time, our sex life had vastly improved, so it was fine with me."

"I wanted to give it a second chance. I wasn't so nervous this time, and I wanted to see if I could get into it. Stan and I got undressed and went into the pool. We arrived late, and it was more crowded than the first time. I remember feeling a bit silly standing in ninety-degree water with my glasses on, stark naked with a plastic glass of white wine in my hand. But then, while Stan and I were talking to this other couple we had met before, I noticed a very good-looking man sitting on the edge of the pool. A girl was going down on him. I guess I was staring because right before he was ready to come he looked right into my eyes and I couldn't turn away. That did something to me, that look. I felt a thrill go through my body, and I had to hold on to Stan's arm, my knees were so weak."

"I saw what happened, and later that evening, I invited the guy into a bedroom with us. We had a threesome, and it was a wonderful experience. And, no, I didn't feel jealous. Sex doesn't have anything to do with love. I know how much I love my wife and how much she loves me. I was happy to be able to give her an experience that would heighten her sexual pleasure."

"So now we are regulars and try to go to as many Wednesdays as we can. But sometimes there's a PTA meeting or we have tickets to a show we don't want to miss. And sometimes Stan has to go out of town on business."

Stan and Judy say that they have met a number of people on their Wednesday evenings who have become good friends. But there are never any sexual encounters with them outside the special environment of that split-level house on the hill.

"People usually get a divorce for one of two reasons," Stan says. "Sex or money problems. We have neither. We have nothing to seriously fight about."

How far can sanctioned infidelity go without causing problems in a marriage? Pretty far, as the following interview makes evident. Sharon and Peter have a good marriage by their standards, but one that many people would find bizarre or shocking. They have been married for eight years and live in a small one-bedroom rented apartment near UCLA, where Peter is a medical student. Sharon was born and raised in Australia, and left home at seventeen to come to the United States, where she studied at UCLA. She works as a part-time waitress by day and as a hooker at night, to support Peter's education. She is an attractive, slim redhead with a classic preppy look. By night she is known as "Kelly."

She explains how this all got started. "About three years ago, I met a girl at college who had been in the business for two years and was planning to retire. We were close friends for a year before I found out about her 'other life.' I was fascinated by how easily she made so much money. She was not a streetwalker; she worked by recommendation only and had a little black book of clients who were discreet and reliable. Since she was retiring and moving back east to get married, she offered to sell me her book for a thousand dollars. I talked to Peter about it, and we decided to give it a try."

"My first reaction was negative," Peter says, "but I knew the girl also and respected her intelligence and ability. She had set certain goals for herself in terms of 'length of service' and finances, and she achieved them. My big concern was the possibility of venereal disease. But all the men in her book were respectable businessmen; many were married or were workaholics who were not technically promiscuous at all."

At first Peter was jealous of these men his wife was having sex with, but gradually he stopped feeling threatened. "So long as she was not emotionally involved with her job, I found I could handle it, and we've proved that it can be done. The money is good and tax-free, and neither one of us is emotionally affected by her work. We agreed that if I should have a change of heart, Sharon would stop immediately. But I know a lot of single men who have girlfriends who sleep with more men in a week than Sharon does, and that's just the way it it. Morality is not what it was twenty years ago, or even ten. We are not puritans or hypocrites, and we simply don't consider the sex act sacred anymore."

Do their friends know about Sharon's profession? "Not one. And we intend to keep it that way. Our friends think of us as an ordinary married couple, and that's exactly what we are."

She gets a little huffy at the suggestion that her work might interfere with her sex life with Peter. "Not at all. That's like asking a gynecologist if looking at women's private parts all day interferes with his sex life. I never have an orgasm with clients."

As for Peter, he has no interest in seeing other women. "Sharon is enough woman for me. Sex is never dull or boring." He smiles. "'Kelly' always has a trick or two if we get into a rut. It's like having several different women in one. Our real concerns have to do with certain goals in life that we're working hard to reach. I think people who put too much emphasis on their sex life are the ones whose marriages stalemate and never ripen and usually end up in divorce. It's like saying, 'If you don't love me passionately, then you don't love me at all.' That won't ever happen to Sharon and me. We know exactly who we are and where we want to go in life together. We have no secrets from each other and no pretense. We know how to share, and we're both too mature to screw up this marriage."

And then there is Magda. A big, buxom blonde with a sultry voice and an air of authority, she is Hungarian by birth. Her family migrated to California when she was six. She speaks five languages and has a slight accent. Her laugh is delightful. For fourteen years she has been married to Stan, a high school music teacher who also gives private piano lessons. He is mild-mannered and dresses conservatively.

Magda is a licensed clinical social worker, experienced in family therapy and counseling.

MARILYN: Why do you consider this marriage to be successful?

STAN: It's my wife's cooking. If you tasted her goulash or chicken paprikash you would know how she won my heart.

MAGDA: He is always kidding. There is more here than paprikash. There is a history of happiness. I am a wonderful wife, true, but that is because he deserves the best. From the day I met him, I knew he was the man for me. I went to pick my younger sister up from her piano lesson, and I arrived early. When she hit a wrong note, Stanley put his hands over his ears, looked up to heaven, and made a horrible face. I started laughing, and have been laughing ever since.

MAGDA: So you believe laughter is the key to a successful marriage?

STAN: It certainly helps. I try to find something to laugh about each day. It helps relieve stress and tension, and it's good for the soul, too.

MAGDA: I agree. Every day I come home from work with a funny story for Stanley, something outrageous. I leave behind me all the pathos that I see on my job.

MARILYN: You have an unusual job. How did you get it?

MAGDA: I was becoming bored and depressed as a social worker, fighting bureaucracy; it's such a frustrating, hopeless thing. I answered an ad which seemed to require my background and experience and found out they were looking for a sexual surrogate. At first I was so shocked. I thought it was some kind of joke. But the people running the clinic were sincere and well qualified. Stanley and I talked it over and decided it would be a good move for me, if only temporarily, to get me out of my depression. I've been working there for over a year, and I love it.

MARILYN: And your wife's unusual profession really doesn't upset you, Stan?

STAN: On the contrary. I enjoy it. Our sex life has improved, and I believe her experience has helped us. I never realized that there could be so many variations on a theme. As I tell my students, practice makes perfect, and we are certainly trying to attain perfection.

MARILYN: Magda, can you go into more detail about how the therapy works?

MAGDA: Clients who come to the clinic for the first time are carefully screened by the administration office. We have about twelve private rooms, all soundproofed for complete privacy. Most of my clients are men, but I have had some women, sometimes couples. We work on a fifty-minute hour.

MARILYN: Aren't you afraid of disease?

MAGDA: Not at all. The clients have to be checked by a registered nurse and submit a certified medical history. With the AIDS scare, condoms are being used. But I rarely have actual intercourse with my clients anyway.

MARILYN: If you don't have intercourse, what do you do?

MAGDA: The most common complaint from men is impotency. Most come to us after having tried a lot of other avenues with professionals who have not been able to help them—proctologists, shrinks, and so on. Many are facing mid-life crisis. With some it is all in the mind. One failure brings on a series of failures, and the pattern is set. It takes time and patience, but I would say seven out of ten can be helped.

MARILYN: Are most of these men married?

MAGDA: About half. The majority of men who come in want to act out fantasies. Things they are too embarrassed to ask their wives or girlfriends to do.

MARILYN: What kinds of fantasy are we talking about?

MAGDA: Bondage and whipping are very popular. They want to be caned, but not too hard. It is more symbolic than realistic. They are men who have problems with their mothers, who feel guilt about the way they've treated their mothers, or sometimes their wives, and want to be relieved of the guilt by being punished.

MARILYN: What do you do if a man wants to whip you?

MAGDA: That is not allowed. I have never had a problem. I have been tied up, which frankly I find very exciting, more than I would have thought. My favorite thing is to dress in costume. I have a wonderful wardrobe of exotic clothes. Some things I have brought home for Stan and I to experiment with.

STAN: She does have some interesting outfits with holes in the best places. It is a definite turn-on for me. You haven't lived until you have seen Magda the gypsy, wrapped in gauze that seems to cover nothing. I have thought many times of taking home movies, but the images in my mind are best.

MARILYN: Do your friends and family know about this interesting profession?

MAGDA: Some close to us do. Most don't. My family would not understand this American occupation.

STAN: Many of my friends know. They are fascinated by Magda's stories. No names, of course. I think she has helped a lot of people. And for us, our male friends who know about it consider me to be the luckiest man in the world. I can only agree.

"My first marriage lasted twenty-eight years. My wife was very proper and I didn't want to insult her, so I got whatever I wanted from prostitutes. Then, when I lost money and couldn't have the kind of prostitutes I wanted to be with, I met girls. I'm still paying palimony—voluntarily—to some of them. I'd travel to Europe with three or four girls at once. I didn't have time to take them all separately."

This is multimillionaire businessman Menshulam Riklis speaking. With his second wife, singer-actress Pia Zadora, things are different. "It's not that I don't want to have affairs," Rik, as Pia calls him, admits. "I'd love to. But I won't pursue it, because my marriage is too important. I run three miles a day to keep young for Pia. That's tough for a guy pushing sixty. I work all day and then fly around the country to be with her on her concert tours. It isn't easy. But I know she wouldn't just run off with some good-looking schlub."

Rik was very taken with Pia the first time he saw her perform. She was then seventeen. He was forty-seven, and he admits that he felt like a dirty old man. "The first time I went out with her everybody laughed and said I should bring diapers. She looked twelve."

Pia herself thought he was too old for her. "But I was fascinated by him. I was too mature for boys my age. We had dinner a couple of times. Then he flew off to Israel for a while. I missed him. He made me feel secure."

They did not, however, have a sexual relationship. "I think he found my being a virgin a challenge," Pia says. "He wanted me to live with him, but he never pushed me. I was living with my parents, and he'd have to take me there every night. If we traveled, my mother or an aunt came with us. Sex wasn't that important. It was the idea of having a trusting relationship. He knew I was the one for him when we first met. It took me about three years. By then I knew he was the man for me. It felt right, because I was so comfortable with him."

"I had a lot of tough moments in the beginning, before we were married," Rik says. "I had a detective on Pia, because what I knew about the other girls I was seeing wasn't very complimentary. I didn't believe a young girl would be devoted to me. I was really fighting my own feelings, because I didn't want to get tied down. I realized you can't understand Pia in the same way as my other girlfriends. When I first met her, she said, 'Do me a favor and don't take me shopping. I don't want anything and I don't need anything.' I bought her a double string of magnificent pearls. She thanked me, got in the car, and gave them to her mother. You cannot buy Pia."

Rik admits that it was Pia's looks that first attracted him. "She was young and beautiful—a European beauty. She's not as pretty as Bo Derek or Morgan Fairchild. But she's put together like God created perfection. I just love to look at her, to watch the way she moves. But I don't sit in the office and think how I can't wait to get home and go to bed with her. The last thing she is to me is a sex object. We have a mission, and that's to see her succeed. She's got everything going for her—she's willing to work, she's got the talent and the backing for superstardom."

I ask Pia if she worries about Rik's promiscuous past, about his taking that up again.

"No, but I think it's important to bring your claws out. If he goes out for a business dinner, I go to the same restaurant with my mother. Or, if I'm out of town, I'll send my mother. Just so that he knows I care enough to be watching. When a man knows that, I don't think you'll have a problem."

While the May/December romance of Pia and Rik causes a certain amount of talk, it is much more accepted in our society than a marriage between an older woman and a younger man. Cynthia Malmuth-Singer is forty-five; her husband, Richard Singer, is thirty-seven. They have been married for five years, lived together for two years before that, and have known one another even longer. Cynthia, who was married twice before and has two sons, runs her own public relations business, and Richard, whose first marriage this is, works in the financial investment business.

Even with a mere eight years' difference in their ages, Cynthia knows what other people think about her marriage to Richard. "They think the initial attraction was physical, that I'm a woman looking for a hot time with a young lover. I've never been attracted to younger men before. I liked older men. Before Rick, I had a relationship with a man twenty years older than myself, and I saw the handwriting on the wall. He was going to be sick, he was going to have physical problems. I must sound like an awful bitch. I'm sympathetic, I ache for people in trouble. But I've witnessed illness, been through illness, and I don't like to be around it. I could see it coming down the road."

Cynthia admits sex is part of it. "I can't say that I didn't think about the fact that I could count on having good sex for a long time with Richard. I'd be a liar. Let's say I married somebody who was sixty. In five years I would be married to a sixty-five-year-old man. I couldn't possibly think that I would have a passionate sex life in the full sense. I remember this older guy saying to me, with tears in his eyes, 'I wish I could be thirty-five for you.' Something happens to men as they get older. And when it does, it's over very quickly."

And what about a man her own age?

"The pits. The most neurotic, usually coming from the same kind of aggravation I've been through. A neurotic wife or two, kids, alimony, analysts. They're hostile, demanding, sexually malfunctioning. I wouldn't touch a guy in his forties."

But it isn't just the sex that concerns Cynthia. She doesn't think older men want to marry an equal. "I think a sixty-year-old man expects a younger woman to be very subservient and very involved with his health and his welfare. If he has money, he wants a hostess, someone who'll look terrific sitting next to him at the opera."

Someone who'll look terrific sitting next to him. All women worry about aging, whether they admit it or not. They've seen too many women discarded for a younger version by husbands who want a "looker" sitting next to them, or in bed with them, someone who will keep their juices flowing. Women who marry a younger man have in a sense put that insecurity about aging behind them at the start. The woman is older—that's a given. She was chosen in spite of or even because of the fact that she is a mature woman. For some women, that in itself removes a common anxiety from the relationship.

Richard is very clear, and as blunt as his wife, about why she is preferable to a younger woman. "I don't have a lot of patience with stupidity, ignorance. That lack of drive and ambition—just take care of me, do this for me. Younger women have a tendency to be too needy, too clinging. Cynthia doesn't try to become an appendage. I don't need another arm. I think *wife* is being reinterpreted. Cynthia has been developing her business for several years, and she doesn't have me asking, 'Why do you want to do that when you could be maintaining a home?' I think the role has expanded. You can be a wife and a person who has a successful business, work as hard as I do—harder on occasions. A wife shouldn't be lesser, nor should a husband. I expected to marry an equal."

"We have a very close marriage," Cynthia says. "But I also have a freedom I'd never had before. I've never been allowed to be who I am. He makes things positive. He gives me freedom, but at the same time I feel like I'm being physically enveloped. I like to look at him. I like to sleep next to him."

The best of two worlds?

"Yes, exactly."

Married twenty-four years, fitness king Jack LaLanne and his wife Elaine both have bodies that look far younger than their ages. Jack is in his late sixties and Elaine in her fifties.

Does being in shape affect your sexuality?

"Absolutely," says Jack. "What's more natural than sex? It's like eating or sleeping. One reason we stay in shape is to be attractive to one another. Some people get flabby and soft and lose their enthusiasm for sex."

How would you feel if Elaine got tired of exercising and keeping fit?

"It'd be her problem, but I wouldn't stop loving her. I don't expect everyone to have my control. I can't be sure that I would respond sexually in the same way, but I doubt that would change. Sex is only one part of the love we feel for one another. You've got to like a person mentally, respect that person, in order to have a good physical relationship. And I feel that it's my duty to keep myself physically attractive, as well."

Has the sexual revolution encouraged older people to experiment?

"We went to a sex movie with a hundred and one positions. We didn't learn a thing."

Do you feel that people can be sexual at any age?

"We had a neighbor who just died at a hundred and two. Three months before he died, he said, "Jack, I don't want to live. I've lost my desire for sex.""

ELBERT HATCHETT: Even after twenty-five years of marriage, sex remains an integral part of our relationship. But the important thing is that when you wake up in the morning there's also something else. Fortunately for us, there is.

LAURESTEEN HATCHETT: As one gets older, one matures in different ways. The bottom line must still be love. He's always been the only man in my life, and I hope I've never let him down.

ELBERT: We've always been open and never felt inhibited. We always did whatever we wanted to do sexually. It's not what it was twenty-five years ago. I thank God for that. Back then all I wanted to do was make love. I'd probably still be making a hundred dollars a week if we hadn't tapered off a little!

The Hatchetts have a very healthy attitude, unworried about the changes the years have brought in their sexual relationship. But many couples do worry a great deal about how to keep sexual interest in the same partner year after year, decade after decade. Let's listen to three couples who have been married for twenty-six, forty-two, and fifty-five years.

First, *Cosmopolitan* editor Helen Gurley Brown and her husband, film producer David Brown. One has to wonder if being married to the editor of sexy *Cosmopolitan* makes it more challenging to sustain sexual excitement. David says that, in their case, "It's exciting because Helen is still a walking time bomb in many respects. She's like a cat—you never know what she'll do or say. That's exciting. Of course, there's nothing more exciting than a new love affair. But there's a sweetness and security and satisfaction in loving a friend, and we've achieved that. It's probably better than the excitement of something new."

"You can't experience that magical kind of sex with one person forever," Helen says. "Maybe for three years after marriage. But if you don't feel the earth shake when your husband walks into the room, you can still have fun in bed. David knows exactly how to turn me on—and I know what he likes. There's no anxiety. And I don't turn him down unless I'm feeling so awful that he probably wouldn't ask me."

Does that mean she will have sex even when she's not in the mood?

"It's like doing anything else that you're not particularly in the mood for at the moment. Maybe you won't have an orgasm, but you'll probably get into it enough so that you won't suffer. I also try to accommodate things David likes more than I do. If you enjoy most of what's going on, a few moments that don't thrill you aren't going to kill you."

"Helen still makes me feel very horny. I like to look at her. I admire her. When I have sexual fantasies, Helen is the protagonist. That's very unusual. I was first attracted by her sensuality and sexuality. It was lust. Then to find out that she was also a good woman and a smart woman—that was a bonus aphrodisiac."

And what in the world does Helen do to keep herself at the center of her husband's fantasies after all this time?

"I treat David like a sex object. I remember how I acted when we first became lovers. Boredom is marriage's worst enemy. I try to keep growing. And I exercise every morning and keep myself as attractive as I can for David."

"Helen has the capacity to turn me on, but that comes at considerable cost to her—the exercise, living on twelve hundred calories a day because I like lean women. She pays great attention to all the womanly things. She does work hard at staying attractive."

"It gets harder for a woman than a man to stay attractive after a certain age."

"But you don't have to be young and beautiful to be sexual—you just have to be alive. But women do have added pressures. If people stop being sexual, though, they lose vital energy in other areas."

"Sex," says Helen, "is like any other activity in that you get rusty if you don't practice it."

Helen's book, *Having It All*, very graphically describes techniques for satisfying a man through oral sex to the point of orgasm. That has to mean that people imagine the Browns' sex life in pretty detailed fashion. But David says it doesn't embarrass him. "Of course we do it, and lots of other people do it. It may seem funny to some people, because I'm not that young and it's like imagining your parents making love."

"I never thought about whether or not it embarrassed David," Helen says. "He read the book as it developed and never expressed any concern. I wouldn't have done the book any differently. It was the culmination of my experiences, and David isn't the only man I've experienced fellatio with."

Asked if they had ever considered swinging, David says, "We couldn't have an open marriage or be swingers. We've got enough to handle by ourselves."

"I've only had experience with one man at a time. The rest always seemed kinky and unnecessary to me, but for those who enjoy it, why not!"

The Browns seems very contented with their lives. "We have a full social life and lots of activities we enjoy," David says. "Helen never wanted children. The only thing we're missing is long weekends. Someday we'll probably give up some of our activities and have more leisure time."

"There is one activity we don't ever intend to give up. Mouseburgers like me are sexy until the end of our lives. I don't intend ever to stop making love."

Edith and George Denny never want to stop making love either. Married for forty-two years, they have two married children and three grandchildren. Both were born and raised in Pittsburgh, but have been living in California for more than twenty years. George is a semiretired insurance salesman with a modest but adequate income; Edith is, and always has been, a housewife. They continue to have an active sex life.

"You know," says Edith, "people who are young believe that older folks lose their sex drive after middle age. That isn't true at all. In fact, in my case I think it's just the opposite. After menopause, I felt sexier than ever. Maybe it was because I wasn't worried about becoming pregnant, maybe because I was so relaxed, probably because George got sexier the older he got. Whatever the reason, it happened. When I hit forty, I thought it was all over, that the sensual sexy feeling would be gone by fifty. At fifty, I was sure it would be gone by the time I hit sixty. Now that I'm over sixty-five, I know it will never be over—till the day I die, I'll be interested in sex."

George agrees. "It's like that song, 'Will you still meet me, will you still greet me, when I'm sixty-four.' It's a Beatles song and I sing it—badly—for Edith all the time. My sex drive might not be as strong as it was when I was twenty-one, but with my experience, I know how to make up for it. We've got a lot of imagination, and we feel freer than ever to experiment with sex."

"George has a collection of porno books that are incredible. It used to embarrass me to even look through them alone, but it doesn't anymore. I think it's exciting, especially when we both read them together."

"We also have a small club of older married couples who live in the building. We meet one night a week in a neighbor's apartment and watch porno movies on a VCR."

"At first, it was awkward sitting in somebody's living room watching these movies with our friends. You should have heard the comments from some of the women. They ranged from 'Oh, that's disgusting' to 'Can you back the tape up? I want to see how they do that again.' We found that after a night of watching, George and I would come home and have terrific sex. We pretended someone was filming us. Now the club is thinking of having movie night twice a week instead of once, since none of us like to go out after dark. A lot of other people in the building think we get together to play cards. They should only know!"

"I think the women in our group who have active sex lives look better than most women do at our age. We seem to have more vitality."

"We heard that having sex uses up about a hundred calories each time. I tell my children that it accounts for the fact that I've kept my figure and still enjoy eating whatever I please."

"I think *eating* whatever we please helps our sex life . . . if you know what I mean."

"George, please! Sometimes he does get carried away."

Violet and Herman Weiss have been married for fifty-five years. Both grew up in New York City, but they have lived in California for thirty years. They have five children, seven grandchildren, and three great-grandchildren. They own a house in Encino, California, and have a houseman who doubles as chauffeur and a full-time house-keeper and a nurse for Herman, who is the victim of three strokes. Violet is eighty-one, a tall, handsome woman with beautiful snow-white hair. Herman, two years older, is almost completely paralyzed and confined to a wheelchair. Although he speaks with difficulty, his wife seems to understand every word he tries to say and can finish sentences for him while he nods his head in agreement.

Violet clearly adores her husband. "I knew when we met that Herman was the only man in the world for me. Through the years I have met many people whom I found to be attractive, but so are paintings, books, music, children. People think that when you get older you stop wanting sex or even thinking about it. That's not true; it just becomes a little less important. But it's still there. Up until three years ago, when Herman had his first stroke, we had a fairly active sex life."

Herman says something and Violet laughs and squeezes his hand. "Herman still enjoys *Playboy* magazine, and I read it aloud to him. He likes Harold Robbins although we both think his earlier books were better. And Jackie Collins can write a pretty juicy novel."

Violet pauses and smiles, looking at Herman. "We can enjoy sex in our minds now. It still has a place in our lives."

I don't think I had that much to do with
Jackson's coming of age. He did it himself. All
I did was listen, really *listen* to what he said
about everything he felt.
—*Karen North*

We have a very deep relationship where we're
bonded. But we also have a very superficial
relationship where we're easily hurt or angry
—we're that stupid, too.
—*Joseph Bologna*

Communication: Laughing, fighting, learning

Dictionaries define communication as "an act of transmitting"; "an exchange of information"; and "a process by which meanings are exchanged between individuals by a common system of symbols." It is all these things and more, but in a marriage it is best viewed as the way in which couples reach—or attempt to reach—mutual understanding. That means not only understanding the partner better, but also, when things are working right, gaining new insights into oneself. It is, ultimately, a learning process in which both partners must collaborate.

Some couples communicate principally through reason and analysis, but fighting is also a way of communicating, one that some couples even in good marriages find necessary even though it carries

175

obvious dangers. Humor is always a help, but some people don't know how to be funny and others don't always get the joke. And there are even those who communicate almost by osmosis, who have to say little or nothing to be understood by their partners.

Communication in a marriage is very personal, and while you will meet couples here who discuss it in quite analytical terms, the subtle mysteries of the process are best conveyed by example. We begin with a couple who have a particular interest in communication in general and have learned to understand one another in a deeply felt way. Psychiatrist Theodore Isaac Rubin, author of nineteen books including the best-selling *David and Lisa*, which also became an important movie, and his wife Ellie have been married for forty years. She is sixty, he sixty-two.

"We have a long history of sharing a lot together," says Ellie. "A lot of hardships, a lot of fun, a lot of youth. We got married very young. We were both in college together, and we fell in love and married."

"When I first saw Ellie, I knew she was for me. It felt so natural, so right. We were good friends first. I liked her as a woman. My father liked women; he had women as friends. He saw those friendships as individual relationships apart from any sexual connection. There are a great many men who do not like women, who do not have the capacity to accept women as friends. That was very true when I met Ellie, and for many men it hasn't changed a bit. When I look at television or go to the movies today, the intercourse between men and women is smart talk. Smartass talk. That's supposed to be communication between men and women."

"We have gone out with couples," Ellie adds, "that do this all the time. It is so boring. They have this adolescent banter they keep up. It is really a way of putting each other down. We don't continue those friendships. We spend a lot of time together instead. It's not that we are constantly stimulating to each other, but I feel angry with myself if I have spent an evening out with people who leave me with a sense of unrest and dissatisfaction. Aside from the adolescent banter, another problem is people who bait you. That is their amusement. What for? I feel as though I've wasted an evening. I would rather be at home, accomplish something I have on my mind to do here, or read. We are comfortable together. Many couples are not, and have to get out with others."

Ellie agrees in principle, but she adds, "I do like to get out by myself more than Ted. The main problem for me is that Ted wants to know where I am all the time. I don't like that feeling. I don't want anyone to know where I am all the time," she says, looking mischievous.

Although she is amused, Ellie admits this is an area of considerable disagreement. "It is annoying. I get angry. He tries not to. And he has gotten better."

"I think safety is a big factor," Ted says. "I get worried easily."

"I could go marketing, and be gone for several hours. I get distracted, attend to other needs."

"I get nervous. This is a rough city, and she is very valuable to me!"

"This is the Russian crisis drama. It goes back to his childhood."

But there is more to it. This was an area in which a communication gap existed. "I used to get more angry," Ellie says, "because I didn't understand where it was coming from. I thought it was just about controlling me. I didn't realize his fear, and that he was just trying to control his environment. So now I will say I am going out for the day without being specific. But he knows I'll be gone all day. I began to understand Ted's feelings more when the kids learned to drive. You are so worried. When they started going on trips, I said call me when you get there. They refused. They said it was embarrassing and uncomfortable."

"If she says she will be back in four hours and is, it is okay," says Ted. "If she says she will be back in an hour and comes back in four, I have a difficult time. No, it is not jealousy, it's possessiveness. Possessiveness from a point of view of dependency. It is very important for me that she is somewhere around. I am more dependent than she is."

"Over the years I have gotten some of his fears. If he is gone a long time without an explanation, I begin to worry. I wasn't like that years ago. I have learned."

Ted disagrees. "She is not a worrier. She may have some Russian Jewish blood, but she is half Rumanian, and that is a big difference. They don't worry the same way, or as much."

There is another area in which Ellie and Ted are different. "I'm more of an expansive person, and she is more reserved. I'll give you a typical example. She's reading a book and I am reading something for my work. I say, 'Let me read this to you.' She will put her book down and listen. But by the third or fourth time, she will say, 'Look, I want to read my book.' I want to share with her as I go along. This is the difference in our personalities. It does present problems. She gets involved in what she is doing, and I'm disturbing her. But I trust her objectivity more than anyone else's, so that when I am working I really need her."

"I would never dream of disturbing him when he was reading. Unless it was an emergency."

"So I would say I want her to be less reserved. We would share more that way, but at the same time I have enormous respect for her reserve. To me, in any successful relationship, the single most important factor is the growth of one's feelings as a result of being together. Greater intensity—more in touch with all feelings. So you become more alive as a result of the relationship. Failure is when two people become alienated from their feelings and function in more perfunctory ways. Going through the motions, without feeling. In a successful marriage, each person has the effect of increasing the spontaneity of the other. In an unsuccessful one, there is resignation and paralysis. Some people achieve that and think they're surviving, but they're half dead. Real peace is peace while you're feeling it all. It is possible."

Communication between the Rubins is reflective and somewhat analytical. The first quality might be expected from a couple who have been married thirty-eight years; the second is perhaps inevitable because of Ted's profession. But communication in a good marriage can also be quite confrontational. In fact, the relationship may run into trouble when one partner ceases to play the "let's-get-it-all-out" game as it had originally been established.

Arthur Forest is a television director with up-and-down periods of success, as is common in that business. His wife of nine years, Marcy, was a model when they met and has subsequently worked in various areas of communications, and the media. It is the third marriage for Arthur, who is in his mid-fifties, and the first for Marcy, who is twenty years younger. They have two children.

It is a marriage that is very verbal—a lot of talking goes on. It was that way from their first date, when they were brought together by a mutual friend.

"I had been through several relationships that had not worked," Marcy says, "and I was not anxious to meet someone in show business, one of those people who go on about Dustin this and Redgrave that. I just wanted to go out with a real man. Our friend said, 'Trust me,' so I did. But I practically gave the man the third degree trying to find out who exactly Arthur was. I didn't want one of those executives on the rise. I definitely wanted an older man, one who had been married, and I preferred Jewish men. They seemed to take women more seriously. Arthur was all three, and he was a regular guy. We had instant rapport and talked all evening long. And there wasn't a single sexual innuendo."

"We were of two different worlds," says Arthur. "The Jewish boy from the Bronx and a Catholic Southern Baptist from New England. She invited me up for a drink, which surprised me, and we talked all night. I kissed her and left, and we agreed to see each other again. I went home and canceled the other dates I had."

Marcy and Arthur are able to be unusually direct with one another about their relationship. "If Marcy wants to do something and I don't, I will do it if she wants it more than I don't. She does the same thing for me. Because we have *decided* to do it this way, there is no resentment. We have made a deal. We have laid it out front. Our friends don't know how to take us, because we express things so freely."

And how do they express anger?

"With anger," says Arthur.

"In front of company or alone," Marcy adds. "I will say, 'Arthur, you shouldn't have done that.' He will say, 'Why?' We go through it and it is over. It is never 'And not only that, but last week you did this and that.' Nothing comes spilling out."

"We don't make digs at each other. If we are annoying each other, we get it out immediately. We may have to excuse ourselves when there are other people around, but we deal with it then and there. Then it is over."

"We were at a party and I said something, and Arthur said, 'Marcy, you are absolutely wrong.' And I said, 'I can't be right or wrong when giving my opinion.' Several of the couples we were with said it really helped them deal with their own problems from that time on."

Taking criticism is hard, but Marcy and Arthur share an attitude that gives them the security to take it. "Living things make mistakes," Arthur says. "And we can learn from our mistakes. Not to be able to accept that is to pretend to be godlike. We both understand that an incident is not going to shake the foundation of my life. I trust my wife to realize I can be wrong, that I'm not some kind of schmuck, I just made a mistake, that's all. Let's admit it and go on to the next thing."

It is significant that the only time the marriage became troubled, it involved a breakdown in this freedom of expression.

"When Arthur turned fifty, he gave up smoking, gained weight, and the flow of jobs wasn't very steady for a while. He was sulking and moody and a real bear to live with. I couldn't communicate with him. I felt I could handle anything as long as we could talk about it, but this guy wasn't talking. The silence was very ugly for me. I thought maybe things were too far gone to save. No sex life, no touching, no talking. He wasn't working, but he went to an office all day and read a novel rather than us doing things together. We could have had fun during that period. I went to a psychiatrist, thinking I would probably be getting a divorce. He said we would have to be treated together."

"We started talking again before the work situation corrected itself," says Arthur. "Actually, I had no reason to worry; my retainer from one show paid all our expenses. But I needed the pressure of work. Now, having gone through all that, if I am not working I love to be home with my family. And I like to give Marcy a couple of days off so she can have her own free time."

"He does so much around here now. When we first married, it was 'The kitty litter needs changing. . . . Yes, Arthur, the bag is under the sink.' He now realizes I can't go to work or go to school and do it all and still be a good companion to him. We also found out we can work together. I worked on the Jerry Lewis telethon that Arthur always directs. And, contrary to what our friends said would happen, it only brought us closer together. It was exciting for me to see the effort Arthur put into achieving the results he did."

So the marriage is in good shape and the talking goes on. But what about the future?

"One of the things we are doing is getting married again next year," says Arthur.

"Do you know why?" Marcy asks with a grin. "It's going to be ten years. Each of his other marriages lasted ten years, and I don't want him walking around thinking there is something he has to do with someone else."

Therapy is usually something that a couple turns to after years of marriage, because they are in trouble, because communication has broken down in some way. They require help to reestablish mutual understanding. But there are couples who seek out counseling of one sort or another for quite different reasons. Sociology professors Jane and Warren Hamilton say that they might not have married at all if they had not had premarital counseling.

"When we met," Jane says, "we'd each been through very rough, emotionally draining relationships. I was terrified of getting involved again. But Warren's tenderness and sincerity won me over bit by bit. It wasn't love at first sight, by any means—at least not so far as I was concerned. But we both cared about people and had the same ideals."

"We were both somewhat wary of commitment. Mutual friends suggested a counselor, and we gave it a try. At first we expected to go three or four times, but it stretched into seven or eight months. It was an enriching, almost adventurous experience, so that by the time we tied the knot, I didn't think there'd be any surprises."

"The only surprise," Jane adds with delight, "is that our relationship kept getting better!"

"We knew about our problems with other relationships and all the strengths and weaknesses we would each bring to the marriage. Jane knew I tended to need order in a disorderly world. I knew she needed to be fulfilled both careerwise and emotionally. We covered everything."

Jane nods. "All our insecurities were out in the open. We knew more about each other than any married couple we were acquainted with at that time. We went over children, relatives, financial goals. We discussed old lovers and what commitment meant to us."

Warren says that the counseling was important to them not so much in improving the eventual marriage but in getting them to the point of marriage. "We were always right for each other. But even so, we might not have married at all. Had we not sought counseling, we might have continued dating forever, until one of us got a job offer elsewhere, and then who knows if we would have stayed together. I think the success of the counseling was that it gave us the security to marry. It was as if we could stand back and look into the marriage that would be."

"And, for the most part," Jane adds, "we liked what we saw. We had a good relationship before. We just wanted to make it even better. We really gained an understanding of where we came from. His upbringing was much more formal, less demonstrative than mine. Not only did counseling help me better understand him, but it helped move him away from the rigidity of his background. We worked on that before—and after—the marriage."

After twenty-eight years of living together not only as husband and wife but often as working colleagues, the Hamiltons are closer than ever. "We're together," Jane says, "because we're separate individuals who mix well together. Many people wonder how we can stand to be together so much, working closely on the same projects at times. I suppose it is quite something to like a person well enough to want to be with him all the time."

"No two people can march to the exact steps every moment, of course," Warren says. "It's like when you're going to have sex. The desire will most likely strike one of us first, but then the desire communicates itself to the other one. Just feeling loved makes you feel loving. We find ways to like the same things—for different reasons. I may be approaching it one way and Jane another, but we're still doing it together."

Not surprisingly, the Hamiltons feel that people with troubled marriages are often afraid of closeness. "I think people put barriers between themselves because they really can't tolerate the closeness. They put other people between them. They put sexual distance between them. They put money problems between them. There are all kinds of conflicts that could be resolved between any two reasonable people. But they're so useful if you have a problem with being close."

Jane adds, "I also think there are a great many marriages in which people act out being parent and child. Very often they alternate between the husband being the child and the husband being the father. And when you are living with a parent, you have difficulty having sex. And then the husband or wife has to go out and play with friends and come home to father or mother. That's all game-playing. It's not about a deep love relationship."

They also feel it is important to get all their feelings expressed when they argue. "I'm very good at that," Jane says. "If I don't do it, it stays inside me. The bigger power is in having self-knowledge. Know as much about yourself and your feelings as possible. I've always felt successful, but I don't know if I could have done as much without Warren or if Warren could have done it without me. The whole is greater than the sum of the parts. Somebody once asked me what was the most surprising thing that had happened in my marriage, and I said that it was the fact that I was loved every day. I didn't expect to be loved every day. I think that's what I feel about our marriage—that sometime during every day I stop and marvel that I feel loved and feel loving."

Warren agrees entirely. "It always astonishes me to be loved so deeply, so unconditionally. I've never been so completely and deeply loved as now. We've both continued to grow and evolve as people since our marriage, and I really feel like I'm a better person."

ROGER CALLOWAY: People say you should find a mate with the same likes. I say it's more important to find a mate with the same dislikes. Jenny and I knew we were made for each other when a business friend called and asked if I'd like to "kill an hour" over coffee. Jenny and I rolled our eyes at each other. I'd have been less upset if the guy had said, "Roger, let's go to the Amazon to get our heads shrunk," and Jenny had exactly the same reaction. We don't have an hour to "kill."

Mention the names John and Bo Derek and the first word that is likely to pop into most people's minds is *sex*. But that is not at all what their marriage is about. You can't blame the public for thinking so, of course. There's the image of Bo Derek in *10* and the fact that John was previously married to two other very beautiful women, Ursula Andress and Linda Evans. Even before that there was a first wife, a ballerina by whom he had two children—one, a daughter, wrote a

Mommie Dearest kind of book, and the other, a son whom John describes as wild, is a paraplegic from a motorcycle accident.

But the headline story is at best misleading. I talked to John and Bo separately, at their request, but on many subjects they said nearly identical things, and I will be quoting them back and forth here. First, they both say the image of John as some kind of Svengali who seduces beautiful women, uses them, and discards them is nonsense.

"From the time I first met John," Bo says, "he encouraged me to be independent and strong. This was before I was well known at all." They met when Bo was seventeen and had a part in a film John directed. "At that time I had no experience, no drive, no ambition. I didn't even know who he was. I was very quiet and very shy, but there was something about John's strength that drew me to him. He treated me as an adult, and no one had really done that before."

During preproduction, Bo became friendly with both John and Linda, but particularly Linda. "She was very supportive. John was tough with me, telling me that I was lazy."

During the shooting of the film, Linda Evans was called away to do a television show, and it was during this period that, as Bo puts it, "Something just happened. It wasn't sexual. We just started spending more and more time together and became very close. Linda eventually became aware of this and left."

"I don't know what happened," John says. "I loved Linda, I was happy with Linda. I just expressed that I wanted to get to know Bo better, and Linda sensed something more and left me."

John and Bo went to Europe, but it was not a happy time. "He and I were very guilty. He really loved Linda, and he didn't really know what he was doing with me. It was a very strange beginning. We didn't get married for a couple of years, and I think we got married just to make everything more understandable. We didn't plan anything, including a career for me."

Even then, the relationship was still muddled. "I was brought up on 'the beach,'" Bo says. "Just go and have a good time. And John was the opposite—very structured. There was something about me that he loved, but on the other hand I frustrated him, and we had a lot of personality problems after we were married. It wasn't sex that got our relationship going. It was really the work. He started making a film, and almost by accident I started helping him make it. And I really began to enjoy it. I sort of woke up. Until then sailing had been my big turn-on, and that attitude drove him nuts. But I began to find responsibility exciting and ended up producing the film. I started to feel the sense of accomplishment. I was needed. I got a lot of very difficult things done. That was an enormous turnaround for us."

Bo feels that her marriage really began when she became more of a person—a responsible person. "There was something keeping us together, but we hadn't really been happy. Our values and needs were too different."

As she became more involved in his work, did she fear displeasing him and do it his way? "On the contrary. He encouraged me to be creative. He was thrilled I enjoyed it and wanted me to keep developing on my own. If I'd wanted a father figure, I wouldn't have picked John—he wanted me to be very independent."

"It delights me to see her mature, become independent," says John. "It gives me a great deal of pride. And it's a lot more fun to look into someone's eyes and see interest and excitement there."

Bo agreed to do *10* largely for the money; she says they had no idea it would be such a big hit. And after that she decided she did want to continue her career. "I felt it was an opportunity that I couldn't pass up, and John realized that, too. But we knew it would be a big interference, because we were really *companions*, the type of couple who go off and study lions or bugs in Africa together. That's us. We live together, work together, love together, play together, and that is very rare."

John says almost the same thing. "We are everything to each other—pals, best friends, lovers. If anything happens, good or bad, she is the first one, usually the only one, I want to go to and tell about it."

"This marriage," says Bo, "has given me the sense of satisfaction that comes from work, from creating, from taking responsibility. It's fantastic for me. I am a different person, and I feel that I am very lucky."

And John? "I am having a love affair with my wife, and neither of us is cheating. That is probably a first in L.A."

I went to this interview with a good deal of skepticism—all those headlines. But they make you believe them. Still, it's impossible to resist pushing things a bit.

"With all these beautiful women in your past," I ask John, "how would you deal with a woman who is aging?"

John, who is sixty, replies, "I will be dead by the time Bo really starts to age. So I have it all worked out."

Violet Weiss says it well: "Herman always believed that putting yourself in the other person's place is important. We always did that with each other and with the children, too. 'If I were you, how would I think, how would I respond . . .' It was an exercise we practiced that became a habit whenever we had a disagreement. It helps to understand another point of view. Being judgmental is unfair to yourself and other people. We've seen too many changes in our lifetime not to realize that there is no 'right way.' The secret is to open yourself up to the other person. If you do that freely and honestly, you will come to know each other so well that it will seem you are one— the male and female part of one. That is one of the reasons Herman and I can communicate so well without words. It doesn't matter that since his strokes he can't speak clearly anymore. It's as if I can read his mind—telepathy, I think they call it."

Casey Kasem, disc jockey and longtime host of the widely syndicated radio show "American Top 40," met his wife Jean on December 21, 1979, and they were married a year later to the day. Jean's career goal had always been news broadcasting, but at her husband's urging she shifted her focus to acting. The change paid off in 1983 when she was cast as the dim-witted, perpetually optimistic Loretta Tortelli on NBC's hit show *Cheers*. The characters of Loretta and husband Nick were subsequently spun off for the series *The Tortellis*.

Like the mismatched Tortellis, Jean and Casey seem in some ways *not* to be made for each other. She is thirty-two and 5 feet 10 ½ inches, while he is fifty-five and 5 feet 6 inches. "Casey and I seem to be somewhat of a sight gag," Jean admits, "but it doesn't bother me for a bit."

At the time they met, Casey was delivering Christmas presents at the office of his ex-agent. "I saw her in the outer room and was very struck by her. Inside I asked if she was an actress and was told no, she was an 'office boy' who delivered tapes for them and had worked there for a while. I went back out a few minutes later and engaged her in conversation. She was so beautiful and fresh and different. After talking maybe five or ten minutes with her, I went home and told my mother and brother, who were in from Michigan for Christmas, how excited I was and that I thought I'd fallen in love."

"It was a very strong connection," Jean agrees. "It was very polite—'Hello, how are you,'—but there was a tension. I felt we were old souls right away."

Casey had been invited to the agent's Christmas party but had decided not to go. "I remember looking through the trash to find the invitation, because I thought Jean was likely to be there." She was. They talked for a long time and were the last to leave. She went home alone, but agreed to a date the night after Christmas, going out not only with Casey but with his mother and brother.

"That went very well," Casey remembers, "and we saw one another every night after that."

It was some time, however, before it became a sexual relationship. "The key for us," Jean says, "is that we became best friends long before we were lovers. I'm so glad that it happened that way. That's much better than trying to become friends after you are lovers."

"Every step we took," Casey agrees, "seemed to be the right step at the right time."

Both Jean and Casey had been married before. Jean's marriage had been a "young mistake." Casey's had lasted seven years and had produced three children of whom he had joint custody, although they lived with their mother. "I have gotten along very well with Casey's children," says Jean. "It helped that they were so young and it was easier to form a loving relationship." But she adds, "Casey had to set me straight about that. I was trying too hard, giving too many presents. I was not their mother and never will be; their own mother is very much alive and involved with them. It was a turning point. Casey's brutal honesty can be very difficult. But it made my relationship with the children much better."

Because they are both strong, highly verbal people, fights do happen. "A marriage is really only a marriage if there is conflict," Jean says. "Otherwise, it would be dull and boring—'Dick and Jane had a wonderful life.'"

"When we have a fight," says Casey, "we realize that talking it through after we've calmed down is sometimes the best way to get rid of it. But because we love one another so much there are other times we don't really have to take that step. We can just forget it."

One area in which there is no conflict is the development of Jean's career. Casey is not only unthreatened by Jean's great success, he is totally unsurprised. "I saw it right from the start. The quality of her comedic timing is so rare that I knew she would make it as an actress. I always felt that her success would be my success. Anything she could do would reflect on my good judgment all the way around, as a husband, as someone who believed in her talent. I recognized that people who have talent thrive on success, and that with success would come much joy that would feed back into the marriage."

The cancellation of *The Tortellis* he sees as only a temporary setback. "I encourage Jean to think positively about the possibility of another series coming along that will be even bigger for her."

"Show business is full of ups and downs," Jean notes. "We help each other with that. We both feel that what makes success worthwhile is the struggle through the difficult periods."

Jean and Casey's lives are far from being focused solely on show business, however. Both are deeply involved in organizations dedicated to world peace and understanding and Third World development, from Jesse Jackson's Rainbow Coalition to the Arab Anti-Defamation League. Says Casey, "Show business can have a false bottom to it. There's nothing wrong with succeeding or making money. But you need more, you need more depth in your life, spiritually and otherwise. I think the way to achieve that is to do something for others that can be significant."

"We are very political and very involved with social causes. We have been brought together by deeper things than even the depth of our relationship."

Both feel that their shared feelings in these areas greatly enrich their marriage. But Casey notes, "It creates pressures, too. It takes time, it takes money. To put real effort into helping others, a couple has to be very much in tune to begin with. It takes two people who, most of the time, can truly understand one another even when the directions they're moving in may not be completely parallel."

Spencer and Diane Christian met during summer vacation while attending college.

What attracted you to Diane?

SPENCER: Unlike most men I know, I've always been attracted to intelligent women. I've always liked strong, independent women who could think for themselves. I can't stand wimpy women who need a man to do their thinking for them. Diane is a thinking person and a strong person. I also find her physically attractive, which is important. But to make a relationship last means finding someone you can share experiences with, someone you can talk to and exchange ideas with. Communication was one of the first building blocks of our relationship.

DIANE: When we first started dating we would talk for hours, and we really felt our relationship was based on all the talking we did.

SPENCER: She was the first woman I'd met whom I could talk to so openly and freely right from the moment we met. We really enjoyed getting into each other's philosophies on life, values, ideals. Even in the most stressful periods we've been able to communicate openly. That's so important in getting beyond problems and solving them.

Did you tell each other everything about your past?

DIANE: He knows everything I did before we got married. It's not that he necessarily asked; I just wanted to tell him. I didn't want to go into a marriage with anything untold.

Is Diane's candor a part of the attraction?

SPENCER: I get a kick out of it now, but when we first met I was a little taken aback. Sometimes she was so honest—not just with me but with other people—that she seemed abrupt and abrasive, which she's not. She's a very sensitive and considerate person, but if you want to know where you stand with her she'll let you know right up front. There were times in the early years of our relationship when I wanted to say and do just the right thing. I didn't want to offend anyone, and I was probably too cautious about that. As a result, I allowed too many people to get close to me. Diane has always been very good at spotting people who just wanted to say they know a celebrity, and she's taught me a lot about human nature.

Do either of you ever hold things back?

DIANE: For a while I went to see an analyst, because I had

anxiety and I didn't know why. After the third session it came out that the real problem was that Spencer wanted a third child and I didn't. Spencer didn't know that. I thought it was just not the right thing to say in a marriage. But once he found out I really didn't want another child, that was the end of it. I saw the analyst for a while, and Spencer would ask me what we talked about at a session. Sometimes I said I didn't want to discuss it and he'd get very annoyed. He was annoyed because we had told each other so many things over the years that he felt I was holding something back. But that wasn't it. I told him, "I didn't say I never want to discuss it, but I'd like to digest it before it comes out of my mouth."

Can you say things to one another that hurt?

SPENCER: Yes, you have to. When Diane had our first child, she stopped working. It wasn't my suggestion, but I agreed it was a good idea. Then, during that time she gained a lot of weight and became physically unattractive. She didn't like herself and her self-esteem started to diminish. At the same time that all these negative things were happening for her, I was getting all kinds of attention and great job offers. I had everything going for me and she had nothing going for her, and she felt even worse for herself. And then I started to feel bad not just because my wife had gotten fat but because her loss of self-esteem made her less stimulating to be with. I admit that there was an element of people saying, "What's he doing with her?" But what was more important to me was that this was my wife whom I loved dearly, who was not taking care of herself and losing the spark that she'd had. I decided I had to be honest with her and tell her exactly what I was feeling. I had to be critical of the things that were turning me off, but I also had to let her know I still loved her and wanted her to recapture the old Diane. There were many, many conversations where we both poured our deepest feelings out, even if those feelings hurt. We worked through the problem, and she lost weight and, more important, regained her confidence. It was a very tough time, but we both feel it strengthened the relationship.

I originally interviewed Bella and Martin Abzug shortly before Martin's death in 1986 of a heart attack. Recently Bella made some additional comments about what the loss of her husband had meant for her.

But let's go back to when I first talked to the two of them. Martin was a very accomplished man, a stockbroker who had also published several novels. But it was Bella who was the star of the family, and that's just what Martin wanted.

I asked them how they had met.

"We met at a concert," Bella said.

"I thought it was at a marriage broker's," Martin said.

"We met at a Yehudi Menuin concert in Florida," said Bella, pinning things down.

"It was a pickup in the back of a bus in Miami. I was going into the army. I was twenty-five and she was eight years younger."

"I was twenty-one. What are you talking about?"

"I thought she was terrific."

"Why shouldn't he have? I had a fine figure and I was well dressed and I was very tan."

Bella agreed to marry Martin two years later—after they had fully discussed their goals in life. "I made it clear I was going to continue law school whether I married or not," Bella said. "We argued out our differences in the two years before we married— which may have a lot to do with why our marriage has lasted thrity-nine years."

"I typed her papers for her."

"He always was a liberated man. But he was very insistent from the beginning that we marry. I was more recessive."

"It's the only time in your life that you were recessive."

"I was in an accelerated law program—very busy."

"She was on scholarship, but when we married, I had to pay the tuition."

"I wasn't in need anymore!"

"Also, she tried to practice law under her own name, but it wasn't permitted."

"The bar wouldn't admit me under my maiden name. I said, 'I'm losing half my identity,' and they said they didn't care."

And so Bella became famous as Bella Abzug. In 1970, after years of helping other candidates get elected to office—all men, Bella notes, many of whom turned out to be something of a disappointment—she ran for Congress herself and was elected.

"I lived in Washington, but I came home on weekends—to be with Martin and our daughters, and to be with constituents."

Martin was already used to taking a lot of responsibility in raising their children. "I had better hours," he says.

"It was difficult, but I tried to make it my business to attend events at school and other social occasions. I was very involved in the parents' association when the children were young. And we spent weekends and holidays with them intensively."

Martin wasn't fazed by the rubber-chicken political dinner circuit, either. "I slept through some good ones. That was my escape."

"I think he did very well, considering they are often boring. He's a jovial, friendly person. But it was optional. Women in politics don't drag their husbands around. The husbands do drag their wives around. I feel sorry for them. When Martin didn't want to come, he didn't."

"People realize that we're both independent types. She has her thing and I have mine. I get a big bang out of watching Bella on TV or making speeches."

"He's fantastic, my biggest supporter. When I practiced law he said I was the greatest living lawyer. When I was in Congress he said I was the greatest living member of Congress. And when I lost elections, he said I was the greatest living statesperson. So I try to be very appreciative and give him lots of love and affection."

Does that include a good sex life, I wanted to know.

"He's already answered that publicly. He was on *Good Morning America* and David Hartman asked why our marriage lasted so long. Martin always has these one-liners that come from nowhere. You never know what he's going to say. So he looked at David Hartman and said, 'Sex.' There's nothing to add to that. It's a compatible relationship on all levels. On another TV program he was asked if it was hard living with a woman who's always running, thinking, going, doing. He said, 'No, there's been excitement every minute. I wouldn't trade her—even for Joe Namath!'"

"Well, Bella's got it all. She's a leader, a great lawyer. But she's also kind, soft, sympathetic. She's there in any emergency."

"Martin's got maturity and strength. One of the problems in society today is that something goes wrong with the maturation of people. Martin's also very capable, very independent. He's not threatened or jealous. He scoffs at these things. He appreciates another person's value."

Just how much Bella valued Martin is clear from her words about him several months after his death, when she herself had lost her 1986 bid for election to Congress from Westchester, New York. "Martin was always there when I came home from the political wars, to talk to, to embrace, and to listen to me rail if I was upset. After losing this last election I really despaired of putting my life together again. Not because of losing the election, but because of Martin not being there. I feel uncomfortable in my own skin now, because with Martin gone part of me is missing."

Karen and Jackson North, who talked earlier about the loss of their thirteen-year-old son, have been married twenty-eight years and are in their late forties. They have two surviving children in their early twenties. Jackson is half Cherokee Indian, born and raised in Oklahoma. He attended Brown University, majoring in political science, but quit after two years. It was at Brown that he met Karen, who was a prelaw student. Jackson is an excellent carpenter, cabinetmaker, and electrician and owns a large, successful hardware store in downtown Los Angeles. Karen, originally from Columbus, Ohio, is a lawyer with a major oil company and hopes to become a judge.

Their marriage was a bit shaky at the beginning, Karen says. "But we have been through so much together and the bond between us had strengthened with the years. I know so many couples who have stayed together because of habit, fear of being alone, and settled for less than they hoped for when passion and youth brought them together. But none of those reasons apply to us. We're together out of mutual respect, admiration for each other, and, most importantly, out of deep love."

"I know I wasn't the easiest man to get along with when I was younger," admits Jackson. "I drank too much, I had a mean temper, and I was angry at the world for reasons I couldn't ever explain. I had a short fuse and was ready to fight about almost anything to get rid of the tension in my body, which felt like it was going to explode. Karen helped me find out who I was and what I wanted out of life, and once I accepted the fact that I was not going to change the world, that I couldn't right all the wrongs I saw around me, I discovered that I could find peace in myself and my family. I was able to become a rational, reasonable man. Without Karen I'm sure I would probably be dead or in jail by now."

Karen, however, refuses to take that degree of credit. "I don't think I had that much to do with Jackson's coming of age. He did it himself. All I did was listen, really *listen*, to what he said about everything he felt. I was just there for him to bounce off. And I let him know I cared about him no matter what terrible demons were chasing him, that I would always be there for him. He thinks I gave him advice, but I never did. Sometimes I suggested alternatives to his way of thinking, but they were just suggestions and I never pushed my point of view."

All I did was listen. Karen may think that's no big deal, but it is often the crucial element in building genuine communication between couples. In troubled marriages, one of the chief complaints is often that the partner doesn't listen. In recent years, there has been a great deal of emphasis on the need for individuals to express their true feelings, to be open and honest with their partners. But no amount of openness is going to make any difference unless there is someone there to receive the message. In fact, the honest revelation that is not really listened to becomes counterproductive. The person who has been doing the revealing inevitably feels cheated if his or her "truth" is not heard.

Karen not only listened, she was *there* when she was needed. Jackson recalls, "Years ago when I first opened my hardware store—that was the late 1960s—a man I was dealing with cheated me out of a considerable sum of money. When I realized what he had done I was furious. It was about midnight, and I drove my pickup truck into his driveway so he couldn't get out and banged on his door, demanding that he come out and fight like a man. Lucky for me, Karen followed me in her car and arrived on the scene a few minutes later."

"I tried to reason with Jackson, but I could see that he was beyond that. The man whose property we were trespassing on threatened to call the police, but Jackson wouldn't stop screaming for him to come out. I sat down on the front porch and started making jokes about what we would say to the police when they arrived to take him away. After a while he calmed down and started to laugh with me. When the police arrived, Jackson was so charming and sweet they couldn't believe he was the man the homeowner was complaining about. Of course, it helped for them to know that I was both his wife and his lawyer. The man refused to press charges, since he knew all too well what Jackson was so incensed about, and I was able to settle the financial matter out of court."

"I want you to know that it's been years since I've even dreamt of behaving that badly," Jackson says. "Having a lawyer in the family does help when you're ready to hit a guy for damn good reason. But I've matured with age and experience. There's more than one way to skin a cat. It's not that I've joined the establishment, I've just learned to cope with it."

Another man who credits his wife with helping him to soothe old wounds is Lou Ferrigno, the bodybuilder turned actor who is best known for playing The Hulk on the television series of that name. Lou, thirty-five, and his wife Karla, thirty-six, have been married for seven years, and have a baby daughter. Karla, a former psychotherapist, met Lou when she was managing a restaurant. He became rowdy, and she threw him out. Later, he returned, and they began talking about the problems he had experienced as a result of his childhood hearing loss. That was the beginning of a special understanding.

Lou's first, brief marriage had been unhappy. "After a divorce," he says, "most men start classifying women. But I didn't have that feeling that all women were the same as my ex-wife. What appealed to me about Karla was that she was a strong woman, she was challenging. She was strong in the way of being honest. A lot of people won't tell you what they're feeling. Later you find a letter on the table, or they take off and have sex with someone else."

Karla remembers her first impressions of Lou. "I saw a pretty macho guy on the outside, but I knew he wasn't. I looked through that and saw a sweet, wonderful man whom I was determined to get. So I started uncovering some of those layers he'd built."

Karla says that she always needed a man who would allow her to be strong. "When I was dating, if I said anything honest to a man, he'd never call again. They couldn't handle it."

"I'm able to give in to her. Certain times she may be wrong. I usually give in to a point, but sometimes I stick to my guns, and Karla respects me for it. Karla didn't want a weak man. She wanted one who was strong enough to let her be strong. And because of her experience in psychotherapy, she's very understanding."

Lou and Karla need to communicate well, since she manages his career and business affairs. "When I met Lou," she explains, "I realized that he was known only as 'The Hulk.' People didn't even know his name. I was determined to change that and to open up all kinds of career opportunities for him. Lou felt comfortable with that. We've always considered each other equal business partners. He has strengths in areas that I don't, and I have strengths in areas that he doesn't. We sit down and talk things out."

That doesn't mean that they don't argue. "There are times," says Lou, "when we hate each other's guts. I don't believe couples who say they never fight." But he doesn't believe in letting his body get angry. "If I have a fight with Karla, it'd be silly to see me using my hands and fists, which some Italian men do. If you have enough strength, you use your mouth, not your hands. Many men use their hands, or screw other women, as a way of getting back. I'd rather hear how upset Karla is, which isn't always easy for me. But once she gets it out, it's over with."

"I'm very stubborn when I start fighting," Karla admits. "I just want to kill. Nobody gets more macho than me! Most people would react with 'I'll show her.' Somebody had to give in to sustain a relationship. Lou has a quality of giving in, and he's taught me to do that more, too."

Lou's sense of humor also comes in handy. "I imitate people," he says.

"He has me in hysterics, and I don't laugh easily. When we fight, Lou keeps at me—he'll kill me with kindness or jokes. After a while, I'll burst out laughing and say, 'I hate you, but this is funny.' Sometimes that'll end the whole argument."

Marianne Rogers has nothing to do with the actual management of Kenny Rogers' career, but she has never hesitated to give him advice. The fact that he has listened has been an important element in their relationship. I talked to them both separately about this issue.

MARILYN: You married Kenny before his first hit, didn't you?

MARIANNE: Yes. But the song "Lucille," which turned his career around, had just been released. It took about six months to start climbing. We never expected the success that came after that.

MARILYN: Were you involved in his change of character and his switch to country music?

MARIANNE: Well, I started cutting his hair and advising him to get a more conservative look. He said he felt more secure with country music, and I definitely encouraged his concentrating on country. I felt that country fans were so much more loyal. He was interested in what I had to say when I started cutting his hair and trimming his beard. I advised him to get a suit—something dressy.

MARILYN: I find that interesting. A lot of women from your southern background would have felt, "Oh, my opinion is not important." But you had a need to have your thoughts respected.

MARIANNE: Oh, yes. I feel the things I say are very intelligent and good advice. Better than a lot of other things he would hear.

MARILYN: So aside from the love and the fun, you had the feeling that this man respected you enough to listen to you.

MARIANNE: That's very important to me. He doesn't have to do what I say, as long as he listens and respects what I have to say. You're right—southern women are not supposed to express themselves. It is not ladylike. Kenny taught me you can say what you feel. You don't have to scream, and you don't have to be a doormat, either.

MARILYN: Kenny, Marianne says that you have helped her express herself more. Are you aware of that?

KENNY: Yes, but it works both ways. Because of her I have learned to communicate, which I couldn't do in the past. I have always been able to articulate, but not really communicate. With people in general as well as Marianne. You have to listen through the words to hear the meaning. "Are you really upset because I'm working too much, and that's why you're telling me to pick up my shoes? Let's not get involved with the shoes if it is something else." By having this communication with Marianne, it helps me listen to my employees better, to everyone in general. I think self-improvement is one of the most gratifying things a person can go through. And Marianne encourages it. She always takes part of the blame. Then I can take eighty percent. The minute I hear 'we' I am ready to take all of the blame. Together we have brought out the best in each other. I wrote a poem for her once. Because she expressed concern about the me that she didn't know. All my marriages, past experiences. She feared another me would surface sometime. So I wrote her a poem about what I would like her to feel: First is for the ego only;/I would rather be last by far./So I say thanks to those before me,/Because I love you the way you are.

I am what I am. I feel she really owes me a debt of thanks to all the other women who put up with the garbage I put them through. In relationships you must be aware of what's the most you can get from it, so you don't have false expectations. You set up realistic expectations simply by discussing it. The bottom line is the least you will expect from this relationship. Don't let it fester. Say what it is when it is happening.

MARILYN: Marianne told me you helped her express her anger.

KENNY: (laughing) Did she also tell you I almost regretted doing that? What happens is that now she comes to me and expresses herself about all the people she's upset about. I get it all, instead of her going to them.

MARILYN: Do you share secret thoughts, fantasies?

KENNY: Definitely. A pretty girl will go by and I will say, "Doesn't she have great hair?" We can share it together as a conversation, instead of me lusting and hoping that Marianne doesn't notice. She does the same thing with guys. She is comfortable and so am I because we talk about it.

MARILYN: What do you take most seriously?

KENNY: The only things I take seriously are Marianne and our son. The minute you place too much importance on success, it will hurt that much more when it's gone. Anybody who is in this business and tells you they don't have an insatiable ego is lying to themselves or to you. That's your motivation. The acceptance by people. The loss is not in revenue, it is the loss of acceptance. That kills you. That's why I keep reaching out to new sources, a Lionel Ritchie, Barry Gibb, Dolly Parton, Sheena Easton. I feel I will get stagnant relying on myself alone.

MARILYN: So if you're going to be alive, you're going to keep growing.

KENNY: That's it. I'm going to try. That's true of our marriage. Our few arguments have strengthened our marriage. We learned that to talk it out—even when angry—is the only way to get rid of it. I live in the future. The past means nothing to me. I've learned from the past. But I don't go back.

NANCY ELLIS: I would say that the success of our marriage is based on our willingness and our ability to discuss our problems openly and never shut down and withdraw from each other when something bothers either one of us. We used to schedule a Thursday-night "rap session" to talk about whatever was bothering us, but now we are able to talk about problems at any time and get them out of the way.

DOUG ELLIS: At first that was hard for me. I consider myself an introvert, and rather than face a problem I would hide my true feelings from myself and build up a resentment that would manifest itself in other ways. I'd become moody or abrupt with the kids or just sulk. Nancy showed me how to handle my anger or frustration, and now I feel a lot better about myself.

We've met a number of couples in this chapter who define communication in terms of talk. But there are couples who communicate very well without discussing their feelings and attitudes in any depth. Eydie Gorme, only half jokingly, says that her marriage to Steve Lawrence has lasted so long because "we've never had a serious conversation." Another couple who don't go in for that kind of thing are Elaine and Arthur, who have been married for eight years. They also lived together for two years before marriage, but, very significantly, as roommates, not lovers.

An art director for a top advertising agency, Elaine is bright, funny, and about forty pounds overweight. Arthur is a junior-college health and physical education graduate, a lover of sports and opera who teaches exercise classes. And it was while taking one of those classes to shed some poundage that Elaine met him. He was warm, friendly, and really tried to encourage Elaine, but it was accidental that they got to know one another better. One day they ran into each other at the gym bulletin board, where both had posted ads saying they had apartments to share. He was then thirty-one, and she was twenty-eight.

Artie gave her a lift home that day, and they talked about their rental problems. A few weeks later they talked again, and found out that neither one had found a roommate. He jokingly said that they should answer one another's ads—and the idea clicked. So they moved in together. Elaine, who was from Toledo, Ohio, rather gingerly explained the situation to her family—who surprised her by being delighted, since they always worried about her living alone in New York. The arrangement quickly developed a typical roommate pattern. He did the laundry and grocery shopping, and cleaned the ovens and kitchen floor. She cleaned the bathroom, took care of the linens, and did the vacuuming and dusting.

Elaine was invited to many dinners and functions as an adjunct to her job, but often didn't go because she disliked attending without an escort. Artie was available and began to go with her. They became very good friends and remained just friends for almost two years. But their feelings for one another were growing, and both were becoming aware of it. With Artie's help, Elaine had also lost a lot of weight and became very attractive. Things came to a head when he got into a fight with a man who tried to make a pass at her. That night they talked about what was happening, and it was the beginning of a very passionate sexual relationship.

Their background helps to explain the fact that they continue to have a relationship that in many ways conforms to the roommate pattern. For while it is common for people to live together before marriage, it is uncommon for a couple to live together for two years without any sexual relationship. And they still have two lives—his and hers.

"We enjoy being on our own, working at or enjoying different activities," Elaine says.

"I love to watch sports," Artie says, "but I don't want to talk about it with Elaine. She isn't interested and doesn't understand the games as I do."

"Silence is a very precious commodity," Elaine says. "We both enjoy it. When you are involved in work—I do a lot of design at home—or just reading a book, and you can say 'go away' to someone without worrying that they will feel rejected, you are very lucky. I think some people are afraid to admit that they would rather be alone often, and would rather not discuss certain areas of their lives, even with their spouses. Artie rarely asks me, 'Where have you been, where are you going, what time will you be home,' and that's a pleasure."

"I never would have thought that I could be married in such an easy way," says Artie. "My parents were divorced, as most of my friends' parents were. My married friends were buying every marriage handbook they could find. I sort of felt marriage was going to slip past me. Everyone seemed to make it so complicated."

Elaine agrees. "Most of our friends discuss their marriages to death! We were very lucky that we first got together without even the slightest thought of being a couple. We got into a pattern of living that worked well as roommates, and it works just as well as husband and wife. 'We love to be together but alone.' I read that somewhere. It describes us."

"I got lucky," Artie says. "I love living with Elaine, but I can't stand talking to her. Only joking. I do love not feeling pressure to be complicated. Elaine is a wonderful companion, and if things stay this good we may both just learn sign language."

Elaine laughs, and Artie hugs her with great affection.

Renee Taylor and Joseph Bologna are comedy writers, as well as actors, and although they do work separately fairly often, a great deal of their work is a joint effort. They've written for the stage, the movies, and television and have also performed in all three media. Married twenty-one years, they have a son, Garbiel, sixteen, and live in California.

Renee was already well known when they met; Joe was writing commercials. They both had the same manager, who introduced them, thinking they might be able to work together. "As soon as I met him I knew I was going to marry him," Renee says. "He was very open. I liked the way he laughed at my jokes; he understood the nature of my material in a very deep way."

Divorced after an early marriage, Renee had been involved with a number of men, but was ready for something more permanent. "I'd decided I wanted someone not crazy. No more exotics, drunks, homosexuals that I'd convert, or men who'd been married five times. I wanted someone to really care about, to marry."

For Renee and Joe, writing is a way of understanding life. "My father was a cheater," Renee says, "and my mother was often infatuated with other men but didn't really confront my father in terms of having a good emotional and sexual relationship. When I was very young, I decided that I was going to write about them and that I wasn't going to be like that. I'd say, 'Her life would change if she could do this, his life would change if he'd do that.' That's what art is, rewriting life. I've been writing my own script by rewriting my mother's life. I have a sense that Joe and I keep writing our relationship."

Writing together involves very close communication, and that spills over into everything else. "In a relationship," Joe says, "you contract into a togetherness, but when you get too tight, you have to expand again, to break away from each other. But you can't go too far. We both have to write on our own, but I get to a point where I say, 'I want to write with Renee again.' There's a security in the two of us being in a room together battling it out. There's a warmth and togetherness in that. When it gets to be too much, you pull back. It's the same in marriage."

"There can be closeness without intimacy," Renee notes. "What we strive for is to be intimate through sharing our own feelings and respecting each other's feelings. We've written with other people as well as each other. It was like an infidelity. 'You're meeting another writer? Who is he?'"

"When we first met, she was my starter and I was her finisher—not just in writing. Renee would want to take a vacation and I wouldn't. Then, once we'd get there I'd plan the whole thing. Now, I understand why I'm a finisher—I'm farsighted. Renee's nearsighted. When I see a project like a garden or a script or a relationship, I see to the end and how much work it is. Renee sees what's in front of her—like with a magnifying glass. She can write a speech for a character and get right in the middle of it and not know how it's going to come out. I can't do that. But over the years, I've developed my way of starting and she's developed her way of finishing."

"We're a team. If he's great, then I'm greater."

"When she's terrific, it makes me better."

"We build on each other. If he's funny, I'll think of something to make it funnier. It goes back and forth. I don't even know what lines I've written or he's written except for a few favorites."

Most couples have different strengths between them, and the recognition of what those strengths are and when they should be applied is what real communication is all about. In good marriages, what happens is very like Joe and Renee's collaboration on a script— the partners build on each other, and each makes the other better.

Joe, in fact, says that they fight while working only when "I want to do it one way, and she wants to do it another."

But fight they do, and they both admit to having anger in them. At one point they became involved in group therapy. They attended groups and even conducted them. "It was that period," Renee says. "We went to est, all those things. We felt we had to get our pain out, our anger. Now, I don't feel that way. I think it's just important for you to know what you're feeling. You can say to people in a nice way, 'You know, I'm really angry with you.' I used to feel I had to show them the extent of my anger. I was very confronting. We were both into all these things, until it got to a point where one of us would say, 'Who cares?'"

"I always say," Joe adds, "that we change and change until we become the people we always were. If you get married under conditions where the real you is suppressed, then the real you comes out, and if the other person married someone who isn't the real you, you're in trouble. But while we've gone through tremendous changes, we have not really changed the essence of ourselves."

"We have a very deep relationship where we're bonded. But we also have a very superficial relationship where we're easily hurt or angry—we're that stupid, too."

"I could say we fight more than we should. But when we have one of those fights there are usually things building up and it clears the air. Renee and I tend to trust anger, emotionalism. We depend upon it to get through to each other. A good creative fight always clears the air. There's a sexual tension in anger—that's terrific. There are other kinds of fights that aren't so terrific—hostile fights. You're upset about something over there and I'm upset about something over here. There's confusion when you're getting out your feelings about something that has nothing to do with each other. One of the things we tried to deal with in the couples groups was how to use anger in a positive way."

"There's so much energy people could use creating," Renee says, "that's wasted on fighting and cheating. It's important to me to have a happy personal life so we can just concentrate on being artists. Show business is a very insecure way of making a living; you can't be insecure in your personal life, too. If I have a bad experience with my career, like not getting a part, the security of a constant love relationship makes me realize that the part wasn't that important. This is what life's about."

When couples are as close as Joe and Renee, there can be problems with a child feeling left out. But they have taught their son Gabriel how to communicate, too.

"I was worried that I wasn't going to be a good enough mother—that my career was too important to me. But he is a terrific kid. He had to move around a lot because of us, and he was great about it. I don't mean being a good sport, but being open—telling us when he was angry, when he didn't want to go. He was another strong person right away, who wasn't overwhelmed by us. When we had all these marriage encounter groups in our home, people screaming, one woman yelled, 'I need love, I need love.' Gabriel had given me a valentine box of chocolates, and after he heard that woman, he slipped a note in it that said, 'I need love, too, Mother.' He's very loving and has a wonderful sense of humor. Joe and I would fight and he'd sit there and laugh. He does impersonations of us. He's given us a lot. He's our greatest creation."

Greatest creation? A lot of parents say that, so I thought I'd talk to Gabriel himself and get the inside scoop.

Gabriel turns out to be very poised. For one thing, he has a firm grip on what it means to be a teenager—it's hell. "I'm going through it; every single teenager in the world goes through it; in Russia they go through it. I take it this way—I'm supposed to go through this stuff. Other teenagers think they're the only ones. A lot of kids my age are really subject to peer pressure and they feel if they can't make friends in Beverly Hills they can't make them anywhere, so they'll do anything to make friends. I don't feel that way because I've lived in different places and I know that if people won't accept me, others will, and I have good friends."

He has also developed a good perspective on his parents. "Since they work together and are married, they can get into an argument when they're really thinking about work. Once they were screaming at each other so loud that I ran in and asked what was wrong. My

Mom said, 'He wants to paint the tiles on the bathroom floor blue!' They were probably thinking about the script, or something else, and arguing about this unimportant thing."

When he was younger, his parents' fights did bother him. "But after a while, I started laughing at them. Then they'd start laughing, too. Their fights are very funny. I used to be afraid when they argued, but not about work, because that had nothing to do with them or me. They scream, or my dad will close the door and my mom will bang on it and yell, 'Let me in!' But they're never angry for more than two or three hours. I like that they get out all their emotions, and I do the same thing."

Even living in Beverly Hills, one of the divorce capitals of the nation, Gabriel doesn't worry about that. "The more they fight, the more I know they're not going to get a divorce, because at least they're paying attention to each other. I told a friend that my parents once argued over a carton of milk and then made up in about two seconds. He said his parents also argued over a carton of milk, but they got a divorce. It's how you take these fights. Do you say, 'Oh, you hurt me,' or just 'So what?'"

Gabriel likes it that his parents talk to him about almost anything. "People think children can't relate to parents, but it's the opposite. So many parents out there just buy their kids presents and don't talk about what they're feeling."

Does he think that coming from a happy family will make him more likely to have a happy marriage?

"It would depend on the girl, but I do think it will help. My parents are lucky that they found each other, because there's not many of that kind around. Not many."

And what is his fantasy image of how his own marriage should be?

"I hope it's exactly like my parents' marriage."

Now, that is what is called communicating your values to your child.

They said it was just an infatuation. My father
said in three years it would be just like my old
marriage, so why bother?
—*Arthur Marx*

Much to the amazement of everyone, I am not
a philanderer. I am not a guy who goes sleeping around. Rather than go to bed with eighty
women, I got married eight times.
—*Mickey Rooney*

Remarriage: Getting it right

We've seen throughout this book that marriages succeed for many
different reasons, although there are certain underlying themes:
genuine caring, mutual respect, a willingness to let the partner be
himself or herself, an adaptability to change. Certainly a marriage in
which one or more of these elements is lacking is more likely to run
into trouble. But it is perhaps the matter of adapting to change that is
most crucial in our speeded-up time. There are many who say that
the divorce rate is so high because people don't try hard enough
anymore and divorces are too easy to get. No doubt there's some truth
in that, but there's another factor that's often overlooked.

It's very simple—we live a lot longer than we used to. Even a
mere hundred years ago, people died much younger than they do

now. The number of women who died in childbirth was very high. If both partners survived to their thirtieth anniversary, it was remarkable. With our enormously increased lifespan, pressures are placed upon the marriage bond that hardly existed before.

Take the issue of keeping sex "fresh" in a long-term marriage. That wasn't an issue a hundred or more years ago, because people just didn't live long enough for it to be a matter of discussion. Of course, an older man who had lost his wife to childbirth or disease might well take a new younger wife. But her youth in itself was expected to provide the old gentleman of, say, fifty-five, with a new lease on life— if it didn't kill him.

But that's only one aspect of the story. Few women worked, and those who did were mostly involved in manual labor, which also increased the likelihood of early death. The very concept of *personal* growth was simply beside the point. Communication between partners, as we understand it, was an alien idea. Thus, in our time, couples face an entire range of issues and challenges that are really very new. We're having to learn how to be married all over again, in a very different context. People can certainly achieve that, as the couples in this book amply demonstrate, but we shouldn't really be surprised that so many people have trouble getting it right. At least the first time.

The large majority of people under fifty whose first marriages do fail try again. And while forty percent of those who divorce once will do so again, we can be slightly encouraged by the sixty percent who remarry successfully. Obviously, some people are learning something. What they have learned, and how they go about applying it to a new marriage, is the subject of this chapter.

Marty Ingels, forty-nine, and Shirley Jones, fifty-one, have been married for eight years. It is the second marriage for both. Marty, a former comic, runs a very successful business providing celebrity talent for commercials. Shirley, who won an Oscar for her portrayal of a prostitute in *Elmer Gantry*, is probably most widely known as a singer and as the star of the television series *The Partridge Family*. She has three sons from her marriage to the late Jack Cassidy, including teen idol Sean Cassidy.

Marty Ingels makes a joke of everything, although as with many good comics, there are some sober truths lurking just below the surface of the humor. Ask him how he and Shirley met and he replies,

"I'd just come out of the hospital after a nervous breakdown. The first place I went was a party at Michael Landon's house. I was coming in and Shirley was leaving and I slammed right into her, knocking her down. Eighty-five commandos wanted to kill me. But Shirley was very nice. I saw an incredible sadness in her eyes. I later found out it was the day her divorce from Jack had come through. I spent the next six weeks trying to get her number. I was obsessed with her. I looked through all her clippings in the library. I stole her pictures and made a collage. When I told people I wanted to go out with Shirley they said, 'Sure, Marty. Maybe Ruth Buzzi is available.'"

Marty finally got her number, he says, by bribing someone at the William Morris Agency. "I had written out a whole script about how sad she was and how I was going to get her a corsage and take her out to the prom and make her feel better. Before I got to the last paragraph, she said yes. I couldn't believe it. I was always one of those guys who wrote poetry and made cards. I never had any confidence on a one-to-one basis. I wasn't one of those surfing guys. But the date went fine. I made her laugh, and she needed that. I never let on what bad shape I was in. I thought I was being very debonair, but she fell in love with the bumbling, fumbling Woody Allen in me."

Shirley has been smiling through all this, and is quick to admit that she loves a certain craziness in a man. "Definitely. I have craziness in me, and I need someone to express it with. I need somebody with a sense of humor. Jack had that, too. Marty and Jack are opposites in many ways, but I fell in love with both of them for some of the same reasons."

Marty and Shirley began a sexual relationship right away. "On our second date, I kidnapped her in a rented mobile home. When I picked her up, she asked what she should wear and I told her to bring a few things. But it had already started. I jumped her on our first date. Outside the restaurant, I told her I had to kiss her that minute. Later on, she told me she'd gotten all excited. She said her knees buckled. Every time I kissed her, I felt her slipping out of my arms."

Marty Ingels forces you to become straight man: "Why did her knees buckle?"

"Three reasons. One, I'm the world's third best kisser. Two, she was about ready to fall in love. And three, she has very weak knee muscles."

The initial sexual excitement continued. "We had a year I can't believe," Marty says. "Two, three times a day. I wanted to say to Shirley, 'Don't get to like this, 'cause the minute I get comfortable that part will fade,' but I couldn't get enough of this lady. She's worked with every big star, but she never had affairs. With her, sex grows as love grows. The more she fell in love with me, the more sexual she became. And yes, it's still there. You could wake her up in the middle of the night and tell her to meet you nude at the picket fence in twenty minutes and she'd get there before I would."

Does he believe in monogamy? "I don't believe the earth animal is made that way, but since I'm committed to the marriage structure, I play by the rules. I'll tell you, though, even if the police arrive at the motel and I'm there with a fourteen-year-old cocktail waitress, Shirley would stay by my side. But, in any fight, the world would side with Shirley."

"Marty says that if the police found him on the floor in little pieces with a noose around his neck and a bullet through his head and I was sitting there with a knife and gun, they'd say, 'This is the most miraculous case of suicide we've ever seen.'"

Before marriage, they didn't exactly live together. Marty's description of his visits to Shirley's home will strike a chord of recognition in any man who has ever courted a lady with children. "It was difficult moving in with Mrs. Partridge. She had three Irish Catholic rock-and-roll football players at home. Shirley must have read in *Reader's Digest* that technically it's considered spending the night if you're there at sunrise. So, every morning she'd shake me and say, 'Marty, it's four-fifty.' I'd say, 'So what, do you have an appointment?' Then I'd get half dressed in one shoe and drive around until the kids' lights went on. They'd come to the door and say, 'Hi, Marty. How come you're standing there in pajamas with no socks?' I'd jump back into bed cursing and growling, and Shirley'd laugh hysterically."

Despite all the fun they were having, Marty didn't really allow himself to think about marriage. "I always felt a relationship would go as far as a woman would let it. People were crucifying me, telling Shirley I'm a user, looking for her money, a star-fucker. And I wasn't sure myself. I had to see a doctor to resolve it. He told me I didn't love Shirley when I first met her. I was too desperate myself, and I found security, Mother Earth, and the success I didn't have. But the joke was on me, 'cause I finally fell in love. She got through my crazy comic outside."

Marty sounds very serious. But it doesn't last. Asked what he and Shirley have learned from each other, he replies, "Shirley's taught me about love, contentment, tranquility, compassion, peace, self-esteem, and I've taught her depression, anxiety, fear, guilt. It's a perfect arrangement."

"Marty always says to me, 'If you could ever have just one anxiety attack—just one little one . . .'"

"Only fifteen seconds' worth—a little breaking-out around the neck area, a short quiver, and a small dizzy spell."

"Actually, when I met Marty, I thought I was having a nervous breakdown because of my divorce."

"That's what I call a Gentile nervous breakdown—you get a thirty-six-minute migraine headache, take two Bayer, medium strength, and it's over. The Jewish nervous breakdown is, you go to Cedars Sinai for a year and a half, your brain is in traction, and you don't recognize your family."

"Marty's very insecure. His background, his guilt, are all different from mine. I enjoy every moment. After we come back from vacation, Marty asks *me* if he enjoyed himself. He's a little paranoid and thinks everyone's out to get him. He thinks I see only the good side in people."

"Shirley thinks if you wait around the house eating a tuna sandwich, opportunity will come knocking on your door. I think you have to go out and kill fourteen dragons a day just to stay alive. Nine years ago I was on the floor. Now I look around and see everything I have—a wonderful built-in family, I'm making more money than I could spend in twenty years, and I'm working in my living room in a nice robe. But I need a doctor to show me how to enjoy it."

One of the differences between them is that Marty's success came late and after considerable failure. For Shirley it was very different. "She took two hundred dollars from her father," Marty says, "and went to New York. She became a star and still had a hundred and ninety-eight left."

"Almost. In one week I had a job in the chorus of *South Pacific*. I was eighteen. Within a year I was starring in *Oklahoma*, bringing it to Europe. That's when I met Jack."

Shirley says that she was very submissive during her marriage to Jack Cassidy. "I did whatever he wanted, because I was so much more successful. He needed the audience and the adulation. I just needed him and the children, but he insisted that I work. He didn't want me to blame him later for ending my career."

"He wanted her to be a star, but it shot him down. For a while I thought I had to be Jack. I got a special robe with an ascot, but it didn't work with this face. She was never impressed by my efforts to become David Niven."

When Marty started dating Shirley, he wasn't in business yet, but he now earns more than she does. "We'd host parties," Marty remembers, "and all these movie stars would throw their coats at me and say, 'Hang this up, kid.' I had too much energy to sit around and be the star's husband. And Jack had lived very high. Shirley was in a bad financial way and wanted to sell the house. I wouldn't let that happen. I went into second gear and fired the business managers and started all over again."

"But he didn't want to become his wife's manager, just that. I still attract more attention, but he's in a position to support me if I stopped working."

Marty's own success is obviously very important to him, but he also takes huge pleasure in having become a part of the Cassidy clan. He tells how he got all his relatives and all of Shirley's together the night that Sean Cassidy appeared at Madison Square Garden in New York. "I rented three buses with bars and seventeen bodyguards. All the old Cassidys and Ingermans got hats with Sean's name on it since we were going to this teenybopper concert. I had thiry-eight Irish Catholics and about twenty-seven old ethnic Hebrews. It took them about two and a half hours to understand each other. Then we were ushered to the first row of the Garden, where for two hours there was wall-to-wall screaming. You can imagine my Uncle Abe [former New York City Mayor Abraham Beame] with all those screaming kids. They all went straight from the concert to Mt. Sinai Hospital! But it works fine. I even got Shirley to be married by a rabbi. The greatest moment of my life was turning around and seeing all the Cassidy boys with little white yarmulkes on their heads. Shirley and I really are an unlikely couple. But she makes things easy for me. I thought after a while I'd see a temper, defenses, criticism. It's never come."

"Marty sometimes says he doesn't deserve a lady who's so devoted. He doesn't think he deserves anything, and that irritates me. But I'm lucky, too. At twenty, I never would have married Marty.

At forty, I never would have married Jack. Marty's what I need. I know he'll always be there for me.'

TED WILKES: I am not sad about my previous marriages. I feel grateful that these two people chose to live with me for the time they did. I was married to my first wife for sixteen years and to my second for five years. Divorce is tragic when there is a sense of a wasted relationship. I don't have that feeling, and I hope they don't either.

Failed first marriages don't always end in bitterness. Often the partners have simply grown apart rather than together. One partner may have changed far more than the other, or both may have developed in such entirely opposite directions that a middle ground no longer exists. Or neither of them may have grown enough, so boredom has set in. And there are certainly those who were never really right for each other to begin with, who married out of sheer immediate sexual passion, which faded with time; who married out of a desire to escape the life they were leading, only to discover that they had stepped into a worse trap; who married because it was "the thing to do," because of family pressure, an unexpected pregnancy, or a fear of being alone. The wrong reasons for getting married are legion.

Unfortunately, a great many people who marry again repeat their initial mistake or make a new mistake, this time for a different wrong reason. On the other hand, those who make good second—or even third—marriages do so on solid grounds: they know who they are and they know how to find out who other people are. Some have grown up, some have grown into the person they were meant to be, but in all cases they have discovered *themselves*. It is almost axiomatic that a good second marriage must be grounded in greater knowledge of the self. For many, that knowledge was gained only in part through recognition of what was wrong with the first marriage. A lot of it may come from dealing with life on one's own again.

Norman Sheresky and Elaine Lewis Sheresky (she uses Elaine Lewis as her professional name) have been married for eight years. He is Jewish, she Protestant, and it is a second marriage for them both. In his mid-fifties, Norman is a prominent divorce attorney;

Elaine, a dozen years younger, is a commercial model with a master's degree in meteorology and aspires to a career in television weather reporting. They have no children.

Divorced or separated women seem to divide into two groups— those who are always on the lookout for a new husband, and those who have taken well to being single. Elaine belonged to the latter group. "When I met Norman, I was not yet divorced from my first husband, but we had been separated for some time and I had my own apartment. I had discovered that single could be fun. You get selfish when you are single. It is real nice to come home and find things exactly where you want them, to follow your own schedule, eat when you feel like it, go to bed when you want. Norman was a blind date. I was meeting a lot of guys, and I didn't really want to go on this date. But I did, and I liked him from the start. By date three I knew I really liked him. I felt there was something special."

They did not live together for a while. They both had apartments, and Elaine found herself running between her place in Greenwich Village and Norman's apartment uptown. "This back and forth became very unsettling for me," Elaine says. "I wasn't thinking of marriage. But something had to change. Norman said okay, and we got this apartment. But things changed radically after a few months. Norman came home one night and told me that we should separate. I was devastated. As far as I knew, everything was wonderful. He claimed he just wanted to "look around." I decided I would move out at my convenience. I would take the time I needed to find a place that was right for me. And I did take my time."

During this period, Norman and Elaine continued to sleep in the same bed, have sex, and spend a lot of time with each other. But Norman also continued to confirm that he wanted Elaine to leave. "He was not kicking me out, but he was clear about his feelings. Finally I found an apartment, and Norman went with me to sign the lease. Right after that I went away on a job for two weeks, and when I came back he asked me to marry him. He said the dignity I showed changed his mind. He'd also been seeing a therapist, talking about what he was looking for in life, and apparently it was me."

Norman and Elaine are both quite astute about why they get along so well together. Elaine was an only child from a lower-middle-class family. Her parents were divorced when she was four, and she did not see her father except on rare occasions. "I had to become self-sufficient at an early age. I felt terrible about my father. I remember telling my friends he was dead. As I look back, I can see that my first husband and I both wanted to be parents, and we constantly fought to control each other. But with Norman, it turns out that I feel I am much more the mother and he is the little boy."

As for Norman, he lost his mother when he was very young, and he admits that he is much more dependent than Elaine is. "I need more affection than she does," he says. "The only difficulty is that Elaine needs to be alone more. But there's a good side to that, too. My first wife and women in general have always seen me as a safe haven, the Rock of Gibraltar. And that's not what I am. I don't have to play that role with Elaine, and that is one of the things that is great."

"Norman doesn't need or want alone time. He hates coming home to an empty house. But I resist letting him get too dependent. I know he would prefer me to spend less time at school and with my work, but he understands my need for it and never tries to stop me."

"I prefer her to work, but not to work to a point where I would be ignored. I think that is a fear on every man's part. I think our relationship really got much better after we were married," Norman says. "I'm sure that's because we always find new things to do together."

"We play together," Elaine says. "Play is working on our electric trains. We built the trains together. I make the trees and houses and clean the tracks and do the wiring."

"First it was the trains, then hooking rugs. And Elaine has worked with me during my teaching programs."

And what about sex in this marriage? Is it still there?

"I have a stronger need for holding and cuddling," Elaine says. "The affection is very important to me. Norman has a stronger sexual drive than I do."

"I like to fuck more than Elaine does, but it works out. We are very happy."

"That's a lawyer's way of getting to the point," says Elaine. "Norman is just a wonderful find for me. If we'd gone to a computer dating service they never would have put us together. Marriage really works when you can have true intimacy and still remain individuals."

"For many years age mattered to me and it made me very tense to date someone younger. But I never dated kids. I only dated successful and very together, secure men. What mattered was what kind of men they were. But their age did create problems with friends who would make certain assumptions. That angered me terribly. I dated men who asked me for dates and whom I wanted to go out with. Guys who were my age or older didn't ask me out, or I would have gone."

This is Polly Bergen talking. As an actress and head of a cosmetics firm, she is known to millions. She is talking about younger men because she married one. Polly is fifty-five, and her husband of four years, Jeff Endervelt, a wealthy and successful attorney who runs several businesses, is forty-five. It is her third marriage and his first.

So Polly is eleven years older than her husband. So what? Countless men's wives are many years younger than they are. Unfortunately, many people in our society, like the friends Polly mentions, 'make certain assumptions' when the woman is older. Among those assumptions—or more accurately, suspicions—may be that the older woman is paying the younger man's keep, or that the man is gay, or that the woman is trying desperately to hang on to her youth. The list is a long one. And often very unfair.

"I come from a close-knit Jewish family," Jeff says. "Everyone always thought I'd be the first to marry, because I'm a family-oriented person, a homebody. But, it just didn't happen. I was always interested in an accomplished woman, and it was difficult to meet such a woman when I was younger. Someone who's just going to be a housewife isn't really attractive to me. With someone like Polly, who's involved in her own career, there's more to relate to. We're both essentially coming from the same place. My mother was a businesswoman. I always knew I wanted that kind of wife."

As for Polly, a third marriage was far from her mind. "That was the last thing in the world I wanted to do. I'd made a very strong effort to get control of my life—to take responsibility for it and learn that I could run it. My second husband had always made decisions for me. Now I'm happy doing it for myself."

Polly and Jeff met on a blind date. "It was strange," Polly says. "We were fixed up by the mother of one of Jeff's old girlfriends. After I'd agreed to the date, I panicked and wanted to get out of it, but I couldn't get Jeff's number."

The date went quite well. "Polly was a good listener, and we had a lot of things to talk about. But it wasn't love at first sight. I liked that she had a good business head."

"And I found Jeff very attractive. But it really bugged me because he didn't call again for some time. I thought it was a put-down."

Jeff admits that not calling was probably a calculated move to some extent. "I knew Polly was a celebrity, used to having guys run after her all the time. I wasn't going to run after her. I wasn't sure if I wanted to go out with her again, but I finally did call and Polly invited me to the movies with some of her friends. The first thing she said when I saw her was that her friends couldn't make it. I thought, 'Good setup, lady.' After the movie, we couldn't find a cab and started running down the block in the pouring rain, laughing. I think that's when I began to have feelings for her. She invited me to watch TV at her place while she packed for a business trip. I thought, 'Okay, lady, if that's the way you want to do it.' I thought this was really the heavy game. Then she left. We went out the night she returned and have been together ever since."

"He stayed that night, and the next day he brought over a change of clothes and a bathrobe. The next thing I knew, he'd taken over a closet."

"Right away we felt enormously comfortable with each other. Our patterns of life are so similar, and we're both essentially homebodies."

"Jeff made me feel very secure. But I suddenly began to feel that we should either marry or he should move out. I felt trapped in a situation I wasn't comfortable with. I'm kind of old-fashioned, and I was involved in business on a very conservative level. I wasn't comfortable traveling with Jeff, but I also wasn't happy that he wasn't invited to functions where only spouses were included."

The one issue that bothered Polly about marrying Jeff was that she would deprive him of having children. With three grown children of her own, Polly did not want to raise another. "I was very concerned about it. I looked at Jeff with young children and thought he was a man who deserves to have a family. I told Jeff that was something he had to think about very carefully."

"I had to deal with it. But maybe she'll change her mind about adoption eventually. It wasn't a hard decision. Polly was the most important thing to me—not children—and she still is the most important thing."

In terms of another important thing, Polly is very succinct. "There's no denying that sex is very important. I don't think I could be married to someone whom I wasn't sexually compatible with. But under no conditions would I marry for good sex. It took me about fifty years to realize you don't have to marry for that."

"I think my wife is the sexiest woman in the world, and we're very, very compatible as lovers. But that's not the reason I married her. It's only a small part of the relationship."

"I really don't know many men who are more interesting than my husband. I know almost no men who are as attractive. But I think the most important part of our relationship is the fact that we are both early risers and neither of us likes to go out at night. Many marriages break up because only one partner wants to go out every night. We'd love to go to bed every night at ten and wake up at seven. Jeff is also the first man I've known who likes to play games. We both adore poker. I taught him to play backgammon, and now he beats me— which irritates the hell out of me. I also love charades, and he's one of those guys who'll make an absolute fool of himself playing charades. Finding someone to play games with is almost better than sex. I could spend my whole life playing poker. I may get tired of sex when I get to be ninety or ninety-five—or slow up a little, anyway."

Polly's business has always required that she do a lot of traveling. "I never traveled enough for it to truly affect our relationship," Polly says. "But Jeff doesn't like my being away. He doesn't like spending one night without me."

"I can spend all day and all night with her, and I love it. She has cut back on the traveling for my sake. But when she has to leave on business, I understand it, and I go with her when I can. I'm enormously proud of Polly. I think she's a very talented, bright lady, and I love to watch her—working or otherwise."

"He gets very turned on when he sees me operate," Polly says with a grin.

They do argue—about politics. "I'm a Democrat," Jeff says. "A moderate, a clear thinker."

"No, I'm a moderate Democrat, and Jeff, who pretends to be a moderate Democrat, is really a conservative Republican."

There is laughter, and Polly says, "I don't think you can marry for the right reasons unless you have spent some time living alone and have learned to enjoy it. You must learn who you are and where you came from. You must be able to marry for the right reasons, not out of fear of being alone or for security. You must marry because you truly want to share your life with someone else."

Edie Chandler is forty-one, two years older than her husband of eleven years, Eric. She has a style of her own that makes her an attractive woman. But Eric is a lot more than just another good-looking guy. He has the kind of drop-dead looks that would make Robert Redford look like a baked potato beside him. That was what attracted Edie to him in the first place. But it is also what later caused problems in their marriage.

Edie, who owns her own catering business, was recently divorced, with two small daughters, when she first saw Eric. "He was a guest at a party I was catering, and I was so attracted to him I would have gone straight into a broom closet with him. He had that effect on women, and yet he had a sweet, almost naive quality. I wondered why he was alone, so I approached him."

"I'm a shy person," says Eric, "and I was pulled in by Edie's magnetism and sheer power of personality. I liked the strong way in which she took care of things, since I'm the easygoing type."

The two shared interests in music, art, sports, and food. Eric brought out Edie's soft side and she brought out his ambition. "I'd done a little modeling in college and then had a series of sales-type jobs, but success wasn't important to me. Once we got serious, though, I felt a need to pull my weight, to make myself something."

"I could talk to Eric about anything—my business, my divorce, our common interests. He had a wonderful relationship with my children that they'd never had with their own father. Eric is so sensitive, he made me see myself in a more feminine way. Half of me thought he was this big adorable puppy and the other half was involved in this intense sexual relationship. He was perfect, and I made him marry me."

"She didn't twist my arm. What held me back was my lack of a secure job that was going somewhere. I didn't want to end up a piece of furniture. I needed to contribute. We talked a lot about this, and

Edie built me up and really motivated me to do better. She got me interested in real estate and we got married a few months after I made my first deal."

Their problems began when Eric became aware of how strictly Edie was keeping tabs on him. "She always had to know who I was meeting and where I was going. We'd go to parties and she'd check out all the women. She was like a shadow. I felt closed in."

"Part of the reason I pursued Eric was his looks," Edie says. "Having a man like that on your arm makes you feel different about yourself. Then, the second he's off your arm, you wonder about everyone else out there thinking the same thing. I'm usually a confident woman, but this was my fantasy man, and I guess I thought I wasn't good enough. The worst thing that happened was when a friend of mine was trying to congratulate me on the marriage. You know how you congratulate the groom, not the bride? Well, my friend told me how lucky I was. She said, 'I've always dreamed about looking up from my bed and seeing a face like that looking down at me.' It set me off. I thought everyone was after him and he must be tempted."

"I wear a wedding ring," says Eric, "and I conduct myself in a manner that says, loud and clear, 'I'm taken.'"

"I trusted him. It was everyone else I didn't trust, even my friends. Sure, I handle myself well in all kinds of situations. But underneath I'm a smart girl with a fixed nose and a stack of beauty clippings two feet high."

"One night, during an argument, Edie started crying, and that's not like her. She mumbled something about 'If you wanted to you could just walk out of here and find someone with a million dollars.' I thought, 'This is sick.' And it got worse. We spent a lot of time discussing how Edie's husband played around, and all the disappointments she had as a kid. Some of the talks were very good, but then she'd bring in all this neurotic stuff, like, 'I had no date for the prom—you wouldn't understand this. So and so never called back—that never happened to you.'"

"It pissed him off when I'd dismiss his insecurities or lack of confidence. I can't believe I was so callous."

"She acted as though I was never hurt or rejected by anybody—like I wasn't a real person the way she was. Do you know what it's like to be used to make someone jealous or dragged around as an escort like a prize dog on a leash? And I'd had my share of women who dumped me because I didn't make enough money. It made me mad when Edie dismissed all that. And it made me mad the way she was talking about herself. She's so attractive. She's got everything going for her. She'd promise to lighten up, but that just meant that she kept it in, her feelings didn't change."

"I was pushing him away, this perfect husband and father and lover. But I couldn't help myself. I'd think, 'I could never find another man who looks like Eric, but he could have anyone.' I'd see women—and guys—stare at him in elevators, stores, on the street. It drove me crazy."

"One night I asked Edie to write down all the things we liked to do together and all the good things about our marriage. We compared notes and had a long discussion. I persuaded her that if I couldn't make her realize her own worth, someone else had to. She had to get professional help. I made her see a therapist, and I went along. I'd told her that I never thought that much about looks, mine or women's. But she'd say that was like a rich guy not thinking about money. Someone had to get her past this obsession."

"I did realize what I was doing to some extent. But it helped a lot to talk it out with someone outside the situation. I had to get beyond my past hurts and look at what I had now. If I hadn't, I know I would have driven Eric way. It would have been my fault. I just couldn't accept that I was this lucky."

"I chose Edie," says Eric. "There's never been anyone else, before or since. I told her that over and over, and it finally sank in, with help from the therapist. She realizes now how much she's given to me and that when I see her I see a very beautiful woman."

"It took a long time," Edie says, "but I understand now that Eric is my husband because he wanted me as much as I wanted him."

"Everyone tried to talk us out of getting married," says Arthur Marx. "They said it was just an infatuation. My father said that in three years it would be just like my old marriage, so why bother?"

Arthur's father was the legendary Groucho Marx, and he was upset for the same reason everyone was. The woman Arthur wanted to marry was his wife's sister Lois. Arthur and Lois had known one another for years as sister- and brother-in-law. Both marriages were in trouble.

"My first wife and I were just drifting apart," says Arthur. "It had been going on for a long time."

"And I was in a marriage where my husband would always answer me, 'How do I know? I have my own problems.' Arthur would stick up for me. He's always been willing to give me time. Arthur likes women; he'd rather be with a woman than out with the boys. Isn't that what a woman loves? With Arthur I am what I want to be."

They did not have a sexual affair until after both had asked their spouses for a divorce. They went to a motel to test their compatibility. "We were there about two hours and decided we definitely were getting married," says Arthur.

"But that one sexual experience wouldn't really have made much difference," Lois adds. "What is more sexual than a man who loves you and treats you the way Arthur does?"

Nearing sixty and on the verge of celebrating their twenty-fifth wedding anniversary, Arthur and Lois still look back fondly on their first months together as a married couple. Both had given up everything financially in their divorces, but the fact that there was little money didn't matter.

"It was fantastic, probably the greatest time in our lives," Lois remembers. "We were completely carefree. All we had was our American Express card. We didn't have a nickel and we never had so much fun or laughed so much. There we were, a perfect age, in our early thirties, we knew what we had, what we loved, and we were together."

"We felt we had it all," Arthur concurs. "We never knew what it could be like before. We were in one room with a tiny kitchen, and we had both come from large, beautiful homes. It didn't matter."

Arthur started working in television as a writer, and then had a big success on Broadway. "Actually, that happened as a result of my observing Lois's daughter, who had come to live with us. I had never lived with a teenage girl before, and I wrote *The Impossible Years* based on that experience."

The play and subsequent film offered a comic look at how kids drive their parents nuts. But there was a serious underside to the real story. "I believe one of the problems of second marriages is the children from the first," Lois says. "They cause trouble. I told Arthur that this 'every Sunday' ritual of his children coming over had to stop. I couldn't handle the sameness of it. Arthur said, 'Fine. You come first, we come first, our relationship comes first.' He never developed the usual Jewish guilt over what he'd done."

"Even so, you're always worrying about them," says Arthur. "Probably too much. About six months after Lois and I had left our homes, I got a call from my lawyer to telephone my seven-year-old son right away. I thought, 'Oh, my God, he's going to beg me to come home.' Then he gets on the phone and says, 'Dad, what's the combination to my bike lock?'"

Now, of course, the kids are long grown up and Arthur and Lois are freer than ever. "I hate routine," says Lois. "I love to run off to this or that, always looking for things to collect. Arthur is thrilled to join me. He loves antiques, loves to travel, loves decorating, and our home is a result of our mutual love for collecting and decorating."

Arthur, once a champion amateur tennis player, is still active on the courts. But it's the things they do together that really count.

"We've spent one night apart in almost twenty-five years," Arthur notes.

"We are really twins," says Lois. "We hate parties and big social gatherings. Arthur keeps saying we have to go out with other people so we will know how great it is to be alone."

Doesn't all this togetherness get on their nerves occasionally?

"We just have blowups," says Lois. "Rules are stupid. He is the Jewish Gary Cooper and I am the taming of the shrew. I just go over and give him a kiss."

"I just overlook things," Arthur says. "When you're getting along so well, you just don't focus on specific problems. She does get mad when I tell her how to drive."

"Everything with my ex-husband aggravated me to death," says Lois. "With Arthur there isn't anything he does that bothers me. Oh, yeah, he gives the dogs too many cookies."

With such a deep attachment to one another, I wonder, is the fear of losing each other something that disturbs them?

"I never think about it," Arthur says.

"I do," says Lois. "You know the saying 'I can't live one day without you'? I think about it. I don't dwell on it. You never know who is the stronger one. I think of myself as the weaker one, that I'd have the harder time. I know men. There is another woman for Arthur. He is attractive to women, and he likes women, and he would find another woman if I went first."

And doesn't Arthur think Lois could find another man?

"I would like her to at least wait until I'm dead," says Arthur Marx.

Bruce and Andrea Dern have been married nineteen years. They have no children together, but Bruce has a daughter, the fast-rising star Laura Dern, from his second marriage, to actress Diane Ladd. Among Bruce's major films are *Coming Home*, *The Great Gatsby*, and *That Championship Season*. Coming from a wealthy family of the sort that required the children to wear a coat and tie to dinner every night, he quickly got a Hollywood reputation as a rebel. Andrea, who grew up on a North Dakota ranch, went to New York as a young woman to pursue a modeling career, promising to return to marry her high school sweetheart. She did, but he was killed in an automobile accident. She then went to Los Angeles, and ended up in an acting class Bruce was teaching.

Andrea initially found Bruce "exciting, but I was petrified of him." As for Bruce, who was in the process of a second divorce, marriage to another actress carried no appeal. "After about twenty hours of consecutive heart to heart over a weekend, I realized she wasn't really interested in becoming an actress. That's when the door really opened up. I said to myself, 'This girl wants to go down the road with me, but not necessarily looking for work.' By the end of that weekend, I knew."

I asked Bruce about his old reputation as a man who needed a lot of women.

"The key to me is that the woman has an orgasm. It has always been that way. If the woman didn't have an orgasm, I wasn't interested in maintaining a relationship. I didn't go back if she didn't have an orgasm. I don't fuck. I'm not a real good fucker. That's why I never got into intercourse, because I found that if I took time to be more loving they would have an orgasm. But since I married Andrea nineteen years ago, I have only been with her. I came into the marriage with it being very important that I literally keep my dick in my pants. I realized my running around had blown two relationships, and I was not going to blow maybe the only chance I'd have at another one. I knew I'd better be more adult than I'd been before."

That was one reason why Bruce did not want to marry another actress. He needed a wife who would go anywhere with him, including long periods while shooting on location. "I don't like to be alone, and I think it's disastrous on location. When one person goes on location and the partner doesn't, you can kiss that relationship good-bye. Movies become family, and for ten or twelve weeks those one hundred or so people live off each other. If their partner isn't with them, they're going to find someone out of those hundred people to share the evenings with."

Andrea says, "I've been around enough movie sets to see what happens. Naturally, I want to be with him, although recently I haven't really loved going on location, because we have a beautiful house on the ocean and sometimes I'd like to stay home and work in my garden. But I go because it's so important to him. He needs me with him, and I'm really flattered that he does."

"She's a famous gardener," Bruce says with pride. "Nationally known. She's also an artist. She does magnificent work, but she will never show it to anybody. Her artistic sense is marvelous and our home looks like a museum—all due to her. She has been offered money jobs as a decorator, but she doesn't want to lay that on us."

"What about money?" I ask. "Can Andrea buy whatever she wants without checking with you?"

"I give her an allowance every month and she does whatever she wants with it. That's her money."

"Is there any 'our' money?"

"No, I make the money, put it in the bank, and pay all the bills. And one of the bills is Andrea. Beyond her salary, we would discuss something that would be beyond her capacity with her own money."

I ask if that ever leads to arguments.

"No. I just give in."

"He's totally easy to please," says Andrea. "He doesn't worry about what he's eating for dinner or things like that. His main concern is his work, and he might be worried about that, but our life together has really been a piece of cake. He makes it so easy for me, I liken my life to living in a hothouse. If I don't feel like cooking, he says, 'Let's eat out.' If I want to go to a movie, he takes me to a movie. He goes crazy at Christmastime and buys all these things and wraps them up and hides them. He buys me big bears."

"Every Thursday," Bruce says, "we have an in-town day. I am her chauffeur and I drive her to the art store. We go to the antique stores, we have lunch, go to the post office, go to the mall. A lot of the time I wait for her in the car. She does drive, but this is our domestic way together. We like to be together."

What about children? Was it a conscious decision not to have any?

"I have no rapport with babies," Andrea says. "I might not even have had children with my first husband if he'd lived. I like kids when they're old enough to talk. I think I've always felt that I really couldn't take the responsibility. I am really impressed by people who have four or five kids."

"We are each other's child," says Bruce. "That's an important part of our relationship. Besides, I'm not great with little kids. When my daughter Laura was little, it was tough for a while. I'm great for an afternoon, but not for having a relationship."

"It was tough because there was hostility between Bruce and Laura's mother for a while, and Laura got in between that. She didn't really feel comfortable with us. She'd come out to stay, then she'd call her mother and want to go back home, and then I'd get mad. All three of us kind of held back. But I always thought Bruce was a great father whenever Laura came over."

"Laura and Andrea get along great now. The closeness came because she became an adult. As soon as we included her into our lives as an adult, she took to it immediately. We are now a family of adults who have fun and who care for each other."

"We don't need a lot of other friends," says Andrea. "We're playmates ourselves, and great pals."

"Our marriage is one of the best," Bruce says. "Every now and then somebody gets lucky in a relationship, and I guess we got real lucky. We met at the perfect time in our lives, and timing is crucial, just like in acting. We were ready to make this kind of commitment. We both needed and wanted it."

For some divorced people, "getting it right" in a subsequent marriage is based on an understanding of what went wrong in a previous marriage or marriages. But it wasn't as simple as that for Waylon Jennings, one of the star "outlaws" of the country-music world for many years, with hits like "Theme Song From *The Dukes of Hazzard*," and his duet with Willie Nelson, "Mammas Don't Let Your Babies Grow Up To Be Cowboys." His first three marriages failed, and although he has been married to singer/songwriter Jessi Colter (who achieved national recognition with her first single, "I'm Not Lisa," in 1971) for seventeen years, it is only in the past few years that marriage has taken on full meaning for him.

"I had a drug problem," Waylon freely admits. "That contributed to the outlaw image. It was always hard for me to conform to married life. Not that I ran around everywhere. It was just hard for me to be responsible. I take a lot of blame for my failures. None of my ex-wives was involved in music, and they couldn't really understand that when you're trying to be successful it's a long hard road."

Jessi Colter was very much a musician when Waylon met her. Born Miriam Johnson, she took her professional name from her great-great-uncle, Jesse Colter, a real-life outlaw who was a member of the legendary Jesse James gang. Jesse herself was divorced, from the great rock guitarist Duane Eddy, but it had been an amicable split. From her point of view, it was a little different when it came to Waylon's past. "He had a very full past as far as women were concerned, and he was just getting over the last relationship when I met him. 'I'm Not Lisa' spoke of that feeling that is easy to come by if you fear that the one you love loves someone else. That's always a fear as you enter a marriage and there's a recent ex."

The fact that there was a musical as well as a marital bond between Waylon and Jessi does seem to have helped. Says Waylon, "I have to have my wife with me. I want her to be with me, and I've always wanted it that way. If you're traveling on the road and your wife's at home, you're going to have problems. I'm helpless if I'm alone and somebody's not there to pick up after me. And I love it when Jessi performs and tears up the audience. There's never been any competition with us as far as our careers are concerned. When 'I'm

Not Lisa' was such a huge crossover hit, people thought it'd make me feel insecure, but I loved it."

Waylon's drug-taking, though, continued to create problems. "I always knew where I could track him down," Jessi says, "and I could count on him in an emergency. But generally his knowledge of anything going on was absolutely nil. Waylon would come home and rest and watch TV and eat. Then he'd leave. It wasn't like wives who have to contend with husbands coming home and kicking the walls and drinking. Waylon never did anything like that. But I'm a person who really likes fun and company and affection and warmth. And when someone has an addiction—their preoccupation with drugs, their marriage to them—there's a definite left-out feeling for people who care about them, left behind, unincluded. When you're taking drugs of any kind, your real choices, your principles, are altered. There's just no telling the limits to which a person can go. That certainly was part of the loneliness, the emptiness, the lack of companionship."

Despite these problems, Jessi had a child with Waylon in 1979, a son they named Shooter in keeping with the outlaw image. Jessi also had a daughter by her marriage to Duane Eddy, and Waylon has five other children by previous wives. Eventually Shooter made a crucial difference in their lives.

"Nobody loved drugs more than me," Waylon says, "and nobody thought they were having more fun than me. But I had a sixth sense that seemed to keep me alive. I think my record was staying up for nine days and nights. I had to hit bottom before I could get off them. Jessi was never anyone who would nag anyone about anything. Somewhere inside her she always had faith that I would finally get off them. I'd been doing drugs for twenty-one years, and I knew my days were numbered. But I knew it would be hard for me to go someplace and be locked in a room. So I decided I was going to Arizona and kind of clean up for a month. My health was terrible. But I told Jessi, 'Get ready, in thirty days I'll be doing cocaine again.' And I looked at Jessi and I saw the strain in her face, and I saw my little boy and I decided I wanted to see him grow up and I wanted to hang around with her. That's when I decided to really get off them. It's been three years now, and I'd never do them again. I feel terribly strongly against it."

To believe him, all you have to do is hear him talk about his son.

"Not too long ago I took Shooter on a trip with me and I took responsibility for him. I gained a lot of respect for being a parent and watching a child. You know, a father often doesn't pay too much attention to that. All he does is say don't do that or come give me a hug. But I wore myself plumb out—not because he's bad, he's a well-behaved child—but just looking around to see if he's all right. The mental strain of knowing you're responsible, not the mother, just wore me out. But I really do believe for people to have a baby at our age is wonderful. It cemented everything that was already there. We're crazy about him and he's crazy about us, and we try to make life as normal as possible. He's not spoiled, and he's a pretty good drummer. In fact, he told me that next year for a hundred dollars he would do one song with me on stage. I was not into being a father when my first children were born, and I missed a lot of wonderful things that I've seen with Shooter."

For Jessi, the last three years have been an answered prayer. "I'd always believed and had faith that God would perform what he'd promised me, which had been the prayer of my heart for years—that Waylon would truly be my husband, and all that that means. After he got off drugs it was so much more than I'd hoped for. At times I've found that what you pray for, when it comes, you need the strength to handle the blessings. I had no idea of how to be a constant companion, yet I'd always yearned for it. But it has happened, and we've found the ability to walk into the newness of our lives. I believe there's a chemistry for married love, and you either have it or you don't. There's a chemistry for long relationships, a potential you start out with. And Waylon and I did have that chemistry to start out with."

"I knew I had to get off drugs," Waylon adds. "Jessi didn't have to say anything. You could see it in her face. I know her very well, and she has such a great heart. It was destroying her seeing me destroy myself. She didn't stay with me because she liked the lifestyle, she stayed with me because she loved me and knew I needed her. It's still a passionate relationship after all we've gone through. You start waking up and saying, 'Look what I've got here!'"

Which sounds a lot like grounds for marriage.

"When I got divorced, I got divorced to get married again," says Gladys Poll.

"I wanted a home. I wanted to be part of a team and I wanted a surrogate father for my son. That was a big guilt for me, taking him away from his father. But I was going to make my life work. I instantly threw myself into any activity where I might find a man—social, political, any kind of gathering. I went out with a new man every week. Except on weekends. Then, anyone who wanted to see me had to have my son along, take us to Madison Square Garden to see a basketball game, whatever."

Although many women who get divorced these days want to strike out on their own, be independent, pursue their own careers, there remain a great many others who, like Gladys Poll, get divorced to get married again. Few of them, however, are as honest and up front about it as Gladys. She gets that from her mother, who is eighty but still roller-skates and drives her own Rolls-Royce. Gladys's mother urged her to have sex before marriage, and she was immediately consulted about how to deal with men after the divorce. Gladys says, "I wanted to find someone very attractive whom I could jump into bed with and he wouldn't tell. My mother was all for my going to bed with all these guys. My mother always said, 'Enjoy life.' I said, 'Where am I going to do this?' She said, 'In the apartment.' I said, 'How can I? The elevator men will talk.'"

Gladys was, obviously, very much of two minds about sexual liberation. But she found what she was looking for, in the person of Martin Poll, producer of such varied entertainment as the *Flash Gordon* television series, Elia Kazan's classic film *A Face in the Crowd*, and the Oscar-winning *A Lion in Winter.* She met him during an Easter vacation she and her son Tony spent in Los Angeles. "Lunch at the Beverly Hills Hotel," says Gladys. "Marty was part of the group. Tony came out of the pool and shook like a baby whale and 'spritzed' everyone. Marty said, 'Get that fat kid away from me.' I said, 'We are a package.' That came as a surprise to Marty. The women he knew did not come packaged with their children. I loved Marty's body as soon as I saw him. This skinny thing. I was dying to go to bed with him. I told him to call me if he was in New York because I wanted to go into the movie business. Of course, I couldn't have cared less about the film business. But he called and came for a drink. We started necking. Then he had to leave, because he had a date. When I saw him again, he probably was sure he had someone who was hot to trot, and he took me to his hotel suite, and I said, 'I don't do those things.'"

Surely, she wanted to?

"But I wouldn't. I was really afraid I wouldn't measure up to the women he knew. I didn't think he would ever see me again if I jumped into bed with him. I was a total dummy. So we dated when he came to New York. Movies, dinner, but that was all. Then he said he was going to Europe, and I said I would love to go with him, and he said he would take me. I wasn't thinking of marrying Marty. I wanted to have an affair with him. It was summer and Tony was in camp, or I wouldn't have gone at all."

Marty wasn't thinking of marriage either. "She was fun, she was amusing. She was different from the women I generally met. But I really live for my films. I didn't think I could fit a marriage into my life again, especially with children involved. When we were returning from Europe, though, I turned to her on the plane and said, 'I've never had so much fun, and I've never been so crazy about anyone since I was nineteen.' A year later we were married. We felt like kids. We walked down the street and held hands. We wrote love letters to each other."

"Even after we came home from Europe I still never thought of marrying him. I was crazy about him, too, but a film producer did not fit my image of the proper husband. Marty was going to be my treat. Not my future husband. But then he went away on one of his trips, and I realized I couldn't even go out on any dates. I just wanted to rush home and wait for his calls. I wrote him eight times a day. It was wonderful. It still is."

Gladys and Marty Poll have now been married ten years. Marty is in his late fifties, Gladys in her early fifties. They both feel lucky. "In my business especially," Marty says, "you don't see many good relationships. And in general, at our ages few people seem to feel the way we do."

Gladys says that she had her first really wonderful sexual experiences with Marty. "Isn't that terrific? We are not aware of our ages. He is like my first love."

This is in fact Gladys's third marriage; her first lasted one week. Both her second marriage and Marty's first were long and troubled ones, and what they have been through in the past enhances what they have now. "We know we have something very good," says Marty, "and we have a comparison. We were not happy before."

"My marriage is my life. He's my prince, my prince charming, my best friend. I preserve him. If I can work a problem out without bothering him, I will—and he appreciates all my efforts. I respect Marty like I did my father. I am proud to be married to him. I love his taste in his work. He is probably the most literate man I ever met. He's smart. He's elegant and refined, and he is not the life of the party. When we decided to marry, I feared that what he enjoyed in me might eventually bother him. That I tell too many stories, talk too much. But he still enjoys me this way. That's what's wonderful."

"Since we have been married," Marty says, "I have opened up a lot emotionally. Things are just more natural with Gladys. She has made a wonderful home for me. A wonderful artistic ambience that works for us. Gladys is very knowledgeable about art, and it is reflected in our home. We spend a lot of time alone. We enjoy being together. We don't need to go out a lot. She has helped me on film projects. She has done research, and I welcomed her participation. On the set she is like a den mother. She travels with me all the time, except when Tony is home from school. She cares all the time."

And what about Tony? Gladys admits she was worried about whether Marty would really be willing to serve as a surrogate father. "Marty had two grown children of his own, and he wasn't crazy about kids. He had to deal with how important Tony was to me."

"It did concern me," Marty says. "I hadn't thought I could fit a marriage into my life again, especially with children. But I wanted to be with Gladys, and having Tony around has turned out to have enriched my life. Tony is Tony Poll. Not legally, but by his own choice, and now I have three children."

And so Gladys, who got divorced to get married, found for herself an exceptionally happy ending.

Marianna Lopez is a small, thin woman in her early thirties, but she looks much older. She was born and raised in a small village in Venezuela and came to California with her first husband sixteen years ago. Her husband beat her, but, as with many women, it took her years to seek help.

"In my country, especially in the villages, the man is the ruler. He can be a tyrant if he likes. I believed it was my lot in life to be with him. I saw many a women worse off than me who accepted their fate—like my aunt, whose husband beat her all the time. It took a long while, living in California, talking to other women, to even think of getting away. I had too much fear. And besides, where would I go in a strange country with no family and a small child?"

A woman from the neighborhood told Marianna about the Battered Women's Clinic. "The first time I went there, I didn't understand the people there, and I was so frightened I went home. The second time was months later, and they sent me to the Battered Women's Shelter with my son. I knew I had to get away. Everyone has a place they reach when they can go no further. I got to the point where I knew for sure that if I stayed one moment longer I would be dead. He did not hurt me as badly that last time, but it made me see. He hit me with an open hand so there would be no bruises. It started because he had a sunburn. He asked me to put lotion on his back. I was in the middle of doing something for my son, so I told him to get the lotion and I would be glad to do it. He hit the ceiling because I won't go for the lotion. Then he beat me. He threw me out into the street naked, and then opened the door and pulled me back in. My son saw it all and tried to help me, and he hit the boy with a stick. I knew then we would have to go."

It was at the shelter that Cesar Lopez, to whom she has now been married for seven years, first saw Marianna. Cesar is of Mexican descent, but is part Indian. He was orphaned at birth and brought up in a facility outside Mexico City called Los Pequenos Hermanos (Our Little Brothers). A small, shy man with a good command of English, he has some training in accounting and works for a firm in the Barrio. He remembers vividly his first sight of his wife. "Marianna is thin now, but when I first saw her she was even thinner. She looked like some of the starving children that came to the orphanage in Mexico. I knew about her from my sister, Bianca, that she lived at the shelter and needed help. I wanted to love and protect her from the moment I saw her."

"Cesar came to me like a miracle. He saved my life and that of my child. I had been at the shelter two weeks, and if it wasn't for Cesar I might have gone back to my husband again."

"At the shelter," Cesar explains, "they ask for about eight dollars a day. Most people don't pay because they have no money. But after two weeks, they ask for about one hundred dollars for room and board. I offered to pay the money, so Marianna wouldn't have to go back. I talked about my life, her life, the future of her child. I told her that abused children usually turn out to be abusive parents. She didn't want that. I said I would help her find a job. I never suggested she stay with me, because I didn't want to make her feel that I, too, would use her in some way."

"I listened to him and tried to believe he was different. A good man. I was suspicious at first. Why was he telling me these things? But he gave me courage. He gave me a sense of being worthy. Something I never felt before."

Marianna did not fall in love with Cesar immediately. "I had no feelings left. I trusted him not to hit me, and that was enough. Only later, when I saw how good he was to me and my boy, did I allow myself to feel anything. He paid for two more weeks at the shelter. The nuns there were very kind. When Cesar and I decided to live together, they helped me to see someone to get a divorce. Cesar and I lived together for six months until the divorce was final, and then we were married."

They live now in a rented house in eastern Los Angeles. Marianna works as a waitress in a Mexican restaurant, and they have a daughter of their own. There are many things, Marianna says, that she admires about her husband, but most of all it is the way he treats her son. "With the baby it is easy to be loving; she is his own flesh and blood. But for my son it is something else. He is not an easy child. He is very angry. Cesar gives him lots of love and support. He has so much patience. I know where he gets it, too. He told me that when he lived with Los Pequenos in Mexico, they had to build their dormitories from rocks on a high mountain. Each boy would run up a steep hill, pick up a heavy rock, and carry it down to the mission. They got half a centavo for every rock they carried. It was endless, heavy work, but the children were happy to do it. How can you not love and respect a man who grows from such a beginning?"

"I learned as a small child," Cesar says, "to love and share with others. We were never too poor to laugh. We were a family, all brothers and sisters, and we were taught to enjoy what we had and to treat each other with respect. I try to do that with my son. He is my son, now."

Remarrying often means accepting a "whole package," as Gladys

Poll put it—not just a new partner, but that new partner's child or children. That can give pause, as it did to Marty Poll. Or it may not even raise a question, as was the case with Cesar Lopez. Either way, it is another aspect of the growth that is required of people who are getting married again. Being a stepparent demands even more maturity than being a parent.

Edward Villella, the former New York City Ballet star who is now a teacher, director, and choreographer, was fully aware of the issues involved when he married his wife Linda, a former Olympic skater and an Ice Capades star, four years ago.

Edward's son by his first marriage lives with his mother, but Linda's daughter was very much a part of the package, and he was sensitive to his stepdaughter's initial wariness toward him.

"She was about three and half when we started living together before our marriage," Linda says. "The first year was a little strained, I thought. I think she was a little afraid of Edward—at least that's what she told me when she was just five."

Edward agrees. "I think she was suspicious of this person who could, theoretically, take the place of her father. I was hypersensitive to that, and it wasn't what I wanted her to do. Nor would I allow myself to be—in any way, shape, or form—her parent. I worked very hard at *not* doing that, at just staying back. I like kids and I have a sense of where they're coming from."

In this case, Edward's standing back had a good, but really unexpected, result. "He's turned out to be a major influence on her life," Linda says. "She's more on the same wavelength with Edward than she is with me or her father. Maybe it's because they're both Libras."

"She's a very sensitive child. We almost think alike—it's very strange. She's a delight to have around. I love to listen to her stories; and she writes wonderfully, paints and designs. She's so inventive. She'll take a scarf and tie it in a way so that it suddenly looks like a costume piece."

Edward is clearly happy to have Linda's daughter as a part of his life, as a friend. But now he has a baby daughter with Linda to whom he will have to be a parent.

Linda says, simply, "It was important for us to have a child between us. I asked him if we could about three days after we married. I wanted to get a pregnancy out of the way. We tried immediately and it took about two months. My first pregnancy hadn't been pleasant at all, but this one was wonderful. Edward was fantastic, so special then."

Edward did not take the prospect of having a child with Linda lightly, however. "Linda's a wonderful dreamer, and I'm a dreamer, too. But the reality was that it was my responsibility. I realized that having a child in New York is a major expense. I'd been very casual about money, and I knew I'd have to add at least twenty thousand a year to continue living the way we wanted to live and have a child. I had to make conscious decisions, to set things up a year or more in advance in terms of work."

The added money is necessary, because for the first time in her adult life, Linda is not working, feeling it is more important to be with her ten-year-old daughter and the baby. She feels that she has made the right decision. "Everyone is so career-oriented now that they always want to know what you *do*. I felt uncomfortable at first about not working, but then I realized that being a mother is what I want to do right now. When the youngest is old enough, I'll work again, probably teaching figure skating, and I won't feel guilty about it."

Thus, for the Villellas, this new marriage is very much a matter of starting over. They are dealing with marriage in ways typical of many younger couples embarked on a first marriage. That is a common pattern among remarried couples when the wife is young enough to bear children. It is as though they feel a need to wipe the slate clean, to go back to the beginning in order to get it right this time around.

LARRY KIRSTEIN: When I got married the first time I told myself I would change the things I didn't like. I never could, and I don't think anyone should get married thinking that. When I married Jane I said to myself, "These are her assets" and "These are a small column of things that will knock the shit out of you." You have to accept that there are things that will bother you.

Some people get it right the second time around. For others, it may take three tries. And then there are those who just keep on getting married and married, divorced and divorced *ad infinitum*.

Enter Mickey Rooney.

One doesn't want to make rash promises, but it looks like his eighth marriage, now in its ninth year, is going to last. Mickey Rooney, the world's most popular movie star in the 1940s, a has-been in the 1960s, and now an award-winning dramatic actor as well as the star of the Broadway hit *Sugar Babies*, appears to have finally settled down with his wife Jan. He's in his mid-sixties, she in her late forties; he has nine children by his seven previous marriages, and she two by her two previous husbands. She's a country singer with a career that allows her to pick and choose what she's going to do, which leaves her time for taking care of Mickey, who clearly needs it.

Mickey Rooney is not an easy person to interview. His answers to questions are often about something else; then he suddenly gets very direct when you least expect it. So instead of attempting a false continuity here, let's just hear a few things he has to say.

"First of all," he says, "not being a philanderer, a guy who's going to sleep around a lot, instead of sleeping with eighty women I got married eight times. I've known people who've been married thirty-five years who finally divorced. They stayed together for the children's sake, and the children never knew that Mommy and Daddy hated each other's guts. It sounds kind of facetious, but I haven't gotten married a lot. I've just practiced a lot."

Do you remember all your other marriages?

"Every one of them. Every moment of them."

Why have you married so many times? Really.

"It wasn't a case of it being a challenge. It was a case of doing the proper thing. Jan and I, for instance, had been living together two and a half, three years before we were married, and finally I said, 'Let's make it legal.'"

Were you afraid of making another mistake?

"I've got news for you. At my age I'm not looking to come home to an empty house and an empty icebox. I'm looking to come into a home that has some feminine charm to it and where there's somebody who cares for me."

Did you marry Jan because she was easy to live with?

"We never got along that well. We had a lot in common and in many areas we were friendly. We got married because we wanted to build a relationship which could *lead* to a good marriage. I think you have to be married to have a really good relationship."

Was it a passionate sexual relationship?

"No. I believe anything that's hot sex or 'Let's get in bed right away' won't last. How many times have you heard a woman say, 'I love him, but I don't like him,' or, conversely, 'I like him, but I don't love him.' It's strange to say, but sex has never been a big part of my life. I'm not one of those kinky guys. I adore women and I love sex, but I can be celibate for fifteen weeks if I'm out on the road. I think sex is different for everybody. Some people like the thrill of 'Quick, lock the door' sex. I do think when it comes down to a formula, though, like 'We always do it Wednesday night,' that can be the beginning of the end. But sex isn't the uppermost part of marriage."

Do you work at this marriage?

"I think if you have to work at a marriage, if everything is laborious, then you have no marriage. But if you mean work as being aware of yourself and the other person, okay. A lot of people are very at home with their own unattractiveness. He breaks wind at the table, she belches. Jan and I are very fastidious, and we're God-fearing. We're clean, attractive people. I'm overweight, but I don't sit at the table and flatulate."

Are you the kind of guy who hates being alone?

"I adore being alone. I read a lot and I paint. I play a lot of golf. I go to the racetrack alone a lot of times. Jan isn't interested in that. Slowly but surely she's beginning to take certain interest in things that I like. Whatever she likes, she does. We're not what you would call a 'divided marriage,' but we're looking at it intelligently. Everyone's an individual, and if you lose that individualism, you have no marriage. I think if you both give enough so that you're not too worried about yourselves, everything else falls into line. I'm behind Jan all the way in anything she wants to do."

You're a more philosophical person than I would have expected.

"Look," says Mickey Rooney. "I'm a man of opposites. I'm an extraverted introvert—a very loud quiet man."

Jan Rooney, like Mickey himself, discounts the notoriety that has accompanied his many marriages. "He first married very young—at a time when you couldn't just live together. You married then, and he was a victim of that. People don't know the circumstances. One of the wives he was married to for only six weeks. She was a friend of an ex-wife who died. Because of that friendship, she conned Mickey into the marriage. There were all kinds of factors. It looks degrading in the public's eyes. When you know the real story, you think differently."

How did you meet Mickey?

"His son, Mickey, Jr., was a good friend of mine, and we worked together musically. We were rehearsing one day, and he said his dad was coming in and wanted to spend some time with him. I didn't want to go, but I did and we had a lovely time. We were all gathered around the piano, laughing and singing. Ironically, before I met Mickey, I was living three doors from a guy who used to tell a different Mickey Rooney story every day. Isn't that strange? And what's stranger is that when I was born, Mickey was in the same hospital because of an injury."

Did you become involved with him right away?

"No. I ran into him again a couple of months later. It was a big party, and we sat down and watched television together and discovered we had a lot in common. We became chummier and chummier after that, but I had no idea it would become serious. I thought we'd just be good friends. Every time he'd come back from the road he'd stay at my house. But I was just taking it day by day. Then he was going to Hong Kong and asked me to come with him, and I did. When we got back, we got an apartment together. After that he was constantly, constantly, asking me to marry him. Before him, I'd never gone out with a man above thirty. It was frightening, to tell you the truth. I wasn't used to an older man. I was skeptical."

Was Mickey's fame part of the attraction?

"Definitely not. His career was down and he had no money. I'm tired of people thinking I was after his money. I had a lot of rich, attractive men after me, but I didn't want them. I was a semihippie."

Did you help him with his career?

"He needed a lot of emotional support, and I gave it to him. He was thinking of moving to Florida, but I had a psychic feeling that if he stayed in California his career would soon reach its pinnacle. There was no way he was going to do *Sugar Babies*. I talked him into it. I told him if he didn't do it, it might be the end of us. He was about to sign a two-year contract for a series as Judge Andy Hardy. I told him, 'Nobody wants to see you as an old judge. They want to remember you as young Andy Hardy. You'll be hurting yourself, and if you do that I won't be able to handle it and I don't know what'll happen to us.' So he did *Sugar Babies*, and it was a huge success."

And what about your own career?

"I've been more interested in encouraging Mickey's. He wanted to handle mine, but he went about it in the wrong way. He frightened people off who were very interested in me. When I told him to drop the ball, he said it was okay, but he was angry with me."

So this marriage does have its tensions?

"It gets a little heavy sometimes. Getting away once in a while is a saving grace for me. I don't know what'd happen if we were together all the time. But I like challenges."

Some people like challenges better than others. There are those who prefer to head off tensions before they get started. One way to do that is to draw up a marriage contract.

Malcolm and Helen Elliott have been married for eight years, and lived together for three years before that. Helen has a fifteen-year-old son by a former marriage who lives with them; Malcolm's two children live with his former wife. The couple also have a four-year-old daughter of their own. Forty-four years old, Malcolm is a successful business manager and investment counselor, while Helen, thirty-seven, designs and is co-owner of a children's clothing line based in Los Angeles. She also receives a monthly allowance from a trust fund set up by her parents, now deceased, and controlled by an uncle.

When they first started living together, the couple signed a cohabitation agreement, which was updated every year and then modified when they married. "At the time we first decided to live together," says Helen, "neither one of us was ready to think about marriage. We had both been badly burned by other relationships. We knew that moving into either Malcolm's or my apartment wouldn't work. Territorial imperatives are always there, and one person is always an outsider. So we decided to lease a house and start from scratch. That's when Malcolm's business acumen came in handy."

"We didn't want money problems to interfere with our love affair," Malcolm explains. "I've seen financial concerns destroy relationships of clients too many times. Between my alimony payments and her trust funds, I thought it best to have it all spelled out. We started by signing the lease of our new house as joint tenants and putting some extra money in a joint savings account so that if things didn't work out, we would both have moving expenses."

Malcolm notes that a cohabitation agreement will hold up in

court, like any other contract, and that such agreements are recognized in all fifty states. He says it is advisable to have a lawyer draw up the contract so that the language is not contrary to public policy. The agreement must also be witnessed by a notary.

"Basically what we did," Helen says, "was to spell out all real property and individual income we had. We agreed to share living expenses in proportion to our respective incomes. Since my first husband was financially responsible for our son, we agreed that Malcolm would not have to be responsible for my son's support."

"Even though that clause was in the contract, I don't think we seriously honored it. I pay for all vacations, summer camp, and guitar lessons. When his natural father's child-support checks are late, we don't worry about it."

The agreement also took into account the possibility of one or the other being out of work for a time. "It's never come up with us," Malcolm says, "but if one of us loses income from unemployment or illness, the expenses become the sole responsibility of the other for six months."

The Elliotts continued the agreement, with some amendments, even after the marriage, because they felt it gave them both a sense of security, although for different reasons. "It worked for us for three years prior to the marriage," Helen says. "It gave me a feeling of self-worth and responsibility. I feel independent, and I like that. I've seen too many women who feel helplessly dependent upon their husbands and who, for that reason, stay in a bad marriage."

"I think the legal responsibility for another person's income can be a psychological burden. Women have been fighting for their rights for years. I think that being financially responsible for themselves gives them a sense of dignity and equality that helps a marriage. I wouldn't want to think that Helen stays with me because I put the food on the table and she's stuck with me."

Helen nods. "Times have changed radically. If I see an expensive dress or piece of jewelry I want, I just buy it. I wouldn't want to ask my husband if I could have it, like a helpless child. If I want to buy a gift for my husband or children, I have a checking account and I can do as I please with it. Nobody knows or cares how much I spend, and there's a certain freedom in that. I feel better about myself, and it shows."

Neither Malcolm nor Helen has much patience with the idea that having a marriage bound by a financial contract is somehow cold-blooded. Like many people who have been married before, they are both realistic and determined to avoid repeating past experiences they found traumatic. "A marriage without a contract," Malcolm insists, "can become a bitter nightmare when it comes to separation or divorce. I'm still living that nightmare with my ex-wife. When I left that marriage, she got everything I had worked most of my adult life for—the house, the cars, the stocks, everything. I was lucky to get out with my football helmet from college and my photograph album. And she still wants more. Every week there's a phone call for some new expense that she considers me responsible for."

"Sometimes I watch him on the phone when it's a call from her. I can see him trying to control himself when she's being unreasonable, threatening to hold back his visitation rights or to turn his children against him. I feel sick to my stomach watching his agony. It just isn't fair. I try to be supportive, but there's not much I can say or do."

"Once when I was on the phone with my ex-wife, trying to get her to be reasonable, I could feel myself losing control. My two kids were planning to spend Christmas out here with us and she was threatening to cancel their trip. Helen came around behind me and massaged the tension in my shoulders. It was so good to feel her with me I think I handled the call better."

The contract the Elliotts have drawn up thus gives Malcolm a defense against past pain and against the possibility, however remote, that it could happen again like that. For Helen, it increases her sense of independence. They fully understand what the contract gives the other; there are no secret agendas here. But there is one small problem. "We have everything all spelled out on paper if we ever did separate," Helen says. "Everything except our season tickets to the Rams games."

"We never added the tickets to our list of jointly owned possessions, but we made an oral agreement to alternate the games. Of course, I get all the games with Dallas."

"Wait a minute!" Helen exclaims. "I never agreed to that."

"There, you see, that proves it! Every marriage, no matter how good the intentions are, needs a written agreement. The only trouble is, it doesn't leave the couple much to fight about. Sometimes a good fight is healthy."

"I hate fights," Helen says vehemently. "You can have the tickets to the Dallas games."

And they are both laughing.

Cara and Jim McClellan have been married for a total of twenty years—but not consecutively. After their first ten years of marriage, they divorced. They then remarried, ten years ago. They originally met, married, and divorced in New York, and migrated separately to Los Angeles in 1970. In their mid-forties, with a grown son and daughter, they now own and operate a travel agency in Hollywood.

An attractive brunette with an outgoing, friendly personality, Cara has worked as a press agent, a childrenswear buyer for a major department store, has owned her own gift shop, and was a partner in a clothing boutique. Jim is slightly overweight, gray-bearded, with a degree in accounting. He was a partner in a New York accounting firm but hated what he did and came to Hollywod to produce low-budget films. After two unsuccessful attempts, he bought into the travel agency and eventually assumed full ownership.

Curiously, considering their backgrounds and talents, their first marriage foundered over financial issues. "We fell in love, got married, and it seemed perfect," Cara says. "All of our friends thought we were the ideal couple. We did, too, until the financial problems started. Neither of us knew how to handle that. We fought constantly over money. I accused Jim of being a failure, and he accused me of being a nag."

"We were both right," Jim says forthrightly. "We loved each other, but we couldn't live together. We separated for a year, and finally Cara went to Mexico for the divorce."

"He sent me a dozen roses while I was in Mexico. The night before I went before the judge he called me at the hotel and promised me that everything would be all right, we would always be friends. I cried myself to sleep, and the next day it was over."

A few months later Jim decided on the move to Los Angeles. "I hated accounting and believed I was a failure. I wanted a fresh start in business, something I thought would be exciting. New York was the scene of my misery; California promised to be the land of milk and honey. Cara and I had stayed close friends. We knew we couldn't live together, but I asked her to come to Los Angeles so we could at least live in the same city."

"I agreed to follow him, partly for his sake and also for the children. They had a good relationship with their father, and I didn't want to see that ruined. New York held nothing for me, either."

Jim had relationships with several other women, but none of them lasted more than a few months. "There was no one I was serious about. Cara was my best friend. We were very close; it was like having a sister. Some of my women friends didn't understand and resented the relationship, but she remained the most important woman in my life."

"During that time," Cara says, "I lived with a man for about three years. Jim and whatever woman he was seeing would come to the house for holiday dinners, children's birthday parties, or just for Sunday dinner. We said we were continuing our relationship for the sake of the children, giving them a sense of family, surrounding them with love from both of us. We didn't realize it was more than that, that we needed each other. In times of crisis, we were always there for each other. When Jim had to go for a back operation, I was there, making arrangements, talking to doctors, sitting in the hospital all day. When I had to have a biopsy for a benign cyst on my breast, Jim took me, stayed with the kids, and was right there until it was over. It was like having a big brother. He was family, and we didn't care what people thought."

Was there any kind of sexual relationship during this period? "It wasn't that kind of love," says Cara. "We would go out together a lot, it's true. He always introduced me as his ex-wife, which raised a lot of eyebrows, but the relationship was strictly platonic. We would discuss the current love in our lives. He always gave me good advice on how to handle men, and I tried to do the same for him about women. Many times I became friends with women he brought to the house, and I remained friendly with some of them after their affair was over."

And how did Jim and Cara's children react to this unusual relationship? Jim shrugs. "I don't think they thought it was unusual at the time. They just accepted the fact that at Thanksgiving dinner, Daddy and his girlfriend, Mommy and her boyfriend, and the rest of the family and close friends we had in Los Angeles would all be together."

"There are so many divorced families in Hollywood that they never had reason to feel we were so different," Cara adds. "Many of their chums and schoolmates had at least two fathers, sometimes even three. Hollywood was the perfect place for our nuttiness. I remember when my daughter was in high school, she did a term paper on her family for sociology. She described our family and went into detail about a Christmas dinner at our house. She got an A on the paper, and the teacher wrote a comment in the margin—he said he would very much like to meet her mother!"

The decision to remarry was spontaneous. In another context, you might say sudden. Jim remembers that they were both between commitments at the time, with no third or fourth parties in their lives. "I was having trouble with my business, and I found myself calling Cara every day. And we would have dinner two or three times a week. It was a relief for me. I didn't have to be 'on' for her, I didn't have to impress her. I could be myself. I started seeing a therapist and began to see how important she was to me, see it in a new way."

"We started talking about how we had both been searching for the perfect mate. Neither of us had even come close to finding the right person. One night he took me out to celebrate my birthday and he introduced me to people as his wife instead of his ex-wife, as he usually did. After the people left and we were alone, he said that the word *wife* sounded right to him. It sounded right to me, too. That night we decided to fly to Las Vegas without telling anybody and make it legitimate."

"Nobody seemed to be surprised," Jim says, smiling. "The kids were very happy and most people said they'd expected it to happen for years and wondered what took us so long to realize it was meant to be."

"In a way," Cara muses, "I regret the years we wasted apart from each other. But I know we needed that time to grow and mature. I think we appreciate each other more than most couples do who have stayed married right straight through."

"The second time we got married for the right reasons. Cara is not only my best friend, which she has always been, she is the great love of my life. We have no secrets from each other, and we know each other better than people who have been married all their lives could. There is security and comfort in that. Most people spend their lives looking for it and never really finding it. We may not have done it the conventional way, but who cares? It turned out right in the end."

✿   ✿   ✿

It turned out right in the end. This could be the motto for successful remarriage in general. But, as we have seen, getting it right is not a matter of conforming to some set of rules that were ignored or misunderstood the first time around. Many of the couples we've heard from did not do it the conventional way. They made their new marriages work because they understood that it was possible for each partner to be himself or herself within the marriage, that allowing the other person to be an individual was not a threat but a stimulus. As in all good marriages, self-respect has led to mutual respect. And that mutual respect serves as a basis for accommodating change. These couples have recognized that marriage is a changing environment, that it has its varying seasons, and that those seasons bring different pleasures as well as different problems.

Certainly at my time of life I want someone
with a sense of humor. That's about all you
have left.
—*Vincent Price*

How can I regret the bad times? They brought
me to where I am now.
—*Brenda Carlin*

The seasons of marriage

When she was sixteen, Peggy Tishman wrote a letter to her best
friend telling her that Alan Tishman was the man she would marry.
Alan, two years older, was not aware that he was engaged. In fact, he
didn't even remember that first meeting. But a year or so later, after
he'd entered Dartmouth College, they attended the same dance in
New York during Thanksgiving vacation, and Peggy was pointed out
to him.

"She was very tall and wore a white flower in her hair. I later
found out she wore it so she could be spotted easily on the dance
floor—she knew all the angles—and I cut in and made a date with
her."

Peggy was already hooked. "You must realize that he was the
best-looking thing that ever walked on two legs at that time."

247

"Thank God I was too stupid to know how she felt," Alan says.

Peggy comes from a wealthy family—they had a cook, a house-keeper, a nurse, and a chauffeur. Alan's family had made a lot of money in real estate, but then lost it in the Depression. The fact that he wasn't wealthy didn't bother Peggy one bit. "He had almost nothing then, and that is about what he had when we married. He seemed to have everything to me. But he wasn't aware of how good-looking he was. He was somewhat shy and had a true ingenuous quality."

They married five years later, after his return from serving overseas in World War II. He was still in the navy, and Peggy got a job as a secretary at the depot where he was stationed. After his discharge, Alan began working in his father's struggling firm for very little money. But the real estate market began to boom in the postwar years, and Alan and his brother steadily built the company up to its present position as one of the most important in the country. He and Peggy had a daughter before the success came, then a son, and finally another daughter.

With the success, Peggy began to get increasingly involved with Jewish philanthropic organizations, not just giving money or lending her name, but putting in long, hardworking days. Early on, she also got a master's degree that allowed her to take on real jobs rather than just volunteer work. In addition to working, she orchestrated an extremely active social life for herself and Alan, sometimes so active it got to be too much for Alan. "He'll say, 'I remember when we were home for dinner alone, back in 1957.' I hear that and I try to slow down. But it isn't easy—I hate to miss an event, a party, an occasion, and that can be very hard to live with. But I hate to go without Alan, and I try very hard not to make appointments with people he really doesn't care for. In fact, he's always been supportive. Whatever I wanted to do was all right with him."

"I was never threatened by her working," Alan agrees. "If Peggy couldn't do her thing she would go bananas. When we argue most vociferously, it is generally about unimportant things. The important things are worked out calmly. I like her control, her strength, her involvement. We have a deep interest in one another, and we want to know about each other's activities."

"We've always talked together," Peggy says. "After our honey-moon, Alan gave me the greatest compliment. He said, 'You are my pal.' He meant you are my friend, my buddy. We still are pals, and we always will be."

It has been a busy, hardworking, successful life, a marriage that has brought happiness to both of them for forty-two years. But despite all their good fortune, all their caring for one another, they could not prevent great personal tragedy from striking their lives. Peggy talks about it with an undercurrent of anger that has not disappeared even after many years. "Our son was killed in an automobile accident at the age of twenty-one," Peggy says. "It was horrible. A drunken woman killed herself, our son, his friend, and badly injured kids in the back of her car. It was the hardest time of our lives, putting the pieces together. Alan was so supportive of me. I was just destroyed, and much as he was suffering, he kept trying to help me get on my feet. He said that he and our daughters all depended on me. 'You can't fall apart,' he said. 'We need you.' And that helped a lot."

One recalls the words of Jackson North: "I don't believe parents ever get over the death of a child." How can they? That is not the way the seasons are supposed to unfold. Everything is rearranged. Something as traumatic as the death of a child seems an affront to the natural order. In a troubled marriage such an event can unleash all the demons that have been lurking beneath the surface, and anger at fate can turn to rage against the partner. In good marriages, people find a way to go on. Every year on the anniversary of their son's death, Jackson North simply holds his wife Karen and lets her cry. And that helps, because they have been through it together, and have one another to hold.

Life goes on. Peggy Tishman speaks of the things that spark a marriage even after so many years: "New ideas, new friends, new trips. Keeping fit, so you constantly feel alive. And just being alone together in old and new places."

Keeping fit, so you constantly feel alive. A lot of people feel that's important at any age. But those words can have quite a different meaning to a couple married for over forty years and to one in the prime of life. Or they ought to. But the seasons of marriage are no more immutable than those of nature—there can be a cold day in July.

Dan is an executive with a small computer manufacturing company and Laurie works as an executive secretary for an independent film producer. They have a ten-year-old son and a daughter who is eight. They have been married thirteen years. Four years ago Laurie had a mastectomy.

DAN: We always had a good relationship, but Laurie's operation increased our awareness of how much we care for each other and how precious our time together is. Sometimes I watch her getting breakfast ready or going over homework with the kids, and I thank God for not taking her from us.

LAURIE: I never realized how meaningful my life was until I almost lost it. I still don't know if I beat cancer, but I have a positive attitude and the prognosis is good. There was some depression after the operation, and both Dan and I saw a psychologist together. I was so afraid Dan would find my mutilated body disgusting that I wouldn't let him see me nude. I wore a padded bra and a T-shirt all the time.

DAN: It wasn't easy to convince her that it didn't change the way I felt about her. What if I had been wounded in the war? Would she love me less? It hurt me to see her withdraw from me, but with the doctor's help, I was patient and she began to trust me again. I remember the first night she really let me look at her. We both started to cry, but she knew I was crying with relief that she was still alive.

LAURIE: During the first year, I thought I wanted cosmetic surgery. I even visited some women who had had nipple transplants, but they looked so artificial to me. Dan and I talked it over and decided not to have it done, and I'm glad now. I love myself and my body, but I don't kid myself—if Dan had not accepted me the way I was, I don't think I could have survived the trauma. Now I can undress in front of him without feeling self-conscious or ugly. I used to watch him in the mirror when I took my bra off, and I saw love in his eyes, not pity or revulsion. I consider myself lucky in many ways. I've heard horror stories about other women whose husbands or lovers left them because they couldn't make love to them anymore.

DAN: Any man who would leave a woman because of a mastectomy didn't love her in the first place and would have left her sooner or later for some other reason. My wife is a brave and beautiful woman, and I'm the one who is lucky to have her.

Married ten years, with children nine and seven, Ann and Neil Yarbro, like Dan and Laurie, ought to be entering one of the most fulfilling periods of their marriage. But a year ago, at the age of thirty-seven, Neil had a stroke. He is not paralyzed, but one side of his body is numb and he is in constant pain. Doctors say he will never make a full recovery but that with proper medication his pain will lessen.

He is still able to work part-time, but the loss of income is considerable. Ann, now thirty-six, used to work part-time herself at a local boutique, but now has taken a full-time job.

Despite the financial difficulties, "Money isn't as important to us as it used to be," Ann says. "I'm so glad Neil is recovering I can't waste energy worrying about money."

"It's funny what a stroke can do to change the way you look at life," Neil adds. "My whole perspective has changed. Money is now just something you use—my goal is no longer to amass large chunks of it. I feel much more relaxed about it. Maybe it's the medication, but I'm more laid back in general, ready to enjoy the simple things, with my family. They're so important to me."

The Yarbros aren't doing much long-range planning these days. "I make sure the insurance payments are up to date," Neil says, "and when Ann suggested we start enjoying our money now, and not wait to spend it on hospitals and doctors, I objected. After all, I'm the one that's sick and I don't want to feel that if something happens to me she will be left destitute. But she convinced me that her theory is right. We do not and never will have big money, so why kid ourselves? Ann is a capable woman, and she has proven to herself and to me that she can take care of herself if necessary. We love each other and the children, and whatever time is left should be enjoyed to the fullest."

These are words one might not be surprised to hear from a man three decades older than Neil. But circumstance has intervened. The seasons are out of joint. The possibility of death is the truth of the matter, despite his youth. But he is not bleak about it, or self-pitying. There are good things that have come out of the situation, especially in terms of their children, and both he and Ann prefer to look at that aspect of it.

"Our daughters seem to be closer together and more protective of each other," Neil says. "I don't see as much sibling rivalry. Disaster has a way of doing that for families. I imagine this family lives as if we have survived an earthquake or an invasion and we are taking care of each other."

Ann agrees. "Before the stroke this family did not really communicate, although we didn't realize it then. We all lived together and went on about our daily business, but we never *listened* to each other. The kids got attention, and we tried to spend as much time together as a family as we could. Now I understand that we avoided discussing serious questions with the children and gave lip service to their questions, their fears, their curiosity, their problems. For instance, when Lisa and Amy were little, Neil bought them a puppy and it was hit by a car and killed. The girls were devastated. We thought we were being protective by not dealing with the subject honestly. Instead of decreasing their anxiety we increased their confusion."

"We're learning to talk to each other about our most hidden fears," Neil says. "We all watched a TV show about an atomic war together. Then we sat down and talked about how this family could survive something like that. We figured out together that the only way would be to help try to prevent one. The girls are now involved in a letter-writing program at school, writing to the President and also local politicians to express their concern."

And so, for the Yarbros, very personal intimations of mortality have led to a greater affirmation of life. Ann and Neil find themselves far more involved with their children than they were before. The disruption of life's seasonal order has led to greater communication. And while we have met many couples in this book who strive to communicate with their children in quite profound ways from the time the children are capable of understanding, it is not at all uncommon for people to discover the secret of being with children much later than the prescribed calendar calls for.

So many people have children carelessly. They do it because they're supposed to, but often they aren't ready. In fact, it may well be that children born out of season, to a couple considerably past the usual age for diaper changing, may be lucky. Kenny Rogers says, "I don't consider myself a stupid person, but I missed out on the thrill of watching a child grow up twice. My career was everything in those days. I'm trying to make it up to my two grown children, but this time I'm going to be a real father with Christopher."

Bill Shoemaker, a fifty-three-year-old jockey who has won more thoroughbred races than anyone, including the Kentucky Derby three times, finds himself in much the same frame of mind as Kenny

Rogers. He has been married for seven years to his third wife, Cindy, now in her mid-thirties, a former model who knew him for years as a friend before they fell in love. He has three children by his previous marriages, but he says, "I was young and didn't pay much attention to them. I am much more involved as a father now." That's especially true with his and Cindy's four-year-old daughter.

"I taught her to call me 'Turkey,'" he says, "and now she calls everybody else turkey."

"The other day she yelled out the door, 'Good-bye, you two turkeys,'" Cindy Shoemaker reports with a grin. "Then she looked at me and said, 'I didn't call you a turkey, Mommy. Daddy said not to call Mommy a turkey.'"

A silly little story perhaps. But also a very significant one. It's not something he would have brought up a few years back in an interview. Then it would have been great horses, great races, history—his history—in the making. He is still racing, still making more history after a brief retirement. But he likes to tell stories about his small daughter. At an age when most men are thinking about grand-children, he has discovered the joy of being a parent. Out of season, perhaps, but he is no less grateful for the opportunity.

After twenty-three years of marriage, Len and Roberta, both forty-eight, have found that a season of greater separateness has not only improved their relationship but in fact preserved their marriage. Roberta lives in a townhouse in Boston, where she owns a boutique. Len, a writer, lives two blocks away in his office.

Both came from conventional families. His parents were Polish-Jewish immigrants; hers are small-town Protestants from Ohio. They met at college and dated for five years before marrying. "In those days," Roberta says, "you didn't think about what a marriage was. We just got married and expected to have one like everyone else's."

"The idea of marriage seems abnormal to me now," says Len. "The thought of one person being everything to you seven days a week is unnatural."

Yet for years they did have a perfectly conventional marriage of the two-career sort. Roberta worked, except for short periods when each of their three children were born. But they found that they were getting increasingly on one another's nerves. The problems came from trivial things, but they began to add up.

"Len has never grown up," Roberta says. "He still rides around on a motorcycle and sings 'I've Gotta Be Me.'"

"Roberta always wanted me to match her. If she was dressed up, I was supposed to dress the same way. Her background was more uptight than mine, and she had to do everything the way the Joneses did. I didn't give a damn what people thought, although I tried not to be actively offensive. But I have to say that Roberta has loosened up over the years."

The ultimate proof of that is their unconventional living arrangement. It began to evolve about six years ago. Says Len, "We were arguing all the time—about how to raise the kids, about what music to listen to, constantly arguing about everything. It got to a point where we were at each other so much that it was upsetting the kids."

"We still liked each other," Roberta adds, "but we couldn't get away from the little things. Basically we got on each other's nerves to the point that we couldn't get past that and have a good time. This grew over the years; it didn't happen all at once."

There was never a deliberate decision to live apart. It just evolved. "I started working very long hours," Len explains. "I also get up very early. So everyone was in bed when I got home and everyone was still asleep when I got up. And the few hours that I do sleep, I snore. Roberta would push me out of bed. I couldn't understand why she had to wake me up. Why couldn't she just go sleep on the sofa? Anyway, I started sleeping at my office sometimes—it's in an apartment. And I did that more and more over a period of years."

"Then you took away your clothes," says Roberta.

"I thought it was silly to come over here in the morning and change and go right back. So eventually I moved over there, and I found that I really liked it. I'm not involved in the nitty-gritty at home. We have different ways of reacting to situations and people, and at this time in our lives we do as we please. When we're out together, I dress as I like and she dresses as she likes. We don't have to be the Bobbsey Twins. We're both ourselves, and we have fun together."

"In the beginning, I didn't understand what was happening," says Roberta. "We really didn't know where we stood with each other. We were both working very hard at the time. I guess we were trying to establish our own identities, which we couldn't do when we were together all the time. We've managed to do that since we've lived apart. I spent years trying to find out who I was, and I never did. Then all of a sudden I got to the point where I was comfortable with myself, and then I could be comfortable with someone else."

They have generally common interests and have not forged particularly separate social lives. "I like some of her friends, she likes some of mine," Len says. "I'll have a function and ask Roberta to come along. If she wants to, she will. The great thing is that I don't have to be part of her and she doesn't have to be part of me on a daily basis if we don't feel like it."

"If I really want him to come, he'll come. There's a backup system of support working here. We always knew we could count on each other. We've always been friends."

"We see each other four or five times a week. Sometimes I sleep over and sometimes I don't. We've gotten back to really wanting each other sexually. But there are times when we'll get into a fight over dinner and I'll think 'I don't have to take this,' and escape."

"I'm glad he has a place to go. It dissipates a lot of anger."

"I call her in the morning. It's so much easier not to have to put up with the things we tolerated for years."

Neither of them feels threatened by the possibility of other relationships. "We've both had a few," Roberta says, "both before and after we started living apart. We admitted that to each other not long ago."

"Roberta started talking about AIDS and asking if there was any danger for her. Everything came out, but the nicest part was that we preferred each other."

"Seeing other people was just another stage like all the others we've been through—being married without children, being married with children, and living apart. So we tried other people, and it was okay but not the fulfillment of some fantasy that a lot of married people think it will be. There's no longing for that. We do prefer each other. This summer we spent a month together in Italy, the longest time together in several years. It was wonderful."

"We accept each other much more than we did. I remember when Roberta became consumed by her business and I felt I'd lost control over her. I admired her success, but it was hard to fake enthusiasm. But I've grown also, so at this point we like being together when we are."

"Even during the worst time we never really wanted to divorce," says Roberta. "What we're doing now works for us. People who rush to get divorced are chickens. They don't have the guts to fight it out. You can walk away from a fight or try to make it work. And we found a way to make it work."

"The biggest problem we had was arguing about how to raise the children, so when we began living separately, they adjusted very well. They hated it when we argued all the time. Now we're all happy, and someday we will live together, but not for now. In a few years I'd like to leave the city and buy a boat to live in—and Roberta can live in a house behind the boat."

Comedian George Carlin's career has had its ups and downs over the years, as has his twenty-seven-year marriage to his wife Brenda. They met in 1960 at a club in Ohio where Brenda was working as a hostess and George was appearing with a comedy team.

"I became interested in him immediately," says Brenda. "He was fascinating and different—a New York kid out of *West Side Story*—and his mind was from another planet. I guess he was attracted to me, because the very first night he came up to me and asked, 'What does a guy do in a town like this after the clubs close?' I said, 'Well, you find some girl with a stereo in her apartment.' And I took him home for two weeks. I don't know if we ever got the stereo on."

Although the relationship was intense, Brenda accepted the fact that she might not see George again after his gig was over. But he wrote and called constantly. "The qualities that attracted me to Brenda were her intellect, her character, and the physical—how she looked. I knew that those things were all there for me."

Within a couple of months they were married. "George didn't ask my father, he told my father," Brenda remembers. At the time of the marriage George was not a big success, but that soon came with regular appearances on *The Merv Griffin Show* and then *The John Davidson Show*. But the success was hard on Brenda. "It affected me very badly, because I felt abandoned. He would do a show, and even though they would have parties and get-togethers to involve the wives and husbands, I was very restless. I wanted to do something, but I didn't know what it was. I even took flying lessons for a while."

Brenda found herself needing to get high. "George was smoking grass when I met him, and I smoked grass with him until our daughter was born. Then I got this attitude that I didn't want it. I guess it was partly being responsible for the baby. But I needed a drink to feel I belonged with George's associates, and then I started on Valium, cocaine, anything that came along. I was very sick, but it took a good five years before I spiraled down to the bottom. My ultimate bottom was backing into the lobby of an inn. It was my last cry for help."

They were living in a conservative California neighborhood. Brenda would have drugs delivered to her. "I was a vegetable. George tried to help. He really wanted to help me, but I didn't recognize—or wouldn't admit—what was wrong. I thought I was going blind and I thought I had a brain tumor."

George was also doing cocaine, but Brenda doesn't think it was her problem that caused that. "The fans, other performers—being out there, it's always handed to you, anything you want." Still, George was not having anything like the problems Brenda was. "For the last two months before I went into the facility, I knew I was going to die," she says. "When I did check in for help, for the first three days they didn't know if I was going to live, and I didn't think I was."

George does not have excessive guilt about what happened. "It's sort of an intellectual feeling where you say if I hadn't done this or had done that maybe it wouldn't have happened. But deep down we know that everyone walks their own trail. I did feel some remorse that I hadn't pushed her harder to take a step for herself. But you can't make a person do that, so I tried to turn my back on it. Maybe I should have tried harder."

"I couldn't have gone to George and said, 'I can't continue this way. I've got to . . .' I didn't have those words. I look at my life now and I look at what it was, and it's like another life, another person. I was there, but I wasn't there. I really felt after I was straight that I'd been given a second chance."

As part of her therapy, Brenda attended Alcoholics Anonymous meetings every day for almost two years. Says George, "I knew her strength of will, the strength of character underneath everything. And I began to see the character and intelligence in many of the people she associated with in AA, and I felt that she was in good hands. I saw her grow week to week, month to month, in her strength and her ability to talk about what had happened. I was very encouraged and just hoped that it would take the first time. For many alcoholics and addicts, it doesn't, and I hoped she wouldn't have to go through a few false starts."

Then, after Brenda had been clean for two years, and George also had been off cocaine for a year, he had a heart attack. "I went through this clinging period then," Brenda recalls. "I didn't want to leave him alone. I was always staring at him. At first I was afraid to have sex, because the heart attack was in my mind all the time. Then gradually I realized he was okay, and I'd see him doing more, and we were able to talk about it."

A turning point came for them when they'd been married eighteen years. "George loves me a lot," says Brenda, "and he would look at me and I would know he understood what I was going through. He would say, 'We have to do something together. Someday we're going to do something together.' And I'd say, yes, yes, never really believing it. Then, in 1978, he decided he wanted to do a cable show for HBO, and I was the coproducer. I was thrown into this job without any previous production experience, and I loved it."

George says, "I felt terrific, because it was the next step in her recovery. It showed that the basic recovery she'd gone through had taken hold and now she was able to use all of herself. I knew that her talents would be well used in production."

They were so well used that for several years Brenda worked for various companies in television production, operating out of an office in her home. "But I became frustrated with it," she says. "I wanted to make more of my own decisions. So last year I bought a small theater near where we live, and put a small staff together, and we are producing some original new plays. We had a very good first season, and one of the nicest things about it is that our daughter, who's interested in serious drama, not becoming a soap star, was in one of the plays. George was very pleased, and he may appear in a play himself next year. It's been positive for the whole family."

George is more than pleased. "That's what partnership is all about," he says, "for each one to have a role and fulfill it. It's a great thing. She's my sweetheart. She's my partner, and she gives me great support in the things I dream about doing. I'm very lucky to have found that combination of qualities I saw in her right away—her character, her intellect—and her looks are still damn good. And she's grown as well, so she's better than ever."

As for Brenda, she has no regrets about the bad times. "How can I? They brought me to where I am now."

Seasons. Spring, summer, winter, fall. But they fool us, don't they? Sometimes nicely. We may not appreciate the hailstorm in August, but what can be more lovely than the rose that blooms in the sun the day after the first snowfall? Passion, we are told, is a thing of youth. Elbert Hatchett says, "We always did whatever we wanted to do sexually. We weren't inhibited. It's not what it was twenty-five years ago, but I thank God for that, because if it was I'd probably still be making a hundred dollars a week!" And we're amused, because, after all, that's the way it goes. Or does it?

Remember the words of Gladys Poll, who had her first truly wonderful sexual experience in her forties when she married for the second time: "Isn't that terrific?" And Edith Denny: "After menopause I felt sexier than ever. Maybe it was because I wasn't worried about becoming pregnant, maybe because I was so relaxed, probably because George got sexier the older he got."

We hear all the time about people who are determined to make their first million before they are thirty, or, conversely, are terrified of hitting fifty. Youth, youth, youth. But splendid as youth can be, it isn't the be-all and end-all. Many people are like fine wines and get better with age. Yes, we've all heard that line before. But it bears repeating, because we tend to be dubious.

As marriages have their seasons, so do remarriages. A couple embarking on a second marriage in their thirties, with careers, kids, and libidos in full swing, obviously have different problems and pleasures than a couple who meet later in life.

Vincent Price and Coral Browne married when the kids were grown, the careers were completely established, the money was in the bank. And though the thrill wasn't gone, it certainly wasn't the number-one priority. Vincent, world-famous for his roles in many of the best-loved horror films, is also a lecturer, author, art expert—he has a dozen careers going at once. While Coral Browne has had a distinguished stage career in Great Britain for forty years, she has come to the attention of a much wider audience in recent years in such television productions as *An Englishman Abroad* and the award-winning film *Dreamchild*.

They met while working on a film called *Theater of Blood.* Says Coral, "I had been happily married for fifteen years until my husband died, and I never thought about marrying someone again. I thought Vincent was an attractive gentleman and fun to be with. I didn't think any more about that, but gradually my feelings and his became much more serious."

When they decided to marry, Coral knew it would affect her work, which was primarily in Europe. "I had an unbelievably successful career in England, and I knew I would be saying no to a lot of jobs because I wouldn't leave Vincent for months on end. I have great love and affection for my husband, so it was not difficult to make the decision that my marriage was more important than my work."

But the timing was also good. At that stage of her life, Coral was ready to sit back a little and put more emphasis on her personal life. "I cut out a lot of work abroad, but I took work here—not always in areas I really wanted to. But I felt all right about it, because I didn't want to be away from Vincent."

Although they try to stay on the same continent, the couple are hardly sitting on the porch taking it easy. "We are both so busy that sometimes it is a surprise when we run into each other—and I get very lonely without him. He is a very gentle and loving husband, almost incapable of saying no. Therefore, I would never want to force him to do what he doesn't want to; it is too easy to get him to say yes even if he doesn't feel that way. I once said to him in the middle of a fight, 'Put yourself in my place,' and he said 'Okay' and started saying everything that would support my side of the argument. We broke up laughing, and that has become a catch phrase that gets us started taking the other's side and laughing our way out of fights. We always laugh together, and that is one of the best parts of it."

Many couples over retirement age spend their golden years boring each other to death. Vincent and Coral never tire of each other's company. "We both work so much that half the time I can't find him. Perhaps that's our secret."

On the other hand, they try to travel with one another when production schedules don't conflict. "I was delighted with his Oscar Wilde show," Coral says. "But I know how lonely theater life can be.

He would have hated to be on the road alone. He would have been miserable—especially since it was a one-man play."

They have friends—mainly from the world of show business, people who are also very busy and find it hard to coordinate schedules—but that's not important to Vincent and Coral. "We are very complete without anybody else—absolutely," she says. "I would like to spend twenty-four hours a day with him wide awake. I adore him."

But even Coral expresses a common wife's lament: "I wish he wouldn't drive himself so hard. He has about fifty careers and is always juggling all of them. I wish he would take life more gently now."

Vincent, whose previous marriage ended in divorce, responds, "It's a great compliment, but slowing down wouldn't work. Both of us love our work, our profession, our life. I did cut some lectures at one point. Then she got three pictures in a row that she very much wanted to do. Actors take their work when it happens, and I need to keep working. We have a wonderful time together, and we are in fact together much more than the businessman and his wife who have to kick the kids out to school every morning."

There are many things Vincent admires about his wife. "If I get a script I give it to her to read, because she is much brighter than I am. Wherever we are, people flock around her like moths to a light. She has friends all over. Coral is one of the wittiest women in the world, and that's one of the main reasons I married her. Certainly at my time of life I want someone with a sense of humor. That's about all you have left."

He admits to being seventy-three, but is quick to say, "I'm going to work until I can't work. I love doing lectures at colleges and I love being with young people and I love new challenges. Coral wouldn't want me to quit, though I must be more selective."

Vincent and his somewhat younger "child bride," as he refers to her, have plans for the future. "We are going to continue what we're doing—live in America, but travel. Coral loves Venice, and we have a marvelous time there. If I want to go somewhere else, we manage to. I do what I love and she does what she wants and we are together. It's wonderful. We both have a very full life. We go our separate ways together."

Vincent Price and Coral Browne found one another relatively late, but they have made their autumn together a splendid one. They feel lucky. Most of the couples I interviewed feel lucky—to have found each other. No matter how many problems they encountered along the way, they still feel lucky. They talk about how much they have learned and grown, how they have sometimes battled and how much they have had to change. "Looking back, I don't really know why she married me," Bob Newhart says of his cherished wife of twenty-three years. "I was a jerk, though I thought I was wonderful at the time."

A good marriage is hard work, most will admit. Still, they feel lucky.

It happened on the beach in the heat of summer. She was twenty-one and he was twenty-nine. His father followed her around and finally said she had to meet his son. This was at a beach club, and it was proper enough to make such an overture.

"They had to practically drag me over to meet him," she says. "I thought he must be some Dracula, but I was polite and I went. I looked up and saw the handsomest man I had ever met."

"She was gorgeous," he says. "I had seen her around before, but I was a little shy. I waited a day or two before calling."

They had a very intense romance right away. But they did not have intercourse before marriage. "She was very strict," he says. "When we were engaged we stayed in the same room once, but she wouldn't let me go all the way."

"What a jerk I was," she says.

That was thirty years ago for Sandy and Jay Originer.

When they first married, Jay was doing well in the construction business on Long Island, while Sandy worked in the fashion business as a stylist. "We met every day after I finished work," Sandy says, "and most of the time we went out to dinner. We were free spirits. We had many friends, we were always out. But we were very strong together. Even though we were very social, we felt no pressure that we had to be, because we enjoyed each other so much."

They waited four and a half years to have a child. That was considered unusual then. Says Sandy, "In my generation you had kids because you were supposed to, and you were supposed to have two. We decided to have one child, because that's what we wanted. We were a very close-knit family."

"If a group of our friends were going somewhere without their kids, we probably wouldn't go. We wanted to stay and be with him."

"You always love your kid," Sandy says, "but Andy was a very interesting kid, and we recognized that. He was more interesting than our friends. At six he played chess. It was wonderful to watch him grow."

And so they changed from free spirits to parents. They wanted to focus on their child, and the shape of the marriage changed. Sandy continued to work, however, and when Andy was eleven, old enough so that she felt comfortable putting additional effort into her career, she started her own cosmetics firm, *Sandy O's Faces*.

Jay thought it was great that she had her own business, and while he says he was not really involved in it, Sandy disagrees. "Jay is very esthetic, and I will come home all the time and report to him about colors or whatever. He is my person to talk to. I may not always agree, but he is my sounding board and he takes it all seriously."

Subsequently, Jay was forced to change his own career. "The building trade got very difficult, and I went into something completely foreign to me—basically sales, and it didn't work out. It was a very difficult time for me. That was when Sandy really showed her true colors. Things were very different. Our lifestyle changed quite a bit."

"We lived too flashy anyway," Sandy says. "We had our health, our looks, our son. We still had lots of fun. I loved my work. So what if you have a little less? Life isn't how much money you have."

"At a time when she could have shown great disappointment in me due to our financial problems, she built me up. It was a bad time for my ego. We were so close to begin with, but I found myself leaning on Sandy emotionally in new ways. Her attitude and spirit pulled me through. Just as I was starting to come back, her business became very successful and friends kept asking if I resented it. How could I? She is me."

Their son Andy is grown and married himself. No grandchildren yet, but Sandy and Jay aren't pushing—they waited awhile themselves. It has been a rich life. There were many rewards, and when there were problems, they overcame them. Jay is thinking of going back into the construction business when he retires from his present job. They have plans for the future, but also a sense of achievement. "What we have now," Jay says, "is better than what we had thirty years ago when we were two kids in love."

Two kids in love—and then marriage, children, a better income, a comfortable retirement, grandchildren. That is the simple arc of marriage, the seasons all in order. There were couples I interviewed whose lives have turned out very much that way. But for a far greater number things have worked very differently. Some of them just wanted things another way. They had children late, or decided not to have children at all. For some, career has been the central focus of their lives, husband and wife alike. They chose to make their marriages work that way—their way.

Many others have been overtaken by events, money problems, illness, enforced career changes, that have made it necessary to discover new ways of living. There are those who failed at earlier marriages and needed another try to get it right. Whatever the circumstances, couples in good marriages recognize that there are two *individuals* involved, and that the interaction of those two separate people makes every marriage unique in some way. These couples don't waste their time worrying about what the people next door are doing with their marriages—they get on with their own.

Above all, couples in good marriages understand that nothing stays the same. As Ted Rubin puts it, "To me, in any successful relationship, the single most important factor is the growth of one's feelings as a result of being together." That is the object; the ways of fulfilling it are myriad.

Change is inevitable. Growth is not. Growth has to be nurtured. Growing together through change, sometimes in spite of change, is what good marriages are all about.

A final interview:
William Masters and Virginia Johnson

William Masters and Virginia Johnson are the most famous names in sexual therapy and research since Kinsey, and frankly I felt a little intimidated about meeting them. I expected them to be somewhat austere personally, and their marriage to be some kind of model arrangement operating on a different level from most people's. Of course I should have known better. They turned out to be real people. And very charming, down-to-earth people.

When I arrived for the interview, William Masters was waiting for me, but Virginia had been held up for a few minutes.

MARILYN: Shall we begin before Virginia gets here?

WILLIAM: Oh, no. She is the boss now, and we can't begin without her.

265

MARILYN: How about some background material?

WILLIAM: I will be sixty-nine next month, and Ginny will be sixty in February. We will have been married for fourteen years in February, but we originally started working together January 2, 1957.

MARILYN: What do you mean she is the boss now?

WILLIAM: Well, in the beginning of our professional relationship, I had the final word and assumed all of the responsibility, and now it is her turn to assume the responsibility.

MARILYN: To me it seems almost impossible to make such a change, emotionally or practically.

WILLIAM: Oh, not at all. We have been full partners all the way.

MARILYN: I thought you said you were the boss at first.

WILLIAM: Yes, at the beginning. Then we became full partners and coworkers for many years, and now it is time for her to be director of the Institute and for me to be a consultant.

MARILYN: How does that work? Did you really change, or is it lip service to a new technical arrangement?

WILLIAM: No, real change has taken place.

MARILYN: For years the final word was yours, and now you are able to accept the opposite situation?

WILLIAM: Sure. Because we both decided to.

MARILYN: What is the root of that, emotionally? Certainly, if people could do things like that in marriage, the nature of most marriages would change.

WILLIAM: People can do that in marriage whenever they want.

MARILYN: But there must be something that precedes this decision. That's the biggie. What is it?

WILLIAM: People must view each other as full partners in life and all ventures, not just as marital partners.

MARILYN: You two work together, so we are talking about a relationship that has two full structures. Are you suggesting that you switched hats in your marriage also, and that married people should do that? Take turns at being the boss?

WILLIAM: I said we did that professionally. In our marriage we have always been two equal partners.

MARILYN: You were married previously, is that right?

WILLIAM: Yes. I have two children, a son and a daughter, from that marriage.

MARILYN: During your first marriage, were you exploring your own notions of human sexuality with your wife?

WILLIAM: No. We were intelligent, not adventurous. One doesn't ever take one's research home and practice it in one's own bed.

MARILYN: No? I would have guessed that you would.

WILLIAM: Well, I'm telling you, you do not. You have a life where sex is with you objectively, and one in which it is with you subjectively.

MARILYN: Why don't they overlap? You are the same person. In keeping with the previous line of stupid questions, how do you go home and get in bed and not deal with what you have been doing professionally?

WILLIAM: You just don't take your work home with you. And this is our work. The two are so separate. Day versus night. The minute you don't keep it separate, you get subjectively involved in your work, and that is deadly.

MARILYN: Now that you have me thoroughly confused, I might as well discard all my thoughtful notes based on your books. You are saying that the Institute for Human Sexuality, which you run, is just your grocery store. It's what you do, and has little or nothing to do with the two of you in a really personal sense?

WILLIAM: You're getting it.

MARILYN: From your position, seeing so many married couples, do you think there is a resurgence of marriage taking place?

WILLIAM: That is a sociological question, and I am not a sociologist.

MARILYN: Well, how about this one. Have women caused a major change in men?

WILLIAM: You bet! There has been a major change in the culture attributed to what is euphemistically called the women's movement. Men are becoming significantly more aware of the female as a partner. Not just as a service organization.

At this point, Virginia Johnson joined us, apologizing for being late.

MARILYN: The boss has arrived. I'm so pleased you are here. I have been having a lot of difficulty separating who you are from what you do.

VIRGINIA: Don't feel badly about that. Even other doctors have that difficulty. It's a natural misconception. You can't fully separate what we do from us, but if you are talking about who we are as individuals, it's as separate as it would be for an artist or any other professional. I must tell you that if I were an artist it would probably affect my sex life a lot more than working here.

MARILYN: How long were you together before you realized you had personal loving feelings for each other?

VIRGINIA: We'd been working together for about ten years. My children from my first marriage were the biggest part of my life. I know that I was not constitutionally geared to live without having children, no matter how difficult it got to be at times, with career and money problems. I don't want to lay this on anyone else, but for me I would have felt like a failure without children. Even when I wanted to go screeching from the room, I knew I had to be a mother.

MARILYN: Did that mother urge of Viriginia's also appeal to you?

WILLIAM: No. It was not unappealing. But I enjoyed her personality. I had fun with her. The more closeness we had, the more I liked her and the more I wanted to be with her.

MARILYN: What was your relationship like at this point?

VIRGINIA: We were still only professionals together. We were warm, friendly, and committed to the same goals.

MARILYN: You were not lovers, not sleeping together, not having an intimate personal relationship?

VIRGINIA: I had a social life of my own, and if I'd been looking for a husband, it would not have been where I was working.

MARILYN: What changed it?

VIRGINIA: It was a very gradual involvement. In order to work with people the way we did, we had to be very comfortable with one another. We had to be able to say anything to each other. That was one of our main strengths. Year after year. When you're doing such critical work, you don't have secrets. And the closeness kept growing.

MARILYN: Let's go back. I keep getting mixed up. One moment I've got it and the next minute I lose it. All that was said before about keeping the work apart from your personal lives—wasn't getting married and having a sex life something that interfered?

WILLIAM: Not in any way, shape, or form.

VIRGINIA: This is a science, a profession.

MARILYN: But you did have sex in your marriage?

WILLIAM: We certainly did, and do. But, I keep telling you, we didn't bring the laboratory home.

MARILYN: Didn't your personal relationship make you better doctors?

WILLIAM: No.

MARILYN: So therefore it could be assumed that you *might* have sexual problems of your own?

WILLIAM: One could.

MARILYN: Do you have sexual problems with one another?

WILLIAM: None.

MARILYN: Did you have sex prior to getting married, and did you live together?

WILLIAM: Yes.

VIRGINIA: But nothing we did or didn't do was because we were in this field.

MARILYN: Okay, let's pretend you are not sexual therapists. When I came here I was unable to separate what you did from who you are. I have just been given a crash course, and I think I do have a new understanding, but it is elusive. So, it's William Masters, the used-car dealer, and Virginia Johnson, the singer. Talk about their marriage. From one to ten, how important is sex in your marriage?

(All laugh.)

VIRGINIA: Sex is an integral part of marriage. You can't put a number on it, though. It's importance, like other aspects, shifts.

MARILYN: What is the "glue" for you, that makes you feel you have a good marriage?

VIRGINIA: Shared goals are binding things, and that is so strong with us.

WILLIAM: I'm thinking, we get distressed by the same things. I think that is important.

VIRGINIA: I think anything can work if two people really try and have personality compatibility. If you have that you can go in many directions.

WILLIAM: We don't have any form that you can package, but aside from personality compatibility, and the ability to share, there has to be a fundamental feeling of respect. I respect Ginny as a whole person.

MARILYN: Are you saying that respect goes along with not trying to change the fundamental person? Some people act as though they are trying to make a short person tall.

VIRGINIA: I am rather unmovable.

WILLIAM: You can bet I haven't tried, because I don't want to change her. Also, we have a wonderful advantage. We knew each other very well before the intense personal feeling began to develop. I believe that is tremendously important in having a chance for a good marriage—to have a friendly working or other relationship first.

MARILYN: How do you continue to enjoy each other?

VIRGINIA: Changes occur all the time—with age, our children, work projects, different programs to work on.

WILLIAM: The intellectual companionship is always stimulating. We are constantly operating on new fronts.

MARILYN: Tell me about the other parts of your life. Do you cook, roller-skate? What do you do on your days off?

WILLIAM: We don't have any days off. My only major outside interest is professional sports, mainly football. I like to watch it, read it, talk about it.

MARILYN: You mean you park yourself in front of the set just like the other guys?

WILLIAM: Absolutely. But I do it in my own room. I also love to go to the games.

VIRGINIA: It doesn't bother me at all. When he is involved with that I know he is happy and content. I need the space.

MARILYN: What are some of the things you try to do?

VIRGINIA: I am an avid reader, including cookbooks. I read them like fiction. I don't cook as much now, but I have since I was a little girl. And I am compulsive about trying to get our home organized. Today, if you are going to have a career, you must trim down, eliminate. I came from an era when you were supposed to run up the little curtains yourself, and within my compulsive nature there is frustration that I don't have time for that. But I'm gradually freeing myself.

MARILYN: Virginia, did you have a philosophy about raising your children?

VIRGINIA: I just loved them insatiably and gave them everything I could to make up for being a career woman. Not lots of candy or pocket money, but a lot of indulgences in whatever they thought was right. Because I was not able to really give them day-to-day direction.

MARILYN: Has that left you with residual guilt?

VIRGINIA: Yes. I feel they would have profited from more time. It doesn't feel too good. They forgive me, they're fine. I'm not. I would like to relive it.

MARILYN: Maybe you will with your grandchildren.

VIRGINIA: I have a granddaughter, and I have learned she is not my daughter. It was a hard lesson to learn.

MARILYN: What about you, Grandpa?

WILLIAM: I love it. The playing, teasing.

VIRGINIA: She is two and a half, and so much fun. Right now she wants him to grow grass on his head.

WILLIAM: I have tried everything else. I might as well try that.

MARILYN: Do you tend to get more of a kick out of grandchildren than you did from your own?

WILLIAM: It is a different type of kick. The ultimate responsibility is not yours.

VIRGINIA: I feel just as responsible as I did. I have things a little out of perspective.

MARILYN: Is there anything you would like to change about each other?

VIRGINIA: Let him go first.

WILLIAM: There isn't anything I don't like. We have misunderstandings and arguments, but that doesn't bother me. If she does something that bothers me, there is tomorrow. I will just walk around the block.

VIRGINIA: I wish he enjoyed the company of other people more, so it would be easier to see more people together. I don't need that much and he will go along with anything, but it is the quality of what he does.

MARILYN: Do you want to protect him from having to do what you know he prefers not to do?

VIRGINIA: Not at all. He just doesn't do it well.

MARILYN: So you're an embarrassment. She can't take you anywhere?

WILLIAM: I have been at times.

VIRGINIA: He is a character. He has this deadpan stand-up

comic humor. But sometimes Bill does outlandish things that don't always strike me as funny. He finally agreed to go to a very important party with me. I very much wanted to go. It was the whole artsy world. We were about the fourth couple to arrive. It was a three-story house that was going to end up full. But we'd hardly hung up our coats when he came up behind me and said in this very soft, gentle voice, "Are you ready to go now?" He was serious. And we did not stay much longer.

MARILYN: Why didn't you send him home?

VIRGINIA: Oh, I would now. But that was in the early days, in my more obedient time.

MARILYN: Are you two affectionate?

WILLIAM: You bet! Very much so. We laugh, we are playful.

VIRGINIA: We are still very sensual. Sex is not treated naturally by many married people. They don't treat it creatively as an expression of how they feel about one another. It becomes a separate performance. When sex and affection are separated, I think that is the beginning of the end. Many women who do not feel respected by their husbands give sex as a duty and can only express affection at certain moments—when they see their mate being a good father, for example.

MARILYN: Do you believe in monogamy?

WILLIAM: Ours is a monogamous marriage by choice. It is an individual decision. I have only one marriage that I am involved in, and I do not feel that I or Ginny or anyone else has a right to impose restrictions on anyone. But monogamy is our choice.

VIRGINIA: As an observer of other people's marriages, unfaithfulness puts them at risk because of the disparity of needs. The people in this country talk about sex a lot, but they really don't choose mates based on their true needs. It's occupation, looks, very limited things. There is so much else that's important. You can't cope with a situation that doesn't represent you. If you want something to work, you had better try representing yourself accurately, as you are, or else it will backfire.

On the way out, Dr. Masters leaned over and softly said, "I can't say this in front of Ginny, but I am married to a woman more intelligent than I am."

MARILYN: She is also very gentle. That is an unusual combination.

WILLIAM: Yes.

MARILYN: You have no difficulty in saying that she is more intelligent than you?

WILLIAM: Why should there be difficulty when it is true?

MARILYN: It is so difficult for many people to admit some of the simplest things about their relationships. Do you feel very fortunate?

WILLIAM: You bet . . . you bet . . . again you bet!

Afterword: A view of the viewer, Marilyn Funt

M: What's with you? Are all your books going to be extensions of your therapy?

M: I can use all the help I can get.

M: But you were so down on marriage. You always said that successful marriage was a contradiction in terms.

M: Exactly. My hostility was too severe, and I knew it. Also, since I have no illusions, I really was a good choice to do this book—I was open to anything.

M: You have spent two and a half years interviewing people who claim they have successful marriages. Have you come up with anything?

M: Yes, a bad case of "overwork." Seriously, though, this trip into the world of the happily married revealed things on two levels for me. One is very personal—I have dissipated much of my own anger and hostility. My marriage and eventual divorce led to very bitter feelings about marriage. "Never again!" I felt. "There is no possibility of a good relationship—just look around you. I will never allow myself to be put in such a position of vulnerability."

M: Do you still feel the same way?

M: No. Or at least, much less. I still may not marry again, but I have spoken intimately with people and have seen how genuinely they care for each other. People who are as concerned about their partner's growth as they are about their own and who have real affection and warmth for each other. These people aren't competing with each other—that seems to be the key. They're not struggling with abstract ideas of independence and control so that whatever one says, the other says the opposite. Their individuality isn't threatened by the marriage. Two independent adults dealing with life in an atmosphere of love and comfort is far safer and more rewarding than one adult and one child or two children battling their way.

M: What effect has that had on you?

M: The effect on me has been a big thaw. I'm relieved to know that relationships can work. I'm relieved to see people love and care, protect and nurture each other with words and physical affection.

I remember when a good friend of mine had a book published, long before my first book. I was still married and desperately hoping for a change in my life. Somehow her success helped me. If she could do it, then somehow I could believe in myself. Meeting all these people with good marriages has helped me in the same way.

M: Can you apply this to your life?

M: I have learned a lot about what is necessary for a good marriage. It is possible for me to have a satisfying relationship with a new person. But I know, now more than ever, that I must have a strong sense of self. I must have a separate identity that won't be dissolved by the union. My work is giving me that—that's where I hope to establish real self-esteem.

Perhaps before I'm on social security I might get it together and share a relationship with someone who can accept an adult in the disguise of a woman.

Also, perhaps I won't need to date "children" to provide me with a sense of control. In a good marriage, each person is "self-controlled," not manipulating the other one. I may not be able to achieve that, but I know that unless I do, I should not marry again.

M: Do these people have to work at making it good?

M: That phrase "work at it" is a drag. You can work at a marriage without having to swallow yourself. You can work at it with love and affection, with ease and playfulness—not with a dogged sense of duty that leaves no joy, no humor.

Those who say, "Why bother if you have to work at it?" do not understand what the phrase means. They probably suspect that they can't truly care for anyone but themselves.

Would that same person object to working at tennis, chess, or painting, would they object to working at being better parents? In that context, they would understand that "working at it" is a process that brings satisfaction and joy. You have to start before you get married, you have to learn what to shop for and who to shop for. I think the crucial issue is that before people get married, they ought to learn about the false assumptions and the mistaken beliefs on which marriages are predicated. Most people marry the wrong person for all the wrong reasons. Attraction is not attachment. When we grow up and find mates, we tend to invest them with fantasy perfections and refuse to accept their imperfections, but realistically that's who they are.

Dr. Albert Ellis said, "Do not ever marry with the expectation that you will be able to change you prospective mate after marriage— to my knowledge no one has yet succeeded in this endeavor."

Our egos really get in the way here—we all have heard this before, but somehow we think we can pull it off.

M: Was that the case in your marriage?

M: Yes. Allen and I couldn't change our "script." So, I went to many therapists to try to change "us." One can't go alone; that is futile. I was so afraid to leave Allen and the children that I left the therapists. It was so much easier. That was until I did meet one therapist—yes, Dr. Portnoy was his real name, Dr. Isodore Portnoy. I did not leave him; two years later Allen and I finally separated.

It is so hard to accept that idea, *not being able* to change someone else, that almost all of us have false expectations, and that is the kiss of death to a successful marriage. "What you see is what you get."

M: Sometimes you are not even aware of how you are trying to change the other person.

M: I don't buy that. I think we know, even if we are not very overt about it.

M: When two people really accept each other, what does it feel like? How does it appear?

M: The respect between the two is very obvious. This respect is not just surface semantics. It is the deep respect that comes from being secure in the knowledge that the person you are married to wants *you* to be who you are. When the true self is accepted, this allows you to do and feel the same for your mate. You can't pretend to feel that way if you truly don't. The corrosive elements of self-deception and resentment will always surface in negative ways, and the seeds of a good marriage will never take root and flourish.

M: Don't you think that if one is unhappy with the facts of their life, that it is better to marry, even if you do not get along that well?

M: I used to think that. I don't any longer. I remember the feeling before I married Allen. He would fill the deadness, I thought—his zest for living, his motivations, his joy at life would become mine. It didn't work—I only became emptier and jealous. A lot of women feel dead—they feel they need a man and generally marriage to make them feel whole. It really is so sad to find out how vulnerable most women still are.

I have come to believe that the right marriage provides a terrific way to live, but we marry too easily—and consequently divorce too easily.

Couples must go through deep soul-searching. They must make an attempt to have many experiences together that are *not* romantic. Some therapists offer formal courses before marriage and also for newlyweds.

M: That's all terrific, but you know the majority of those getting married will not do that.

M: I feel it should be made available and provided free by the state and federal government. We have to do a lot to get a driver's license, so why not some preparation for a marriage license?

The harmful consequences of divorce, *especially* to children, are so great that I think the states would save a lot of money in the long run if they provided certain forms of free premarriage counseling as a prerequisite for a marriage license. Few things in life are more worth saving than a good husband-wife partnership. Perhaps if people did not get married so easily they would not get divorced so easily. For really bad marriages there are no choices. I am not dealing with those at this point.

The couples in this book have shown me how rewarding marriage can be—it really seems to be the best arrangement for child-rearing and personal nourishment. I don't mind telling you how many times I left an interview deeply depressed and jealous that I did not have what they had. I might never have. Also, I felt sick to my stomach when I realized how much pain we caused our own children, and it broke my heart to think that we left them with such a black image of marriage.

I came from a home where there was no divorce, but where there was a very unhappy marriage. As Maggie Scharf says in *Intimate Partners*, the early themes of life keep repeating the patterns.

One of the main reasons I did this book was hopefully to give my kids another message, however indirectly. Perhaps in some way this book will make up for the hurt of their divorce. Yes, it was their divorce, too.

M: Are you thinking about remarriage?

M: Not really. Well, sort of, perhaps later on . . . I can't answer that question. I am more mixed up now. Before doing this book I was dead set against remarriage. Now I would really like it, but it still seems so impossible. But at least the antennae are opened.

M: Has Allen remarried?

M: No, and that may be part of it. After sixteen years of marriage and eight years of divorce, we seem to be getting along. We are both very involved with our children, and since neither of us has new families, we must be closer than many divorced mates.

We even see other occasionally, with and without the kids. We talk often and continue to fight, but mainly on the telephone. I think our contact is in some respect reassuring to our children—except my son keeps reminding me that I *am* divorced, and am "allowed" to *pursue* men.

M: Your book doesn't offer up specific advice—any rules, any exercises for staying together.

M: I beg your pardon. My book is full of advice and ideas for staying together, but not in the conventional self-help-book way. I am not a good self-help-book type.

The concentration and lack of anxiety that is usually necessary to try to use the advice makes me very nervous!

This book is the Park Bench School of Marriage Counseling.

Just listening to other stories and other ways people have coped has always given me fresh ideas about helping myself and my situation.

I hope those who read this book will benefit in the same way.

M: Do you really think the couples you talked to told you the truth, especially about infidelity?

M: I may sound naive or dumb, or both, but I believe they did. Of course, there are some cases where that is not so. *Remember*— these are *all* very good marriages, and the truth often serves no purpose but to be destructive, and has nothing to do with the big picture.

M: In a world where the following titles are on the best-seller lists—*Men Who Hate Women; Smart Women, Foolish Choices; Women Men Love—Women Men Leave; Women Who Love Too Much; Men Who Can't Love*—do you think marriage has a chance?

M: Books deprecating men are big hits, but they keep the war going. Both women and men feel the same way. Most want to be independent and loved. The issues are far more complex than these "commercial grabber" titles suggest.

Also, many of these books hurt women—they can do a lot of damage by making women feel even more fearful and diminishing their fragile self-esteem.

Soon we should be hearing from the men: *Women Who Don't Love Enough and Make Foolish Choices; Women Who are Left Because They Can't Love Too Much; Women Who Hate Men and Their Mothers.*

Look, we live in an imperfect world, and the only thing we can be sure of is death and taxes.

M: I believe I heard that before.

M: I didn't say it was original.

M: Can you define the ideal marriage?

M: Are you saying can I spell out the rules in a book? Of course not! Every loving couple is different, except in one way, and that's finding that the more they share the more they love each other.

M: Sounds terrific.

M: Yeah, doesn't it!

M: Seriously, though, one of the most interesting aspects that really impressed me is how commitment flows naturally from sharing difficult times.

It seems that coming through very tough periods together adds dimension to a relationship and really strengthens the bond. "We did it together." Starting a business, getting a child off drugs, coming out of bankruptcy, putting your kids through college, starting second careers, even surviving the loss of a child. The tough times can destroy a weak marriage. But for a couple who know they really belong together, these times can be strengthening—even exhilarating. "We made it and we're still together!" That has a special magic. The building of a personal history accrues interest . . . interest that is not "simple" but compounded through the years. Eda Le Shan said it beautifully: "After being married for forty-three years, I have learned the meaning of love. Love is simple. It's dreaming for someone else as well as yourself." We can identify that feeling with our children, but when we can feel that way for a mate, we are truly in the "business of marriage."

People embrace marriage as a union that promises protection against the outside world. That is asking too much from it.

Perhaps just being close and *comfortable* and building a life together is all it's about, and that's not bad!

As a veteran of an unhappy marriage, and an observer of many happy ones, I realize that there is nothing worse than a bad marriage and nothing on this earth better than a good one.

I really have to go.

The words of singer/original thinker Carly Simon say it for me:

What we have to do with this world is call for action, and call for everyone to help. I think the spirit of our community has to be born again in a very large, large way.

One thing everybody can do is make the community of their family a better place. They can start with allowing the differences between people to exist.

That's also part of the trouble between nations. We have to accept the fact that other people's points of view are okay, so we can live together. If two members of a family disagree, it is much better to work through the disagreement than to decide one member of the family should move away.

I can't agree with her more! Will you excuse me . . . I must get to my singles-over-forty wilderness and vegetarianism film-editing group. Who knows? Mr. Right may be sitting next to me chomping on an organic celery root.

Index